Ethnic Chinese in
Contemporary
Indonesia

Ethnic Chinese in Contemporary Indonesia

EDITED BY
LEO SURYADINATA

CHINESE
HERITAGE
CENTRE 華裔館 *Singapore*

and

ISEAS

INSTITUTE OF SOUTHEAST ASIAN STUDIES
Singapore

First published in Singapore in 2008 by
ISEAS Publications
Institute of Southeast Asian Studies
30 Heng Mui Keng Terrace, Pasir Panjang
Singapore 119614

E-mail: publish@iseas.edu.sg　　•　*Website*: bookshop.iseas.edu.sg

ISEAS Library Cataloguing-in-Publication Data

Ethnic chinese in contemporary Indonesia / edited by Leo Suryadinata.
   1. Chinese—Indonesia.
   2. Chinese—Indonesia—Politics and government.
   3. Indonesia—Ethnic relations.
   I. Suryadinata, Leo, 1941-.
DS632.3 C5E852   2008

ISBN 978-981-230-834-4 (soft cover)
ISBN 978-981-230-835-1 (hard cover)
ISBN 978-981-230-836-8 (PDF)

Typeset by International Typesetters Pte Ltd
Printed in Singapore by Utopia Press Pte Ltd

CONTENTS

LIST OF TABLES AND FIGURES

TABLES

FIGURES

PREFACE

On 19 July 2007 the Chinese Heritage Centre (Singapore), Institute of Southeast Asian Studies (Singapore), and NABIL Foundation (Indonesia) organized a joint one-day seminar on "Ethnic Chinese in Indonesia in an Era of Globalization" in Singapore. The purpose of the seminar was to provide comprehensive and up-to-date information on the topic to the educated layman in Singapore by fully examining the position of ethnic Chinese in Indonesia before and after the fall of Soeharto, with special reference to the post-Soeharto era.

To reach a wider audience, the organizers have decided to publish ten papers from the seminar. All of the papers have been extensively revised and they will be useful for readers who want to know the current situation of the Chinese in Indonesia.

I would like to thank the paper-writers for revising their papers and the Institute of Southeast Asian Studies Publications Unit for agreeing to publish these papers.

Professor Leo Suryadinata
Editor

CONTRIBUTORS

Aris Ananta, Ph.D., Senior Research Fellow, Institute of Southeast Asian Studies

Bakhtiar is a statistician at the Statistics Indonesia, Jakarta.

Evi Nurvidya Arifin, Ph.D., Visiting Research Fellow, Institute of Southeast Asian Studies

Charles Coppel, Ph.D., Associate Professor, School of Historical Studies, University of Melbourne, Australia

Aimee Dawis, Ph.D., Lecturer, Faculty of Communications, University of Indonesia, Jakarta

Marleen Dieleman, Ph.D., Formerly Assistant Professor, Leiden University; Currently Visiting Fellow, Business School, National University of Singapore

Eddie Lembong, Drs, Former General Chairman, Chinese-Indonesians Association (INTI), and Founding Chairman, NABIL Foundation, Jakarta

Jamie Mackie, Emeritus Professor, Department of Economics, Australian National University

The late **Wladimir Sachs**, Ph.D., Professor, Associate Dean of Research, ESC Rennes School of Business, France

Susy Ong, Ph.D., Metro TV Jakarta, Indonesia

Natalia Soebagjo, M.A., Co-founder and Vice-Chair, Centre for Chinese Studies and Lecturer, University of Indonesia, Jakarta

Leo Suryadinata, Ph.D., Director, Chinese Heritage Centre; Adjunct Professor, S. Rajaratnam School of International Studies, Nanyang Technological University

Frans H. Winarta, Ph.D., Leading Human Rights Lawyer, Jakarta

GLOSSARY

Cina   An old Indonesian/Malay term which was used to refer to the ethnic Chinese and China; it became derogatory in the twentieth century, especially after the Sino-Japanese War, in Indonesia. In 1967 the Soeharto regime adopted the term to replace Tionghoa (ethnic Chinese) and Tiongkok (China). See also Tionghoa.

Cukong   A Hokkien term (*zhu gong*) to refer to a boss. During the Soeharto period, it was used to refer to a Chinese businessman who collaborated with a government high official, including military generals.

Era Reformasi (or Reform Era)   A term used to refer to the post-Soeharto era.

Imlek   This term is often used together with Tahun Baru Imlek in Indonesian, which means Lunar New Year. It is also called "Chinese New Year".

New Order (or *Orde Baru* in Indonesian)   A term used to refer to the Soeharto period (1965–98).

Old Order (or *Orde Lama* in Indonesian)   A term used to refer to the Sukarno period (1957–65).

Pembauran   Originally means "mixing", sometime it is also used to mean "assimilation" by some Indonesians.

Peranakan   An Indonesian/Malay term which originally refers to the descendants of mixed marriages between foreign males and Indonesian/Malay females. In the nineteenth century in Indonesia the term *Cina*

	Peranakan is used to refer to Chinese Muslims and in the present day usage, it refers to the descendants of old established Chinese who are local born and speak Indonesian/Malay or a local dialect in their daily life. It is also a form of self-identification.
Pribumi (Pri)	An Indonesian term which refers to the indigenous population.
Non-Pribumi (non-Pri)	A phrase used in Indonesia to refer to non-indigenous people, usually it means ethnic Chinese Indonesians.
Tionghoa	A Hokkian term to refer to the ethnic Chinese in Indonesia. It was popularly before the New Order. But the Soeharto regime abolished the term and replaced it with a derogatory term Cina for the ethnic Chinese and China. It is now becoming popular again among the *totoks* and some *peranakans*. See also Cina.
Totok	An Indonesian term which originally means pure blood; in the twentieth century, it was used to refer to the new Chinese migrants to Indonesia who were foreign born and were culturally still Chinese. In the present day usage, it refers to the migrant Chinese or their immediate descendants who still speak (some) Chinese. It is comparable to *Sinkeh* or *Singkeh*.
SBKRI	Surat Bukti Kewarganegaraan Indonesia, or the document proving the Indonesian citizenship. This document was required by the Indonesian authorities to prove their citizen status before applying for passport and other official documents.
Sinkeh (Singkeh)	Liternally means "new guest" (*xinke*) in Chinese. See also totok.
Undang-Undang Dasar 1945 (UUD 1945)	The 1945 Indonesian Constitution, which is also a current constitution; it has been amended four times since the fall of Soeharto to make it more democratic.
WNI (Wargnegara Indonesia, Indonesian citizens)	This term is often used to refer to Indonesian citizens of Chinese descent as "indigenous Indonesians" are automatically Indonesian citizens.

1

CHINESE INDONESIANS IN AN ERA OF GLOBALIZATION: SOME MAJOR CHARACTERISTICS

Leo Suryadinata

Indonesia is the largest country in Southeast Asia, and the absolute number of Indonesian Chinese was believed to be the largest in the region; that is, between three and five per cent. Recent studies based on the census show that the number is not as large as previously estimated (between 1.5 and 2 per cent), but it is still large enough for them to play a significant role in various fields, especially in the economic, social, and cultural fields, if not in the political field.

Due to political and economic reasons, the Chinese in Indonesia became the target of mob violence in May 1998, when anti-Chinese riots were rampant with looting, raping, and killing taking place. This May tragedy shocked the world. However, with the fall of Soeharto, the conditions of the Chinese in Indonesia have vastly improved, and many are of the view that they never enjoyed such a position in the Indonesian recent history. What are the real position and conditions of the ethnic Chinese in Indonesia?

As I see it, the Chinese in Indonesia have the following major characteristics.

Heterogeneity of the Ethnic Chinese in Indonesia

Chinese Indonesians are not a homogeneous group. They are divided by culture, political orientations, economic background, and citizenship.

1

Culturally, the Chinese were divided in the past into locally born, Indonesian-speaking *peranakans* and foreign born Chinese-speaking *totoks*. But nowadays the absolute majority is either *peranakans* or peranakanized *totoks*. In terms of religion, some are either Buddhists, Confucians, or the followers of a mixture of Buddhism, Taoism, and Confucianism; some are Christians, and others are Muslims. Politically, they are divided into pro-Jakarta, pro-Beijing and pro-Taipei, but the majority is pro-Jakarta. Economically, they are also divided into upper class, middle class, and the lower class, and it appears that the middle class forms the majority. In terms of citizenship, they are divided into Indonesian citizens and foreigners, with the majority holding Indonesian citizenship.

Despite the heterogeneous nature of the Chinese community, the Indonesian authorities in the past, if not now, considered them a homogeneous group. They regarded the ethnic Chinese to be loyal to China (especially Beijing), not to Jakarta. They considered the Chinese a "foreign minority" who should become part of the indigenous population through total assimilation. This is particularly the case during Soeharto's rule.

LEGACY OF THE SOEHARTO ERA

Soeharto's Assimilation Policy: The thirty-two years of Soeharto rule has had a major impact on the Chinese in Indonesia. The three pillars of Chinese culture were eradicated: Chinese schools were closed down, Chinese mass media were banned, and ethnic Chinese organizations were dissolved. In addition, the name-changing policy was introduced. Chinese Indonesians were advised to change their names into Indonesian names. What is an Indonesian name? Anything as long as it is non-Chinese.

Indigenous Indonesian nation: During the Soeharto era, the ethnic Chinese were expected to be absorbed into an Indonesian nation, defined by the government as the *pribumi* (indigenes)-based nation. To become members of this "indigenous nation", the Chinese Indonesians were expected to abandon their "Chinese-ness". To a large extent, a large number of Chinese Indonesians have been Indonesianized, if not indigenized. Put differently, many *totok* Chinese, especially their children, have been peranakanized, while peranakan Chinese have been further Indonesianized.

The Soeharto government intentionally confined the Chinese to the economic sector and made it difficult for them to enter other sectors. As a result, the Chinese have inadvertently become richer, and their economic power has become stronger. During the New Order, one could find Chinese economic elite, but no Chinese political elite, meaning, ethnic Chinese political leaders. Those Chinese who were interested in politics could only join three New Order political parties or "broker-type" organizations. These political leaders did not represent Chinese Indonesians. Not surprisingly, after the fall of Soeharto, there were no recognized Chinese political leaders who could lead ethnic Chinese-dominated parties.

ETHNIC CHINESE ORGANIZATIONS

The fall of Soeharto has given rise to three Chinese cultural pillars: Chinese organizations (both ethnic political parties and ethnic Chinese NGOs, Chinese clan and alumni associations etc.); Chinese Mass Media (*Guoji Ribao* and six other Chinese dailies); Chinese education.

Let us first examine Chinese organizations, both political and NGOs. Almost immediately after Soeharto's downfall, new political parties were formed. More than 100 parties emerged, of which three were ethnic Chinese-dominated parties: Partai Reformasi Tionghoa Indonesia (Parti), Partai Pembauran Indonesia, and Partai Bhinneka Tunggal Ika Indonesia (PBI).

Soon after its establishment, the Partai Pembauran Indonesia was dissolved due to a lack of support; Parti is also a political party only on paper as it could not participate in either the 1999 or 2004 general elections; this was because it failed to fulfil the requirements of the General Election Committee. Only the PBI took part in the 1999 election and won a seat in the national parliament and a number of provincial parliamentary seats in West Kalimantan and Riau. The party was soon divided and a new Chinese-based political party, the Partai Perjuangan Bhinneka Tunggal Ika (PPBT), was established, that competed with the PBI. Nevertheless, both the PBI and PPBT were unable to contest the 2004 election as both did not meet the requirements of the General Election Committee. The ethnic party approach has failed and many Chinese Indonesians have adopted a non-ethnic Chinese party approach to assume political positions, especially at the national level. One of the major reasons is that Chinese Indonesians form a very small percentage (about 2 per cent) of the population, and they are also heterogeneous in their cultural and political orientations. Moreover, the thirty-two years of Soeharto rule have eliminated Chinese political leaders, with only economic elites surviving during the New Order.

As Chinese Indonesians are ideologically and culturally divided, some ethnic Chinese disagreed with the establishment of ethnic Chinese political parties; instead, they set up non-party Chinese organizations. The first Chinese Non-Governmental Organization (NGO) formed was the Paguyuban Sosial Marga Tionghoa Indonesia (PSMTI, known as *Yinhua*

Baijiaxing Xiehui). Later, the organization split up and a new NGO, known as Perhimpunan Keturunan Tionghoa Indonesia (abbreviated as INTI or *Huayi Zonghui*), was set up. There were also other smaller Chinese NGOs, including Gandi, Solidaritas Nusa-Bangsa, SIMPATIK etc., which were formed specifically to combat racial discrimination in Indonesia. Among Chinese NGOs, the most important are the PMSTI and INTI. Both were established in Jakarta, but they have numerous branches in major cities all over Indonesia.

The post-Soeharto era has also witnessed the rise of Chinese clan associations. Almost every major clan such as Hokkien, Hockchia, Hakka, and Cantonese associations have been revived, and some clans, for instance, the Hakka, have three rival associations competing to represent the dialect group. According to one source, there are more than 400 ethnic Chinese associations, including many clan associations, in Indonesia. But it is worth noting that these clan associations are small in terms of membership and that their members come from the older rather than younger generation.

It should be pointed out that after the fall of Soeharto, one can see the emergence of the *peranakanized totoks* who have been involved in politics. For instance, Nurdin Purnomo (Wu Nengbin) and Susanto T. L. (Lin Guanyu), are *peranakanized totoks*; they are different from the pre-Soeharto Chinese politicians who were *peranakan* in their background. These *peranakanized totoks* are bilingual in that they still speak Chinese dialects, but are able to speak Indonesian as well. Many were Chinese-educated, or received some Chinese education up to junior or senior school level.

Due to the small number of Chinese Indonesians and their divided political orientations, no ethnic Chinese party was able to win the election in Indonesia. As stated earlier, many Chinese Indonesians have abandoned the "ethnic approach" to politics and adopted the "non-ethnic approach". They joined the *pribumi*-dominated political parties and were able to become members of parliament. It is also quite obvious that more Chinese Indonesians are now participating in politics, especially at the local level. Many Chinese Indonesians have become local parliamentary members and a few have become district chiefs through the election process.

CHINESE EDUCATION AND CHINESE LANGUAGE TEACHING

The fall of Soeharto is also a watershed for Chinese education. Following globalization and democratization, the new government of Indonesia permitted the revival of Chinese education. However, this has not been followed by the re-emergence of pre-Soeharto, full-fledged Chinese-medium schools. The reasons are complex.

There have been significant social changes in the New Order. The Chinese community has been Indonesianized. *Totok* children have been *peranakanized* and have lost their command of the Chinese language. Furthermore, Chinese Indonesians have become attracted to the English language. Well-to-do Chinese send their children mainly to Singapore and the West for their education. Children of those less well-off have continued their education within Indonesia. As such, the Chinese have been integrated into the Indonesian system. Even the Batam International University, which was established after the fall of Soeharto, was an Indonesian-medium university specializing in IT and business. No Chinese studies department has been set up in the university.

It should be noted that after the fall of Soeharto, some Chinese Indonesians, especially those who were ex-graduates of Chinese-medium schools, were eager to re-establish the pre-Soeharto schools. These Chinese-school alumni are economically well-off and would like to see the re-emergence of such schools in Indonesia. To my knowledge, there were numerous discussions within ex-Chinese school alumni associations in Jakarta and elsewhere on this subject, but no agreement was reached. Many Chinese Indonesians, including those ex-Chinese school graduates, encountered difficulties in re-establishing such schools. First of all, the Chinese society in Indonesia has been Indonesianized or *peranakanized*, and they have different educational needs. The pre-Soeharto education environment no longer exists. Even those Chinese who were Chinese-educated during the pre-Soeharto era have become Indonesian citizens and their children have received Indonesian and English education.

These Chinese Indonesians recognize that to live in Indonesia, they need to adapt to the Indonesian situation. Pre-Soeharto Chinese schools will have difficulty in attracting students as the majority of Chinese Indonesian children no longer speak and write Chinese. Finding teachers and textbooks will also be problematic. Many have eventually decided to establish trilingual schools where Mandarin, Indonesian and English are all taught in the curriculum. These schools are mainly primary schools and their standard of Chinese language is not high. There is the hope that after many years, these school children will be proficient in three languages and will form the backbone of the Chinese Indonesian community. According to one researcher, there are at least fifty such trilingual schools in Jakarta alone.

As a matter of fact, the so-called trilingual schools can be divided into National Plus Schools and International Curriculum Schools.

National Plus Schools

Let us first look at the National Plus schools which form the majority of such schools.

As stated earlier, during the Soeharto era, all schools in Indonesia, whether public or private, were national schools. With the exception of the Special Project National Schools (SPNS) which existed from 1968 to 1975, all schools in Indonesia were not permitted to teach Chinese as an extra-curricular subject. The fall of Soeharto has seen the rise of the so-called National Plus schools, which is slightly different from the SPNS in the sense that the teaching of Chinese is integrated into the curriculum. Nevertheless, only about four hours a week are given to the teaching of Chinese language as a subject.

In fact, the curriculum of these schools is identical to that of the national schools, except that Chinese language is offered as a subject. There were not enough local Chinese-language teachers and a few Chinese-language teachers were recruited from China. I visited one such school in Jakarta (Bukit Mulia Indah) which is sponsored by the Fuzhou Association. The school is a National Plus school, first established in 1993 as a primary school.[1] In 2002, the restriction on the teaching of Chinese was relaxed and the demand for Chinese language learning increased. In response, the Bukit Mulia Indah School opened extra-curricular Chinese classes for children and adults, with Chinese teachers directly employed from China.[2] It was reported that the response from the local Chinese community was encouraging.

International Curriculum Schools

During the New Order, Soeharto only allowed international schools to be established for embassy children. However, towards the end of the New Order, he permitted the Taiwanese community in Jakarta to set up an international school, especially for Taiwanese children, using Mandarin as the medium of instruction. Local Chinese were not allowed to attend this. However, after the end of the New Order, there was liberalization of international-curriculum schools, and these schools were established by both Indonesians and foreigners. The most well-known are perhaps the Jakarta International School and the so-called Nasional High (which is affiliated with the Chinese High School in Singapore). These two international schools use English as the medium of instruction, but also offer the Chinese language and Indonesian. Chinese Indonesians are allowed to study in these schools and after graduation they can continue their studies in Western universities.

Students of these two schools are either foreigners, or they come from well-to-do Chinese Indonesian families. They can afford to pay the high fees charged at these schools. It is also interesting to note that even the Taiwanese school in Jakarta is allowed to take in Chinese Indonesian students after the fall of Soeharto.

Chinese Language Learning Centres

In fact, a large number of the so-called Chinese schools in Jakarta are "Chinese Language Learning Centres" rather than regular schools. These centres teach Chinese to children and adults, and their number has rapidly increased after the fall of Soeharto. In major cities such as Jakarta and Surabaya, such centres are growing in number in major shopping malls which Chinese Indonesians often visit. They recruit teachers from China and even have links with colleges or universities in mainland China. They often organize groups to study the Chinese language or to improve their Mandarin in mainland China. I have visited a few shopping centres in Peluit and Muara Karang (both in Jakarta) where such centres operate.

Chinese as a Foreign Language in State-run National Schools

The most important achievement for Chinese Indonesians is their success in getting Chinese to be taught as a foreign language in Indonesian state-run schools and ethnic Indonesian-run schools. This is a significant development as during the New Order, the Chinese language and characters were banned. The fall of Soeharto has changed the linguistic landscape of Indonesia. The Chinese language is permitted to be taught in state-run secondary schools.

The initiative was taken by an organization called "National Coordinating Body for Mandarin Education" (Badan Koordinasi Pendidikan Bahasa Mandarin, BKPBM), which was set up by Chinese-educated Chinese Indonesians on 18 January 2004.[3] This was originally a small committee which coordinated Chinese-language teachers in Indonesia. It was first formed in April 2001 and it helped organize Chinese-language examinations for Chinese-language teachers in Indonesia. When it was transformed into the Coordinating Body, it began to cooperate closely with the Indonesian Ministry of Education. This Coordinating Body is now chaired by Kakan Sukandadinata (Yang Jianqiang), a leading Chinese businessman who was a graduate of the *Chung Hwa Chung Hsueh* (Hua Chung) in Jakarta prior to the New Order. This Body is in charge of coordinating Mandarin seminars and assists in the training of local Chinese-language teachers. It also liaises between the Indonesian Ministry of Education and Hanban of the People's Republic of China (PRC). As Indonesia badly needs qualified Chinese-language teachers, and there are not enough local Chinese teachers, many Chinese Indonesians are sent to China for training; Hanban (the executive body of the Chinese Language Council International) also sends Chinese teachers to ease the shortage in Indonesia.

It is interesting to note that Hanban has helped to establish Confucius Institutes overseas in recent years to teach the Chinese language and culture, but no such institute has been set up in Indonesia as Confucianism is regarded as a Chinese Indonesian religion (*Agama Konghucu*). If this institute were to be set up, people might think China is promoting Confucian religion in Indonesia.

The teaching of Chinese in Indonesia has just started and it is still too early to judge if this will be successful. Some Chinese Indonesians have taken this opportunity to promote Mandarin. However, due to the importance of English and Indonesian, they would like to promote three languages at the same time. This is not easy but it has become a fashion now in Indonesia to have trilingual schools or trilingual education.

CHINESE LANGUAGE MEDIA

After Soeharto stepped down, one of the Chinese cultural pillars, Chinese newspapers, has also been revived. Initially, Chinese periodicals were published to meet the demands of the Chinese educated. Gradually, Chinese dailies also emerged, mainly in major cities such as Jakarta, Surabaya, and Medan. The most well-known Chinese dailies are *Guoji Ribao*, *Yindunixiya Shang Bao*, *Heping Ribao*, *Shijie Ribao*, and *Qiandao Ribao*. The first four are published in Jakarta while the last one is in Surabaya.

It should be noted that the post-Soeharto Chinese newspapers tend to be "multinational", as they are linked to foreign newspapers. For instance, *Guoji Ribao* is linked to the American *Guoji Ribao*, while *Shijie Ribao* is linked to Taiwan's *Shijie Ribao*. The ex-Indonesian military controlled newspaper, *Yindunishiya Ribao* (Harian Indonesia), has also recently been purchased by the Malaysian *Sin Chew Jit Poh* (Xingzhou Ribao) and has become *Yinni Xingzhou Ribao*.

It is also worth noting that the control of foreign newspapers in Indonesia has been relaxed, and even Mainland Chinese and Hong Kong Chinese newspapers are distributed freely in Indonesia. For instance, *Guoji Ribao* of Jakarta also carries the overseas editions of *Renmin Ribao* (People's Daily of the PRC) and *Wen Wei Po* (Wenhui Bao of Hong Kong). These two mainland Chinese newspapers were distributed together with *Guoji Ribao* as its "supplements".

The competition among Chinese dailies has been very keen and only a few newspapers can survive. The largest newspaper at the moment is *Guoji Ribao*, which publishes around 30,000 copies per day. However, due to the shortage of readers, writers, and advertisements, many Chinese dailies have been forced to close down, the cases in point being *Long Yang Ribao* in Surabaya, and *Xin Shenghuo Bao* and *Shijie Ribao* in Jakarta. The last one was the most recent casualty.

The size of the Chinese newspaper readership is declining and many are worried about the future of Chinese-language dailies. It has been suggested that Chinese dailies face three challenges: shortage of readers, newspapermen, and funds.[4] This is due to the closure of Chinese schools in Indonesia and the suppression of Chinese culture in general during the Soeharto era. Readers are mainly older Chinese who had gone to Chinese-medium schools prior to the Soeharto period; meanwhile young Chinese readers have not emerged. The only source of new readership is made up of new Chinese migrants (*Zhongguo xin yimin*) who are still small in number.

Chinese-language television station has also emerged. The most well-known is *Metro Xinwen* (Metro News) in Jakarta which broadcasts in Mandarin. This is affiliated with *Media Indonesia* and the broadcasting hours are limited.

ETHNIC CHINESE RELIGIONS

In fact, there is another Chinese cultural pillar, or the fourth pillar, which is often forgotten, that is, ethnic Chinese religions.

The Confucian Religion (Matakin), which was de-recognized by the Soeharto regime in 1979, also gained prominence after the fall of Soeharto. Indeed, during the Abdurrahman Wahid (Gus Dur) presidency, he and his cabinet members attended the celebration of the Chinese New Year (in February 2000) in Jakarta, which was organized by Majelis Tinggi Agama Khonghucu Indonesia (Matakin). Wahid also abrogated the Presidential Decision no. 14/1967, which prohibited Chinese Indonesians from celebrating Chinese festivals in public.[5] On 31 March 2000, his Minister for Home Affairs, Surjadi, issued a new instruction (no. 477/805/Sj) repealing the 1978 Circular (Surat Edaran) which recognized only five religions, excluding Confucianism.[6] During the Megawati presidency, she moved one step further to declare Lunar New Year Day, which is often known as Chinese New Year

Day, a national holiday in Indonesia.[7] The declaration of Lunar New Year Day as a national holiday was appreciated by most of the ethnic Chinese. But some were unhappy because the Lunar New Year Day was made into a national holiday based on its link to the Confucian religion, not the ethnic Chinese. But there is a dilemma here for the Indonesian government: if the national holiday is linked to an ethnic group, many Indonesian ethnic groups would also like to make their ethnic New Year days Indonesian national holidays.

With regard to the position of Confucian religion, the national government appears to recognize this religion but many local authorities do not consider Confucianism a religion. Confucian marriages are not automatically recognized and many local authorities have refused to let ethnic Chinese print "Confucian religion" on their Identity Cards.

However, another ethnic Chinese religion, "Chinese Buddhism", enjoyed more freedom during the Soeharto era and continues to develop after the end of the New Order. During the Soeharto period, after Confucianism was de-recognized, and Taoism was quietly banned, Chinese temples were required to be transformed into *vihara* (Buddhist temples) and some non-Buddhist idols in the temples were removed. However, this measure was not very successful. After the fall of Soeharto, Chinese temples have enjoyed more freedom again.

CHINESE ECONOMIC STATUS

During the Soeharto era, Chinese Indonesians were channelled to the economic sector, giving rise unintentionally to the emergence of Chinese economic power. Nevertheless, certain economic areas were still closed to the ethnic Chinese. For instance, patrol kiosks. After the fall of Soeharto, restrictions have been relaxed. Furthermore, direct foreign investments are welcome. Ethnic Chinese businesses in Indonesia have benefited from this liberalization as many foreign companies have been eager to form partnerships with them.

The liberalization of economic policies has also given rise to the emergence of new Chinese entrepreneurs. In the list of Chinese conglomerates, one comes across new names which were not known during the Soeharto era. However, old conglomerates still exist although their ranking order in wealth has dropped; some of the top positions are now occupied by new players (see Table 1.1).

It is known that among Chinese Indonesian businessmen, the most successful are those who still have a strong Chinese cultural background.

Table 1.1
Indonesian Conglomerates in 1994 and 2002 (Top 12)

1994	Company	2002	Company
1	Salim Group	1	Gedung Garam
2	Sinar Mas Group	2	Djarum
3	Gadjah Tunggal	3	Sampoerna
4	Pasopati/Nusamba	4	Kalbe (indigenous)
5	Lippo Group	5	Panin
6	Astra Group	6	Rodamas
7	Barito Pacific	7	Lippo
8	Bank Danamon	8	Central Pertiwi
9	Austindo Group	9	Bhakti
10	Bank Bali Group	10	Ramayana
11	Panin Group	11	Tempo
12	Bakrie Group (indiginous)	12	Wicaksana (indigenous)

Source: Leo Suryadinata 2002, pp. 276, 282.

During the Soeharto era, the Hockchia group dominated the business scene, but after the fall of Soeharto, non-Hockchia businessmen began to emerge, sharing economic wealth/power with the Hockchia. This phenomenon requires more research.

It appears that ethnic Chinese business in Indonesia has grown rapidly in an environment of globalization and democracy. Chinese businessmen are often members of the Indonesian middle class as they have also been concentrated in urban areas. The concentration of the Chinese in urban areas is linked to recent Indonesian history. Since the end of 1959, foreigners (read: ethnic Chinese) were prohibited from engaging in retail trade in rural areas, resulting in the rapid reduction of Chinese dwellers in villages. This development has tended to produce what is known as an "ethno-class", i.e., ethnicity coinciding with class status. It is still too early to talk about ethno-class in Indonesia, but the Chinese as an urban middle class have attracted the attention of many observers. I have not been able to get the latest information about the economic status of the Chinese Indonesians from the 2000 Population Census and 2005 Mid-term Census. A result of the study of those documents may be able to help us answer the above question.

THE STATUS OF CHINESE INDONESIANS

Since Indonesia attained independence, the Indonesian Government has inherited the Dutch colonial policy and laws of divide the population into indigenous and non-indigenous groups. The indigenous population has more rights than the non-indigenous population; the Chinese have been regarded as part of the non-indigenous population. The Indonesian terms used for indigenous Indonesians are either Indonesia *asli* or *pribumi*. In the un-amended Indonesian Constitution of 1945 and various Indonesian regulations, "indigenism" was clearly reflected. However, after the fall of Soeharto, the concept of "indigenism" has gradually been abandoned, at least in some official documents. For instance, during the Habibie presidency, he issued a Presidential Instruction abolishing the use of *pribumi* and *non-pribumi*. But in the Amended Indonesian 1945 Constitution, the term "Indonesia asli" still remains although the clause on it being a requirement for being an Indonesian president was amended. It is no longer required that an Indonesian president should be an indigenous Indonesian (Indonesia asli); being a natural-born Indonesian citizen is sufficient. In order words, a natural-born Chinese Indonesian is eligible to be elected president of the Republic of Indonesia.

The most significant change, according to many observers, is reflected in the 2006 Indonesian citizenship law. On 11 July 2006, the Indonesian Parliament amended the 1958 citizenship law. The new law, which was promulgated on 1 August 2006, has been hailed as a victory for democracy as it abandons the male-centred principle and the indigenes and non-indigenes dichotomy. The principles of both *jus sanguinis* and *jus soli* have been adopted by the new law. In other words, children of foreigners who live in Indonesia will be eligible to apply for Indonesian citizenship. Foreigners who marry Indonesian women can also become Indonesian citizens. The most important feature of this citizenship, according to Frans Winarta, a leading human rights lawyer in Jakarta, is that a natural-born citizen is an *asli* (indigenous) Indonesian. Chinese Indonesians who are citizens of the Republic of Indonesia are considered to be indigenous Indonesians. However, this interpretation occurs in the Explanatory Note rather than in the Law itself and there has been a debate on this term.[8]

Another observer, Drs Eddie Lembong, also pointed out that on 29 December 2006, the government abrogated the Colonial *Staatblad* which requires non-indigenous Indonesians (read: Chinese) to be registered separately.[9] This new decision has made Chinese Indonesians equal to the so-called indigenous Indonesians. Nevertheless, some observers have noted that these new laws and regulations have not been popularized and implemented. In other words, discrimination is still being practised in many areas. Still, from the legal point of view, some of these laws are "revolutionary".[10]

SINO-INDONESIAN RELATIONS AND CHINESE INDONESIANS

Sino-Indonesian relations began to improve with the normalization of ties in 1990. After the fall of Soeharto, it appears that the relations have further improved. This is due to the fact that China considers Indonesia a major country in Southeast Asia that is crucial for its security, as well as a source of natural resources. And Indonesia, in this era of globalization and the rise of China, has also modified its attitude.

China was keen on establishing the China-ASEAN Free Trade Area (CAFTA), and in 1999, Zhu Rongji, then Prime Minister of the PRC, proposed the concept of CAFTA at the ASEAN leaders' informal meeting in Singapore. But there was no agreement on the matter. Some ASEAN states, especially Indonesia, did not support the concept. However, when Zhu attended the 7th ASEAN Summit in Brunei Darussalam and proposed the idea again in early November 2001, the concept was accepted fully by the member states, including Indonesia, despite its earlier position of maintaining its distance from open approval. The readiness of ASEAN (including Indonesia) to accept this concept was partly due to the rise of China as an economic power and partly due to the rather poor economic conditions in many ASEAN countries after the economic crisis. A lot of direct foreign investment had gone to China instead of ASEAN. It was hoped that CAFTA would improve economic relations between ASEAN (e.g. Indonesia) and China.

In April 2005, during the 50th anniversary of the Afro-Asian Conference (also known as the Bandung Conference), Chinese President Hu Jintao visited Indonesia. On 25 April, he and President Susilo Bambang Yudhoyono issued the "Joint Declaration between the Republic of Indonesia and the People's Republic of China on Strategic Partnership".[11] This was hailed as the most significant strategic partnership ever offered by Beijing to a Southeast Asian country. In July 2005, Yudhoyono visited China and concluded more deals with Beijing. Although there are economic contents in the new partnership, its strategic and security aspect is the most significant and interesting.

In the spirit of the Joint Declaration, the PRC is no longer considered to be a potential threat by the Indonesian authorities and Chinese Indonesians will therefore cease to be a "security risk". However, it is still not clear how far the agreement will be implemented and whether the security cooperation will be smooth.

Concluding Remarks

Indonesian policy towards ethnic Chinese has drastically changed after the fall of Soeharto. The Chinese Indonesians, for the first time in Indonesian modern history, are enjoying tremendous freedom. Both their legal and cultural positions have vastly improved. Their ethnic rights have been gradually restored, at least on paper. The assimilation policy has been officially abandoned and the Chinese cultural pillars, in a rather different form, have been revived. A policy of cultural pluralism has been adopted and the ethnic identity of Chinese Indonesians has become stronger. Many Chinese Indonesians who lost their Chinese culture, especially the language, have begun to learn Chinese again. Nevertheless, Chinese Indonesians remain divided by culture, religion, economic status, and political orientations. But due to the rise of China and revival of Chinese ethnicity, many indigenous Indonesians are likely to regard Chinese Indonesians as a community again.

Globalization and democratization have encouraged a sense of ethnicity and the Chinese Indonesian ethnic identity may become stronger. This Chinese ethnic identity, if politicized, may come into conflict with the "indigenous Indonesian" identity. It is also worth noting that Chinese Indonesian economic status has grown in the era of globalization. Although not all Chinese Indonesians are rich, they nevertheless form a major component of the Indonesian middle class. They are often perceived as an ethnic class in Indonesia and this is quite dangerous.[12] When the gap between the rich and the poor widens in the era of globalization, ethnic Chinese may become victims of ethnic and political violence again if the Indonesian economy runs into difficulties.

The rise of China in recent years has had a major impact on the Chinese in Southeast Asia in general, and in Indonesia, in particular. China as an economic power has been able to export cheap commodities to Indonesia, affecting the manufacturing sector in the country. Many small and medium enterprises (SMEs) were unable to compete with Chinese goods and were transformed into trading companies. Only a few Chinese MNCs are still able to compete with the PRC. In addition, Chinese soft power has also attracted many Chinese Indonesians and the so-called indigenous Indonesians. The Chinese language is becoming popular. Some Chinese Indonesians have become re-oriented towards China, especially culturally and economically.

This re-orientation towards China is not a problem in the era of globalization, but will become a problem again if there is economic difficulty or economic disaster in Indonesia.

Globalization and democratization have given rise to a resurgence of the ethnic Chinese identity. There is ethnic consciousness and many ethnic Chinese have begun to be proud of their ethnic background. Chinese religions (Chinese Buddhism, Confucian Religion and Taoism) are attracting followers. The increased wealth among the Chinese communities has also given rise to envy among the non-Chinese. It appears that the social gap between Chinese and non-Chinese grows. In February 2002, for instance, there was a survey by *Tempo* which shows the growing social distance between the Chinese and non-Chinese. Perhaps, this does not apply only to the Chinese and non-Chinese; even among "indigenous Indonesians", the ethnic gap is also widening.

Globalization and democratization have generated a pluralistic Indonesian nation. The government has recognized the rights of ethnic cultures (including the Chinese culture), but it appears that there is still a gap between the government policy and indigenous Indonesian attitudes in general. If the above survey can be used as an indicator, one can argue that the largest number of Indonesians (indigenous Indonesians) still expect the Chinese Indonesians to be integrated, if not assimilated, into the so-called *pribumi* nation.

Notes

1   "Jisiangshan Jijinghui Huadong Jianjie", in *Jixiangshan Jijinghui (Yajiada Fuzhoutongxianghui) Ershi Zhounianhuiqing Tekan 1986–2006*, p. 60.
2   Ibid.
3   Chen Tiandi, "Pojie Yinni Huaren Jiaoyu Shizi Liliang Buju Cheng Juida Wenti", <http://oec.xmu.edu.> (accessed 15 June 2007).
4   "Yinni Huawen Baoye Miandui 'San Shao' Kunjing", in *Yinni Jiaodian* (Indonesia Focus), June 2005 (Hong Kong), p. 48.
5   See "Keputusan Presiden Republik Indonesia Nomor 6 Tahun 2000", issued on 17 January 2000.
6   See "Pencabutan Surat Edaran Menteri Dalam Negeri no. 477/74054 tanggal 18 November 1978".
7   "Keputusan Presiden Republik Indonesia Nomor 19 Tahun 2002 Tentang Tahun Baru Imlek", issued on 9 April 2002.
8   Law on Citizenship of Indonesia 2006 has the following provision: "Those who become Indonesian citizens are indigenous Indonesians and other non-indigenous Indonesians acknowledged by law as citizens" (Article 2). The term "indigenous Indonesian" in this article provoked public debates as the state still differentiates

between "indigenous" and "non-indigenous" Indonesians. However, the term "non-indigenous Indonesian" was later clarified as follows: "The meaning of 'indigenous Indonesians' are those who become indigenous citizen of Indonesia since their birth and have never become other citizens of their own free will." See Frans Winarta, "Are Chinese Indonesians Still Discriminated Against?", paper presented at the international conference on 19 July 2007, Royal Plaza Hotel, Singapore.

[9] "Pemberdayaan Potensi Etnis Tionghoa Sebagai Komponen Bangsa Dalam Rekonstruksi Nasional: Khusus Dalam Bidang Kehidupan Politik", a speech delivered at Hotel Nikko Jakarta, 10 May 2007, in connection with the 7th anniversary of *Harian Indonesia Shang Bao*.

[10] The term "revolutionary" is used by Frans Winarta in his above paper when he refers to the 2006 citizenship law of Indonesia.

[11] For the full document, see <http://www.Indonesian-embassy.or.jp/menue/information/state/joint-decl> (accessed 9 December 2005).

[12] Ethnicity and class are often separated. But with globalization and democratization, some observers have noted that there may be a convergence between ethnicity and class. A quantitative and qualitative study should be conducted on this issue.

2

CHINESE INDONESIANS IN INDONESIA AND THE PROVINCE OF RIAU ARCHIPELAGO: A DEMOGRAPHIC ANALYSIS[1]

Aris Ananta
Evi Nurvidya Arifin
Bakhtiar

Introduction

In spite of the joy ethnic Chinese in Indonesia have known in the last eight years, the size of their population remains debatable. Not surprisingly, it was difficult to find accurate statistics on Chinese Indonesians. It is not easy to produce the statistics because there is still no consensus on who Chinese Indonesians are, even among Chinese Indonesians themselves. Ethnic Chinese have been living in Indonesia for many generations and have experienced many different political attitudes towards them.[2]

Furthermore, it was even a political taboo to produce statistics on the ethnic composition in Indonesia during the Soeharto period (1967–98) for the sake of nation building under the slogan of *Bhinneka Tunggal Ika*, or unity in diversity. Everything related to Chineseness had also been seen with suspicion. Not surprisingly, the political system had resulted in an unwillingness and a lack of confidence among Chinese Indonesians to identify themselves publicly as Chinese during 1967–98. This attitude towards the

Chinese and Chineseness aggravated the problem of producing statistics on Chinese Indonesians.

Soeharto's fall from power was a turning point for the Chinese in Indonesia. The country under President Abdurrahman Wahid (Gus Dur) took a positive step by abolishing some of the discriminatory laws against Chinese Indonesians. The Chinese Lunar New Year, known locally as *Imlek*, had been freely celebrated until the abortive 1965 coup when it was banned for about three decades. It was later made an optional holiday under the presidency of Gus Dur. His successor, Megawati Sukarnoputri, further made it an official national holiday in 2002 and it has been celebrated throughout Indonesia since then. Lion dances and red lanterns proliferate in many cities during Chinese New Year celebration. Mandarin courses, for example, have also been mushrooming and there have been many non-Chinese Indonesians taking the courses. More importantly, the new law on citizenship passed in 2006, seen as a revolutionary step in ending discrimination against certain groups of Indonesians,[3] including Chinese Indonesians, has legally allowed Chinese Indonesians to hold several government posts, including the possibility to be the president of the Republic of Indonesia. The law removed the distinction between "indigenous" and "non-indigenous" Indonesians by redefining "indigenous Indonesian" to include all citizens who have never assumed foreign citizenship.

With this new and positive attitude towards the Chinese and Chineseness, Chinese Indonesians now have the confidence to state who they are, though they themselves may be confused in their understanding of their ethnicity. The Chinese in Central Java, for example, may identify themselves as Indonesian, Chinese, or Javanese — but they may also use a different identification depending on the situation. Chua (2004) hinted that the only clear thing distinguishing them from the *pribumi* (indigenous) were their skin colour and eye shape. Koning (2006) argued that some of them may not define themselves as Chinese though there is no political pressure to do so. This is the case not because of their lack of confidence, but because they feel they do not belong to it. Turner and Allen (2007) interpreted this phenomenon as the emergence of the process of re-identification among Chinese Indonesians. It is no longer an enforced assimilation.

Therefore, statistics on Chinese Indonesians after Soeharto stepped down, particularly after 2000, may not suffer from the problem of understatement because of their unwillingness and lack of confidence among Chinese Indonesians to state publicly who they are. Rather the statistics will exclude those "Chinese" who, even without any political and social pressure being applied on them, do not feel they are Chinese.

However, the debate on identity is not strictly limited to Chinese Indonesians. It also applies to other ethnic groups in Indonesia, and even to many ethnic groups in other parts of the world. In this chapter, we will not delve into the debate on the identity of Chinese Indonesians. We utilize the definition of ethnicity used in Indonesian surveys/censuses data — that is, the concept of self-identification. The ethnicity of a person is defined according to what the person identifies himself/herself. This is the same concept used in the 1930 census. This concept has also been widely used in many other countries. Our discussion on Chinese Indonesians in Indonesia as a whole is a revision and an extension of Suryadinata, Arifin, and Ananta (2003), who utilized the published data of the 2000 Indonesian Population Census to examine the statistics on Chinese Indonesians.

In this chapter, we improve on previous statistics on Chinese Indonesians by working directly with the raw data of the 2000 Indonesian Population Census, although the revision does not change most of the conclusions in Suryadinata, Arifin, and Ananta (2003). The statistics presented here are not only limited to the size and percentage of Chinese Indonesians in relation to the total population, but also cover their geographical distribution, provincial concentration, as well as their age structure. We also produce the first estimate on the number and percentage of Chinese Indonesians in 2005 at the national level by working directly from the raw data of the 2005 SUPAS (*Survai Penduduk Antar Sensus* — Intercensal Population Survey).

Another feature of this chapter is the comparison of the number and distribution of Chinese Indonesians with that of two other foreign minorities, the Indian and Arab Indonesians, in 2000. In addition, we examine the religious composition of each of these three ethnic groups.

Because Indonesia is a large and heterogeneous country, the demographic characteristics of Chinese Indonesians vary from one region to another. Hence, another feature in this chapter is the examination of the demographic characteristics of Chinese Indonesians in the province of Riau Archipelago, the province bordering Singapore. This is one of Indonesia's mineral-rich provinces — an important source of bauxite, granite, and crude oil. It has a bright economic prospect, particularly with the much anticipated implementation of special economic zones in Batam, Bintan, and Karimun in the province, with its higher per capita income and income growth rates than those at the national level. Furthermore, as will be shown later in this chapter, in terms of size, Chinese Indonesians cannot be regarded as a small minority in the province of Riau Archipelago. The discussion on Riau Archipelago in this chapter is a deepening of that in earlier papers on Riau Archipelago (Ananta and Bakhtiar 2005; Ananta 2006; and Ananta and Arifin

2007), with particular attention to Chinese Indonesians. For example, we examine the sociocultural background such as religion, migration status, and education of Chinese Indonesians in this province.

DECLINING NUMBERS AND PERCENTAGE OF CHINESE INDONESIANS

The first available statistics on ethnic composition were from the 1930 Population Census. In the 1930 census, the ethnic Chinese, regardless of their "nationalities", were classified as "foreign oriental" and they were registered separately from the "indigenous population". The 1930 census, as argued by Mackie (2005), was less than perfect and was not based on full enumeration of the population outside Java, but simply on officials' estimate. After that there was no other survey/census which collected data on ethnicity. During the Megawati Sukarnoputri presidency, Badan Pusat Statistik (BPS-Statistics Indonesia) had a mandate to gather information on ethnicity under the 2000 Indonesian Population Census. Though this census also has limitations and weaknesses, as discussed in previous studies (Suryadinata, Arifin, and Ananta 2003; Hull 2001; Surbakti, Praptoprijoko, and Darmesto 2000), it remains an important source of information for a better understanding on ethnicity in Indonesia in general, and ethnic Chinese in particular. Moreover, this is the first population census in Indonesia with a 100 per cent enumeration sample.[4]

It was the 1930 census, undertaken by the government of the Netherlands East Indies, that provided a quantitative figure of 1.23 million ethnic Chinese in the later called Indonesia, or 2.03 per cent of the total population.[5] This figure was perceived to be fairly accurate (Mackie 2005). During the census, there were also difficulties in defining who the Chinese were. The 1930 Population Census then took self-identification as the means to collect information on the Chinese and other ethnic groups.

With the absence of such surveys/censuses between 1930 and 2000, various estimates on the number of ethnic Chinese in Indonesia had been made. An estimate for 1961 by Skinner (1963) came up with a range of between 2.3 million and 2.6 million people in Indonesia identifying themselves as Chinese. These constituted between 2.4 and 2.7 per cent of the total Indonesian population. Suryadinata (1978) estimated that the number of ethnic Chinese in Indonesia in early 1970 was about 2.8 per cent of the total population, that is, 3.6 million ethnic Chinese. This estimate was lower than the previous number stated by Adam Malik (1973). He stated that the ethnic Chinese in 1973 numbered five million persons. Turner (2003) indicated that the Chinese in Indonesia comprised approximately 3.0 per cent of a total population of about 231 million. It was approximately 6.9 million. Another estimate, Jacobsen (2003), cited a higher percentage of ethnic Chinese. He argued that in 2003, the Chinese in Indonesia formed around 3.5 per cent of a total population of about 220 million, or an absolute number of 7.7 million in 2003.[6] Regardless of the year, the often quoted proportion of ethnic Chinese to the total Indonesian population was between 4.0 and 5.0 per cent (Mackie 2005). Furthermore, recent news published in *Xinhua* mentioned that ethnic Chinese in Indonesia formed around 5.0 per cent of the 225 million of Indonesia's population, or more than ten million Chinese.[7]

The preliminary estimate based on the thirty-one volumes of the 2000 Indonesian Population Census provided a figure much below 3.0 per cent on the proportion of Chinese Indonesians (Suryadinata, Arifin, and Ananta 2003).[8] However, because of the limitations of space, the volumes only published statistics for the eight largest ethnic groups in each province. Therefore, they could only find statistics on Chinese Indonesians in eleven provinces where Chinese Indonesians were one of the eight largest ethnic groups in the province. From these eleven provinces, covering more than 68.0 per cent of the total population, the number of Chinese Indonesians amounted to 1,738,936 persons, or 0.86 per cent of the total population of about 201.2 million. In 2000, foreign ethnic Chinese constituted only 0.05 per cent of the total population in Indonesia. Despite their foreign citizenship, these ethnic Chinese might have been born, grown up and worked in Indonesia. They might have adapted themselves to many local cultures and spoken Bahasa Indonesia instead of their dialects. Even when foreign ethnic Chinese are included, ethnic Chinese in Indonesia only formed 0.91 per cent of the total population in 2000.

However, because this calculation had not taken into account the possibility of the existence of Chinese Indonesians in the other nineteen provinces, an earlier study conjured up two scenarios for estimating the percentage of Chinese Indonesians in those provinces. One was that Chinese Indonesians in the nineteen provinces constituted 0.6 per cent of the total population in the nineteen provinces. In the second scenario, Chinese Indonesians formed 2.0 per cent (Suryadinata, Arifin, and Ananta 2003). In this study, the authors assumed that 25.0 per cent of Chinese Indonesians did not want to identify themselves publicly as Chinese. This assumption was made because some Chinese Indonesians might still be unwilling or lack the confidence to identify themselves publicly as Chinese, even though Indonesia's political system had changed after Soeharto stepped down and more favourable attitudes towards the Chinese had already been emerging. This might be particularly true in 2000, just two years after the 1998 May violence against the Chinese.

Using the two scenarios to estimate the percentage of Chinese Indonesians in the nineteen provinces and the assumption of their unwillingness and lack of confidence, the authors in the earlier study concluded that the number of Chinese Indonesians ranged from 2.83 to 4.01 million, or from 1.40 to 1.99 per cent of the total population, with 1.50 per cent as the most likely figure. Refer to Suryadinata, Arifin, and Ananta (2003) for a detailed discussion on this estimation.

In this chapter, by estimating directly from the raw data of the 2000 Population Census which covered all thirty Indonesian provinces, we produced more accurate statistics on Chinese Indonesians without having to make any assumptions on the presence of Chinese Indonesians in the nineteen provinces. We found that there were 2.41 million Chinese Indonesians in 2000, or about 1.20 per cent of the total Indonesian population (see Table 2.1).

We have also used the same scenarios as in Suryadinata, Arifin, and Ananta (2003) to take into account the possibility of their unwillingness and lack of confidence. Assuming that 25.0 per cent of Chinese Indonesians did not want to identify themselves publicly as Chinese in 2000, we estimated that there were 3.22 million Chinese Indonesians in 2000, forming 1.60 per cent of the total Indonesian population. If we included Chinese foreigners, ethnic Chinese formed about 1.65 per cent of the total population. This new and more precise estimate was within the range estimated earlier by Suryadinata, Arifin, and Ananta (2003).

However, at this stage, an important question remains — to what extent are Chinese Indonesians still unwilling and lack the confidence to publicly identify themselves as Chinese? The assumption of 25.0 per cent is perhaps very high. A study conducted from mid-1980 to mid-1982 during the Soeharto era by Tan and Soeradji (1986)[9] found that ethnic identification among Chinese Indonesians was relatively high. Only 17.0 per cent among female Chinese respondents stated "sometimes something else", meaning that sometimes they identified themselves as Chinese, but at other times, as belonging to other ethnic groups. Only 4.1 per cent of female Chinese respondents identified themselves as other ethnic groups in Indonesia. The percentage was even smaller among male respondents. Male Chinese Indonesians seemed to be more likely to identify themselves as Chinese publicly.

Moreover, as time passes, with the continuously rising positive attitude towards Chineseness in Indonesia, and the rising confidence among the

Table 2.1
Number and Percentage of Chinese Indonesians:
Indonesia, 2000 and 2005

	2000	2005
No Assumption		
Number	2,411,503[b]	2,311,715
Percentage	1.20	1.06[c]
Assumption[a]		
10%		
Number	2,679,447	2,568,572
Percentage	1.33	1.18
25%		
Number	3,215,337	3,082,286
Percentage	1.60	1.41
Total Population	201,241,999	218,068,288[d]

Notes:

a = This is an assumption on the percentage of Chinese Indonesians who did not want to identify themselves publicly as Chinese.

b = The statistics for the year 2000 are calculated directly from the raw data of the 2000 Indonesian Population Census.

c = The "1.06%" in 2005 is calculated directly from the raw data of the 2005 Intercensal Population Survey, which excluded the province of Nanggroe Aceh Darussalam and the regencies of Nias and South Nias in the province of North Sumatra.

d = The statistics for the total population of Indonesians in 2005, already including Aceh, Nias, and South Nias, is cited from <http://www.datastatistik-indonesia.com/component/option,com_tabel/task,/Itemid,165/>. A special census for Aceh, Nias, and South Nias has been conducted in 2005 (SPAN 2005).

Source: Authors' own calculations.

Chinese Indonesians to state publicly who they are, we believe that less than 10.0 per cent of Chinese Indonesians did not want to identify themselves as Chinese in 2005. If they did not identify themselves as Chinese, they did so of their own accord without any political pressure — therefore, these "Chinese" were not included in the statistics on "Chinese Indonesians".

Working directly with the raw data of the 2005 SUPAS (Intercensal Population Survey), which are the latest available data, we estimate that there were 2.31 million Chinese Indonesians in 2005, forming 1.06 per cent of the total Indonesian population. This figure was even much smaller than our estimate for 2000. In other words, the number of Chinese Indonesians declined from 2.41 million in 2000 to 2.31 million in 2005, and the percentage declined from 1.20 to 1.06 per cent. These two estimates were made without any assumption of the unwillingness and lack of confidence among Chinese Indonesians.

However, as shown in Table 2.1, we also make the 25.0 per cent assumption in 2005 so as to compare this to our estimate for the year 2000. In this unlikely scenario, the number declined from 3.22 million in 2000 to 3.08 million in 2005; and the percentage declined from 1.60 to 1.41 per cent. With the more realistic 10 per cent assumption in 2005, the decline was larger — the number declined from 3.22 to 2.57 million; and the percentage, from 1.60 to 1.18 per cent.

In summary, one clear conclusion is that the number and percentage of Chinese Indonesians in Indonesia declined during 2000–05. The decline will be larger if we incorporate the possible disappearance of those Chinese Indonesians who are unwilling and lack the confidence to identify themselves publicly as Chinese. The question is the extent of the decline as well as the determinants of the decline.

One possible explanation for the decline is that the fertility rate of Chinese Indonesians continued to be very low, particularly relative to other ethnic groups. This explanation is supported by the facts presented in Figure 2.1, showing the age structure of Chinese Indonesians. The much smaller percentage of population aged 0–4 than those of older groups (5–9 and 10–14) indicates an impact of declining fertility rate in the past decades. Furthermore, a study conducted in the early 1980s by Tan and Soeradji (1986) showed that the number of children born among Chinese Indonesians had already been relatively low — it was also the lowest among the four main ethnic groups in their study.

The second possibility is that there was a large outflow of Chinese Indonesians to foreign countries. They emigrated to study, work, or join family members elsewhere. The third possibility is a rising number of "Chinese" Indonesians who did not feel they were Chinese. The fourth possibility is that there was an underestimation for the 2005 statistics because the data-set was collected in a survey, rather than a census. The fifth is a combination of the four possibilities.

Whatever the explanation for the decline in the number and percentage of Chinese Indonesians in Indonesia during 2000–05, the information from the 2005 data has improved our understanding of the number and percentage of Chinese Indonesians in Indonesia. Our conservative estimate, still assuming some unwillingness and lack of confidence among Chinese

Figure 2.1
Age Structure of Chinese Indonesians, 2000
(in percentage)

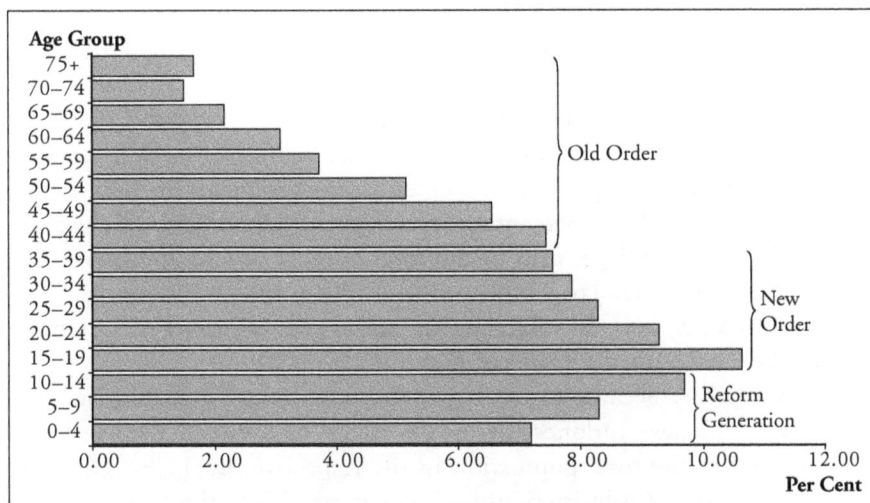

Source: Calculated from the raw data of the 2000 Indonesian Population Census.

Indonesians, is that the percentage of Chinese Indonesians to the total population of Indonesia was at most 1.60 per cent in 2000. It is more likely to be below 1.60 per cent. Furthermore, it is likely that the rate has declined to 1.18 per cent in 2005.

WHERE DO CHINESE INDONESIANS LIVE?

To some extent the current geographical distribution of Chinese Indonesians in Indonesia follows the historical background of the settlement of the first Chinese migrants. The Hokkien, Teochiu, Hakka, and Cantonese — predominantly from the two Southeast China provinces of Fujian and Guangdong — were the four ethnic groups of the first Chinese migrants to Indonesia. The Hokkien entrepreneurs dominated the economies of Eastern Indonesia, Central, and East Java. They also dominated the western coastal areas of Sumatra, while the Teochiu concentrated themselves in the east coastal areas of Sumatra, including the Riau Archipelago. Apart from these areas, the Teochiu also settled in Kalimantan. The Hakka established themselves in Kalimantan and the Outer Islands. The Cantonese were the other significant Chinese migrants to settle in the Indonesia archipelago. It was in the seventeenth century when the Chinese first arrived in Indonesia. They settled in the city of Batavia (now Jakarta) on the island of Java to take advantage of the many business activities there (Turner 2003).

In 2000, Jakarta was still the province with the largest number of Chinese Indonesians. As shown in Table 2.2, about one fifth of Chinese Indonesians lived in Jakarta, the capital of Indonesia. Other provinces on the island of Java had relatively large percentages of Chinese Indonesians. The province of East Java had 7.92 per cent of the total number of Chinese Indonesians in Indonesia; Central Java, 6.86 per cent; West Java, 6.77 per cent; and Banten, 3.73 per cent. In total, almost half (45.92 per cent) of all Chinese Indonesians lived on the island of Java.

Nevertheless, because of the large total population in the province, the number of Chinese Indonesians on the island of Java did not contribute significantly to the total population in the respective provinces. They were small minorities. Only in Banten and Jakarta did Chinese Indonesians constitute more than 1.0 per cent of the total population of the respective provinces. In Jakarta, they constituted 5.83 per cent of the total population of Jakarta; and in Banten, 1.11 per cent.

As seen in Table 2.2, West Kalimantan was the province outside Java having the largest number of Chinese Indonesians. Unlike in Jakarta, the number of Chinese Indonesians in West Kalimantan accounted for a much bigger proportion to the province population. Chinese Indonesians constituted nearly 10 per cent of the province's population.

North Sumatra was another province with a large number of Chinese Indonesians. The number was close to that in West Kalimantan. However, because of the relatively large number of population in the province of North Sumatra, Chinese Indonesians only constituted 3.1 per cent of the province's population. Perhaps, most Chinese Indonesians lived in the city of Medan, the population of which only accounted for 16.55 per cent of the province's population.

In terms of percentage to the province's population, Chinese Indonesians were not small minorities in three provinces: two on the island of Sumatra (Bangka Belitung, 11.75 per cent, and the Riau Archipelago, 9.73 per cent) and one on the island of Kalimantan (West Kalimantan, 9.62 per cent). Some socio-cultural backgrounds of Chinese Indonesians living in the Riau Archipelago are discussed later in this chapter.

Table 2.2
Number, Percentage, and Geographical Distribution
of Chinese Indonesians: 2000

PROPINSI	Number of Chinese Indonesians	Percentage to Total Population in the Province	Geographical Distribution (per cent)
Nanggroe Aceh Darussalam	5,877	0.34	0.24
North Sumatra	353,525	3.07	14.66
West Sumatra	15,029	0.35	0.62
Riau*	195,254	4.11	8.10
Jambi	32,643	1.36	1.35
South Sumatra	75,275	1.10	3.12
Bengkulu	2,691	0.17	0.11
Lampung	35,603	0.54	1.48
Bangka Belitung	105,614	11.75	4.38
Jakarta	486,487	5.83	20.17
West Java	163,255	0.46	6.77
Central Java	165,531	0.54	6.86
Yogyakarta	11,331	0.36	0.47
East Java	190,968	0.55	7.92
Banten	90,053	1.11	3.73
Bali	10,630	0.34	0.44
West Nusa Tenggara	5,727	0.15	0.24
East Nusa Tenggara	4,346	0.11	0.18
West Kalimantan	359,202	9.62	14.90
Central Kalimantan	3,856	0.21	0.16
South Kalimantan	10,374	0.35	0.43
East Kalimantan	28,238	1.16	1.17
North Sulawesi	3,117	0.16	0.13
Central Sulawesi	11,468	0.57	0.48
South Sulawesi	36,937	0.47	1.53
Southeast Sulawesi	2,192	0.12	0.09
Gorontalo	1,225	0.15	0.05
Maluku	1,920	0.17	0.08
North Maluku	700	0.10	0.03
Irian Jaya	2,435	0.14	0.10
INDONESIA	2,411,503	1.20	100.00

Note: * Riau is referred to the "old" Riau, which splits into two provinces (Riau and Riau archipelago) in 2003.
Source: Calculated from the raw data of the 2000 Indonesian Population Census.

OLD ORDER, NEW ORDER, AND
REFORM GENERATIONS

As mentioned earlier, Chinese Indonesians had been under unfavourable political and social pressures during the New Order (1967–98) of the Soeharto government. How big was the size of the New Order generation of Chinese Indonesians in 2000? Assuming that they started realizing the pressure from the New Order when they were ten years old, this generation should include those born ten years before the start of the New Order, in about 1957, up to those born in 1988, ten years before the end of the New Order. In other words, the New Order generation of Chinese Indonesians was born between 1957 and 1988, after the independence year of 1945.

This generation may have different perceptions of their Chineseness from those of earlier and later generations of Chinese Indonesians. In 2000, members of the New Order generation were between 12 and 43 years old. There were about 1.95 million Chinese Indonesians aged 10–44. This figure can be used as an approximation of the size of "New Order" generation, which constituted more than half (60.7 per cent) of all Chinese Indonesians. About 242,000 or 17.5 per cent of the New Order generation were 15–19 years old. They formed the largest age group among the New Order generation (see Figure 2.1).

The Old Order generation of Chinese Indonesians, under Soekarno, born before 1957, may have bitter experiences, particularly with the post-1965, 30 September coup. About 500,000 people were killed in the 1966 anti-Communist purge. This number includes a great number of Chinese Indonesians. They were massacred because of PKI's close association with PRC (Cribb and Brown 1995). This generation has witnessed the tragedies and many were already at least 43 years old in 2000. In total, there were approximately 0.77 million Chinese Indonesians aged 45 years old and above. This figure may be used to indicate the size of the Old Order generation of Chinese Indonesians, which formed 23.8 per cent of all Chinese Indonesians in 2000. By assuming an average life expectancy of 75 years, the Old Order generation will completely disappear by 2032.

Unlike the Old Older and New Order generations, the Reform generation, starting from those born in 1988, is still insignificant. In 2000, there were only 0.50 million Chinese Indonesians under ten years old, forming a still small percentage of all Chinese Indonesians. However, the Reform generation will keep rising in both absolute size and percentage, indicating the rising importance of this new generation of Chinese Indonesians. It is interesting and important to keep monitoring and analysing the development of these three demographic generations, especially their dynamics, including the possible interaction and inter-influence among them.

CHINESE, INDIAN, AND ARAB INDONESIANS

In addition to Chinese Indonesians, there are two other Asian "foreign minorities" in Indonesia, namely the Indian and Arab Indonesians.[10] It is, therefore, useful to compare the three groups. Indian Indonesians were involved in plantations as blue collar workers/labourers during Dutch colonization of Indonesia (Mani 2006). Like the Chinese, Arab Indonesians were considered "middleman minorities" (Coppel 2002).

In 2000, there were 34,685 Indian Indonesians, constituting a tiny 0.017 per cent of the total Indonesian population. At the same time, there were 87,066 Arab Indonesians, forming 0.043 per cent of the total Indonesian population — more than double that of Indian Indonesians. The number of Chinese Indonesians was at least twenty times the total number of Indian and Arab Indonesians. As is the case with Chinese Indonesians, the number and percentage of Indian Indonesians declined during 2000–05. The number dropped to 13,084 and the percentage to 0.006 per cent in 2005. The percentage of Arab Indonesians also declined to 0.040 per cent of the total population of Indonesia in 2005. The number of Arab Indonesians, however, rose slightly to 87,227 in 2005.[11]

It is clear from the above figures that Arab and Indian Indonesians are very small minorities compared with Chinese Indonesians. Coppel (2002) argued that the relatively small number of Arab Indonesians, particularly relative to Chinese Indonesians, was one of the reasons there were no anti-Arab violence during twentieth century and afterwards, although Arab and Chinese Indonesians shared the same economic interests. Another reason was that Arab Indonesians, as shown in Table 2.3, were almost exclusively Muslims, and tended to live in *Kauman* (areas around the mosque) — this fact made them relatively easily accepted by the Muslim-majority Indonesian population. In contrast, only 5.41 per cent of Chinese Indonesians were Muslims. They were also more likely to live in *Pecinan* (Chinese commercial and residential areas), separated from the majority population. However, with the advance in development, rising population, geographic mobility, and democratization of the society, this pattern of seggregation has become less obvious.

A similar reason may be offered for the absence of anti-Indian violence in Indonesia, although Indian Indonesians are also perceived to be mostly rich. The number of Indian Indonesians was even much smaller than Arab

Table 2.3
Religions of Chinese, Arab, and Indian Indonesians:
Indonesia, 2000 (in percentage)

Religious follower	Chinese	Indian	Arab	Total Population*
Muslims	5.41	29.91	98.27	88.22
Christians	35.09	11.09	0.66	8.92
Buddhists	53.82	16.96	0.93	0.84
Hindus	1.77	40.08	0.08	1.81
Others	3.91	1.96	0.07	0.20
Total	100.00	100.00	100.00	100.00

Note: * Cited from Suryadinata, Arifin, and Ananta 2003.
Source: Calculated from the raw data of the 2000 Indonesian Population Census.

Indonesians. Politically, it was too small to cause social instability. Moreover, 29.91 per cent of Indian Indonesians were Muslims.

The distribution of religious followers among Chinese, Arab, and Indian Indonesians was different from one another and from the total Indonesian population. Indonesia is a country with Muslims as the big majority, accounting for 88.22 per cent of the total population in 2000. However, there was a sizeable number of Christians, forming the second largest group of religious followers, constituting 8.92 per cent of the total Indonesian population. The Buddhist was a tiny minority, contributing to only 0.84 per cent of the Indonesian population, or 1.7 million in 2000.

About half the Chinese Indonesians in Indonesia were Buddhists and around one third were Christians (Protestants or Catholics). In other words, almost 90.0 per cent of Chinese Indonesians were either Buddhists or Christians. It is a markedly different pattern from that of the Muslim-majority population of Indonesia as a whole. Yet, Muslim Chinese are not a small minority among Chinese Indonesians — they accounted for 5.41 per cent of Chinese Indonesians.

On the other hand, the distribution of religious followers among Arab Indonesians was highly unequal. They were almost exclusively Muslims, as there was only a very tiny percentage of non-Muslim Arabs. In contrast, a relatively more equal distribution of religious followers existed among Indian Indonesians. The largest percentage was Hindus, but they constituted only 40.08 per cent of all Indian Indonesians. Muslims were the second largest (29.91 per cent), followed by Buddhists (16.96 per cent). There was also a sizeable number of Christians (11.09 per cent) among the Indian Indonesians.

Similar to that found among Chinese Indonesians, the geographical distribution of the Indian Indonesians may have remained the same from 1930–2000. As described in Mani (2006), in 1930, most British Indians, about 20,100, were concentrated in Sumatra. A sizeable number of Indians can be found in Java and Madura, followed by Borneo (Kalimantan), and Celebes (Sulawesi).

We also found that in 2000 the largest number of Indian Indonesians lived in the province of North Sumatra, and they constituted 63.56 per cent of the total Indian Indonesian population. Medan is known not only because of the contribution of Chinese Indonesians, but also for its colourful ethnic composition — the Bataks, Malays, Chinese Indonesians, and Indian Indonesians. Kampung Keling, or Little India, is considered the "home" of the Indian community in Medan, whose members are mainly the descendants of South Indians who came to work in the plantations in the nineteenth century (Mani 2006). The existence of the Sri Mariaman temple in Medan is a reminder of the South Indian heritage, and the temple has become one of Medan's tourist attractions. Kampung Keling remained relatively safe even when ethnic riots occurred in Medan in 1998. (Gunawan, 2007).

Indian Indonesians in South Sumatra were the third largest in Indonesia, forming 3.59 per cent of the total population of Indian Indonesians.

Table 2.4
**Provinces with the Five Largest Numbers of Indian Indonesians:
Indonesia, 2000**

Rank	Province	Number	Geographical Distribution (per cent)	Percentage to Population in the Province
1.	North Sumatra	22,047	63.56	0.19
2.	Jakarta	3,634	10.48	0.04
3.	South Sumatra	1,245	3.59	0.02
4.	East Java	1,164	3.36	0.003
5.	West Kalimantan	1,150	3.32	0.03
	15 other provinces	5,445	15.70	–
	Indonesia	**34,685**	**100.00**	**0.02**

Source: Calculated from the raw data of the 2000 Indonesian Population Census.

Altogether, Indian Indonesians in these two provinces on the island of Sumatra already contributed to two-thirds of the entire population of Indian Indonesians. The relatively close proximity between Sumatra and South Asia was perhaps an explanation of the relatively large percentage of Indian Indonesians living in Sumatra. In other words, the geographical distribution of Indian Indonesians is very unequal.

The second largest number of Indian Indonesians was in Jakarta, where it formed 10.48 per cent, much below the 63.56 per cent in North Sumatra. However, it should be mentioned here that even in North Sumatra, the contribution of this ethnic group to the province's population was very small, only 0.19 per cent. The contribution was even much smaller in Jakarta (0.04 per cent). They were really a very small minority.

In contrast, as indicated in Table 2.5, the geographical distribution of Arab Indonesians was more equal. The largest number of Arab Indonesians was in East Java, where they constituted 26.13 per cent of the entire Arab Indonesians. The four largest numbers were all found on the island of Java. This indicates that Arab Indonesians mostly settled in Java while Indian Indonesians settled in Sumatra. The province of South Sumatra had the fifth largest number of Arab Indonesians. Though Arab Indonesians can also be considered a small minority, they were still larger in numbers than Indian Indonesians.

Table 2.5
Provinces with the Five Largest Numbers of Arab Indonesians:
Indonesia, 2000

Rank	Province	Number	Geographical Distribution (per cent)	Percentage to Population in the Province
1.	East Java	22,747	26.13	0.07
2.	Central Java	10,751	12.35	0.03
3.	Jakarta	10,202	11.72	0.12
4.	West Java	7,251	8.33	0.02
5.	South Sumatra	6,417	7.37	0.09
	15 other provinces	29,698	34.11	–
	Indonesia	**87,066**	**100.00**	**0.04**

Source: Calculated from the raw data of the 2000 Indonesian Population Census.

Case Study on the Riau Archipelago

Living in an Economic Magnet

The province of the Riau Archipelago was formed in 2002 from the province of Riau. Since its establishment, the province has expanded its administrative areas into six districts, especially because of the separation of the regency of Lingga and the city of Tanjung Pinang from the regency of Riau Islands. This expansion occurred during the administration of the current governor, Ismeth Abdullah, who is the first directly elected governor in the country. This province, especially in Bintan, was the only bauxite-mining area in Indonesia. Mining began in Bintan in 1935. The only Indonesian granite producing quarry is on the island of Karimun. The province has also produced crude oil since the nineteenth century (Esmara 1975).

Regardless of its wealth in natural resources, the Riau Archipelago in 2005 contributed only a small portion, 1.80 per cent, of total Indonesian GDP.[12] However, the economy grew relatively fast, at 6.57 per cent in 2005, higher than the 5.60 per cent in Indonesia as a whole. Among all districts, the city of Batam had the highest growth rate of GDP (8.29 per cent), followed by Tanjung Pinang (6.58 per cent) in 2005.[13] Per capita GDP of the Riau Archipelago was 32,148,725.23 rupiah in 2005, which was about 2.5 times that in Indonesia as a whole.[14] It was about US$3,384, just behind Singapore, Brunei, and Malaysia in Southeast Asia.[15]

This trend is likely to continue and the contribution of the Riau Archipelago to Indonesia's GDP will become increasingly important, particularly as a result of the impending implementation of the special economic zones in Batam, Bintan, and Karimun.

Mostly Locals

Increasing migration to this province has been a logical consequence of the Riau Archipelago being an economic magnet. The close proximity to Singapore and Malaysia may be one of the determinants for the rising migration to this province. The establishment of BIDA (Batam Industrial Development Authority) in 1971 was the main magnet of the migration to this province. Within five years, its population grew rapidly at 4.85 per cent per year to about 1.3 million people in 2005. In terms of the size of its population, this province has about a quarter of Singapore's population, but it has wider land. As seen in Table 2.6, the city of Batam had the fastest population growth rate among the districts in the province and accounted

Table 2.6
Numbers and Growth Rate of the Population:
The Riau Archipelago, 2000 and 2005

	2000[b]		2005[c]		Annual Population Growth Rate (per cent)
	Number	Per cent	Number	Per cent	
Karimun	164,770	16.48	200,645	15.75	3.94
Natuna	78,081	7.81	88,503	6.95	2.51
Batam	437,358	43.75	616,221	48.36	6.86
Riau islands	319,482	31.96	368,858	28.95	2.87
Riau islands[a]	–	–	117,959	9.26	–
Lingga	na	na	82,941	6.51	na
Tanjung Pinang	na	na	167,958	13.18	na
Total	999,691	100.00	1,274,227	100.00	4.85

Note:

a = Riau islands after Lingga and Tanjung Pinang became separate districts. Based on Peraturan Pemerintah no. 5/2006, the regency of Riau Islands was renamed the regency of Bintan.

Sources:

b = Compiled and calculated from Suryadinata, Arifin, and Ananta 2003.

c = Compiled and calculated from <http://www.datastatistik-indonesia.com/component/option,com_tabel/task,/Itemid,165/>.

for nearly half of the province's population. This fast growth was mainly contributed by the migration to this city, and offset the relatively low fertility in this city.[16] Batam was the second largest city in Indonesia in terms of the percentage of migrants in the population — migrants constituted 43.64 per cent of Batam's population in 2000.[17]

Moreover, within the province itself, people have been moving from one area to another. Many permanently lived there, some made this province their temporary homes, and some commuted to this province on a daily basis. In other words, the Riau Archipelago is a dynamic province with increasing population mobility.

As examined in Ananta (2006) and shown in Table 2.7, about one-fifth of the population in the Riau Archipelago were recent migrants to the province, meaning, they came from outside the province during 1995–2000. The

Table 2.7
Inter-provincial Migrants for the Five Largest Ethnic Groups by Type of Migration: The Riau Archipelago

Ethnic Group	Recent Migrants (1995–2000)	Life-time Migrants
Malay	6.61	15.40
Javanese	31.63	64.76
Chinese	5.64	14.74
Minang	36.41	77.13
Batak	44.65	80.16
Total	20.67	43.28

Note: The boundary for defining migration status is the provincial boundary.
Source: Calculated from the raw data of the Indonesian 2000 Population Census, cited from Ananta 2006.

percentage of migrants is even higher if we look at their places of birth. 43 per cent of the Riau Archipelago's population were born outside the province. Table 2.7 presents inter-provincial migrants for the five largest ethnic groups in the province: the Malay, Javanese, Chinese, Minangs, and Bataks.

The majority of Chinese Indonesians enumerated in 2000 were non-migrants. A very large majority (85.3 per cent) of Chinese Indonesians were born in the province and a still larger majority (94.4 per cent) already lived in the province five years earlier. The Malays, who are often said to be the *putra daerah* ("son of the soil"), had a similar experience as Chinese Indonesians — they are mostly non-migrants/ locals. Malays who were born in the province accounted for 85.6 per cent of the Malays there and 93.4 per cent already lived in the province since 1995. In contrast, the percentages of non-migrants among the Javanese, Minang, and Batak were smaller. In other words, these three groups were mostly migrants in the province. In summary, based on the two types of migration, similar to the Malays, Chinese Indonesians were mostly non-migrants. Probably, Chinese Indonesians can also be considered local, rather than *pendatang* (visitor).

Even if Malay and Chinese Indonesians in Riau Archipelago are not migrants from other provinces, have they moved across districts within the province? Table 2.8 provides a decomposition of the types of migration among migrants into three groups: intra-provincial migration (moving from one district to another within the province), inter-provincial migration (coming from other provinces in Indonesia), and international migration

Table 2.8
Decomposition of Migration by Types for Each of the Five Largest
Ethnic Groups: Province of the Riau Archipelago, Indonesia, 2000
(in percentage)

Ethnic Group	Intra-provincial Migrants		Inter-provincial Migrants		International Migrants		Total
	Recent	Life-time	Recent	Life-time	Recent	Life-time	
Malay	30.94	30.39	68.42	69.25	0.64	0.36	100.0
Javanese	4.35	4.11	95.37	95.80	0.27	0.09	100.0
Chinese	35.25	46.64	62.38	50.76	2.36	2.60	100.0
Minang	3.91	2.20	95.93	97.76	0.15	0.04	100.0
Batak	2.41	1.23	97.50	98.74	0.09	0.03	100.0
Total	9.50	10.31	89.67	89.16	0.83	0.52	100.0

Note: Recent migrant is a person who lived in a district in the province of the Riau Archipelago in 2000, but did not live in that district in 1995. Life-time migrant is someone who lived in a district in the province of the Riau Archipelago in 2000, but was not born in the district.

Source: Calculated from the raw data of the Indonesian 2000 Population Census.

(coming from other countries). Using the criterion of place of residence in the five years prior to 2000, we see that the majority of migrants originated from other provinces in Indonesia. Only 9.5 per cent migrated from other districts within the province. International migration accounted for a very tiny portion of the migrants.

The dominance of inter-provincial migrants was very obvious among the Javanese, Minangs, and Bataks, with more than 95.0 per cent of the migrants being inter-provincial migrants. Although the percentage of inter-provincial migrants among Malay and Chinese Indonesians was also larger than intra-provincial migrants, the percentage of intra-provincial migrants was sufficiently large among Malay (30.94 per cent) and even Chinese Indonesians (35.25 per cent). In other words, compared with other ethnic groups, Malay and Chinese Indonesians tended to move from one district to another within the province itself. The same conclusion can be drawn from analysing their places of birth (life-time migration) presented in Table 2.8.

In summary, migration from other provinces was dominated by ethnic groups other than Malay and Chinese Indonesians.

Not A Small Minority

The migrants into this province have changed the ethnic composition. Esmara (1975) indicated that around 1970, there was already a high proportion of non-citizen residents in the former province of the Riau and most of them lived in the current province of the Riau Archipelago. He further mentioned that foreign residents were almost entirely ethnic Chinese and many had family ties in Singapore and Malaysia. However, we have found that the number of foreigners in the Riau Archipelago were very insignificant in 2000. Among this insignificant number, about half came from PRC and a quarter from Singapore, although there was no information on whether the Singaporeans were Chinese, Malay, Indian, or of other races.

As discussed in the previous section, the Javanese, Minang, and Batak were important ethnic migrants in the province. The influx of these ethnic groups and others might have changed the ethnic composition of the province significantly. In 2000, the Malays, the so-called *putra daerah* — often claimed to be the "owner" of the Riau Archipelago — were not the majority ethnic group, although they were still the largest group, followed by the Javanese (mostly migrants) and Chinese Indonesians (mostly non-migrants). Chinese Indonesians accounted for 9.7 per cent of the total population in this province, making them the third largest ethnic group (see Table 2.9).

With this percentage, therefore, Chinese Indonesians in this province may not be considered a minority. If they were, they would be a large minority. Moreover, the proportion of Chinese Indonesians varied across districts, ranging from a relatively small percentage of 2.5 per cent in Natuna to a

Table 2.9
Ethnic Composition in Urban and Rural Areas:
The Riau Archipelago, 2000 (in percentage)

Ethnic Group	Rural	Urban	Total
Malay	72.01	26.53	37.44
Javanese	11.70	25.51	22.20
Chinese	5.38	11.11	9.73
Minang	0.99	11.84	9.24
Batak	0.80	11.38	8.84
Others	9.12	13.63	12.55
Total	100.00	100.00	100.00

Source: Calculated from the raw data of the 2000 Indonesian Population Census.

relatively large one of 13.8 per cent in Karimun. In between, they accounted for 6.2 per cent in Batam and 12.7 per cent in the Riau Islands.[18]

Based on the 2000 data, the ethnic composition tends to become more heterogeneous as the district becomes more attractive to migrants. Suryadinata, Arifin, and Ananta (2003) showed that the Malays in Batam were not the largest ethnic group, but the fourth after the Javanese, Minang, and Batak, with each forming a sizeable portion. An exception was in Natuna, at the far end of the province, where the Malays were the majority accounting for about 85 per cent of the population. As shown in Table 2.9 the proportion of Chinese Indonesians was not so much different from those of the Minangs and Bataks, the ethnic migrants from Sumatra. Yet, in the rural areas, the percentage of Chinese Indonesians was much larger than those of migrants from other provinces in Sumatra (such as the Minangs and Bataks).

However, with the increasing flow of migrants from other provinces dominated by non-Malay and non-Chinese, the percentages of both the Malay and Chinese Indonesians in this province will shrink as the economic development of this province gets underway, particularly when the programmes on the special economic zones prove successful. The decline in percentage is probably due to the higher influx of non-Chinese Indonesians into the province. Furthermore, just like Batam (the previously uninhabited island which has turned into the most densely populated area in the province), Karimun and Bintan will probably change tremendously. The percentage of Chinese Indonesians (and also Malays) in these districts may have declined during 2000–07, and will continue to decline further.

The ethnic composition is very different in terms of rural-urban location. The Riau Archipelago is highly urbanized, with a 76.0 per cent urbanization rate, i.e., 76.0 per cent of the population lived in urban areas in 2000. Table 2.9 shows a difference in the ethnic composition of urban and rural areas, with urban areas showing a more equal distribution of ethnic groups, and each group forming a sizeable portion. The Malays in urban areas were also the largest group, but the percentage was just slightly above the second largest ethnic group, the Javanese. On the other hand, the Malays in rural areas were a very large majority, forming 72.01 per cent of the total rural population. Chinese Indonesians in urban Riau Archipelago accounted for more than 10 per cent, while in rural areas they were just half of the urban proportion. This difference in percentage of Chinese Indonesians in urban and rural areas is somewhat expected as it carries a historical burden. Under the Dutch, ethnic Chinese and two other foreign minorities, the Arab and Indian Indonesians, were subject to different sets of regulations and restriction. They had to apply for a special pass if they wanted to move and do business in rural areas.

Buddhists and Low Education

The migrants also play an important role in changing the structure of human capital in Batam in particular, and the Riau Archipelago in general. Batam, the district with the largest flow of migrants from other provinces, had the highest percentage of people with senior high school education or at least twelve years of schooling (Ananta, Arifin, and Suryadinata 2004).

Table 2.10 shows three categories of educational attainment. The first is those with less than primary-school education. The second is those who attained the *wajib belajar 9 tahun* (nine-year compulsory education), finishing with SMP (Sekolah Menengah Pertama — Junior High School). The third is those with at least SMU (Sekolah Menengah Umum — Senior High School or equivalent). The table shows that about one-third of the population here completed at least senior high school, much better than in Indonesia as a whole, where only 16.9 per cent managed to complete at least senior high school (Ananta, Arifin, and Suryadinata, 2004).

As shown in Table 2.10, ethnic migrants, especially the Batak and Minang, had a higher educational level than others. Chinese Indonesians in this province had a relatively low educational level. The majority only managed to finish junior high school at best. The educational achievement

Table 2.10
Educational Attainment of the Five Largest Ethnic Groups:
Province of the Riau Archipelago, Indonesia, 2000
(in percentage)

Ethnic Group	Less Than Primary School Education	Primary or Junior High School Education	At Least Senior High School Education	Total
Malay	44.18	38.49	17.28	100.0
Javanese	25.13	35.79	39.06	100.0
Chinese	42.45	43.91	13.57	100.0
Minang	23.54	25.80	50.62	100.0
Batak	20.54	14.29	65.15	100.0
Total	34.52	35.06	30.37	100.0

Source: Calculated from the raw data of the 2000 Indonesian Population Census.

of Chinese Indonesians was just similar to that of the Malays. They were in the two lowest educational strata.

In terms of religion, Buddhists were the second largest group of religious followers in the province of the Riau Archipelago, after Muslims. The percentage of Buddhists in the Riau Archipelago was 8.90 per cent, much larger than the 0.84 per cent in Indonesia as a whole. The percentage of Buddhists was even larger in urban areas.

With more than 80.0 per cent of Chinese Indonesians in the Riau Archipelago being Buddhist, the second largest religious group among Chinese was Christian (Protestants and Catholics). It can be mentioned here that not all Buddhists were Chinese — 2.49 per cent of Buddhists were Malays. Unlike the non-Muslim Malays among the Malays, Muslim Chinese were not a very small minority among Chinese Indonesians. As seen in Table 2.11, they constituted 4.44 per cent of the total number of Chinese Indonesians in the province.

Given the further development in the province, we speculate that new arrivals of Chinese Indonesian migrants to the province has been and will be more likely to be Christians and/or from more educated groups. Further studies should explore this possibility.

Table 2.11
Religions of Ethnic Groups:
Province of the Riau Archipelago, Indonesia, 2000
(in percentage)

Ethnic Group[1]	Muslims	Buddhists	Protestants	Catholics	Hindus	Others	Total
Malay	98.29	0.59	0.57	0.48	0.06	0.02	100.00
Javanese	97.01	0.19	1.45	1.26	0.06	0.03	100.00
Chinese	4.44	84.76	3.92	3.17	2.63	1.09	100.00
Minang	99.42	0.07	0.35	0.13	0.01	0.01	100.00
Batak	26.92	0.27	64.11	8.55	0.02	0.13	100.00
Total[2]	80.72	8.90	7.38	2.46	0.37	0.17	100.00

Notes:
1. These are the five largest ethnic groups in the province of the Riau Archipelago.
2. "Total" refers to the total of population, including those outside the five largest groups.

Source: Calculated from the raw data of the Indonesian 2000 Population Census (Ananta 2006).

Concluding Remarks

It is not easy to define who ethnic Chinese are and even to estimate their number. This is one of the problems in producing the statistics on ethnic Chinese in Indonesia. Moreover, Indonesia is large and heterogeneous. So is the group of ethnic Chinese, whatever the definition and measurement. There has been a paucity of statistics on ethnicity, including ethnic Chinese, in Indonesia after the 1930 census. It is not surprising that, without any available statistics, all figures mentioned during discussions on ethnic Chinese in Indonesia were based on guesses or extrapolations from the 1930 data.

The breakthrough was made in the 2000 Population Census. The census was also the first with a 100 per cent enumeration, and a much better coverage and accuracy than earlier censuses. As in the 1930 Population Census, the 2000 Population Census also used the concept of self-identification — the ethnicity of a person is defined according to what the respondent said about herself/himself. Therefore, in these two censuses, a respondent is categorized as a Chinese if she/he said that she/he was a Chinese.

Suryadinata, Arifin, and Ananta (2003) is the first statistical study on ethnicity and ethnic Chinese in Indonesia, optimizing the availability of information on ethnicity in the 2000 Population Census. They worked from the thirty-one volumes of books published by Statistics Indonesia, and estimated that the percentage of ethnic Chinese was between 1.5 and 2.0 per cent, with a better estimate at 1.5 per cent, or 3.01 million people.

In this chapter, we have re-examined the statistics by working directly with the raw data of the 2000 Indonesian Population Census. We also used the raw data from the recent 2005 Indonesian Intercensal Population Survey to strengthen and sharpen our conclusions on the percentage of Chinese Indonesians in Indonesia in 2000, as well as to find out the figures in 2005. The results of our re-examination on the 2000 Population Census support and strengthen the earlier findings (Suryadinata, Arifin, and Ananta, 2003). We conclude that 2.0 per cent is certainly too high for the percentage of Chinese Indonesians in 2000. The percentage was at most 1.60 per cent in 2000. It could even be lower than 1.60 per cent. Furthermore, the percentage seemed to have declined during 2000–05, and the question is to what extent the decline has been. It may have declined to 1.18 per cent in 2005, and the number, from about 3.22 million in 2000 to about 2.57 million in 2005.

There were five determinants for the decline in the number of Chinese Indonesians in Indonesia during 2000–05. The first possibility is the relatively low level of fertility among Chinese Indonesians, particularly compared with other ethnic groups in Indonesia. We guess that their fertility was already below replacement level in early 1990s, and it may even have occurred earlier than 1990. The second possibility is a large outflow of Chinese Indonesians to other countries — for studying, working, or joining family members elsewhere. The third possibility is an underestimation in the 2005 statistics because the data-set was collected in a survey, not a census. The fourth possibility is a rising number of Chinese Indonesians who did not feel they were Chinese. The fifth is a combination of the first four possibilities.

With the raw data of the 2000 Indonesian Population Census, we also find that the percentage of Chinese Indonesians was much larger than those of two other foreign minorities, Indian and Arab Indonesians. The percentages of the two other foreign minorities were minuscule, much smaller than 1.0 per cent, especially for Indian Indonesians. Arab Indonesians were almost exclusively Muslims. On the other hand, only slightly more than half the Chinese Indonesians were Buddhists, and there was a substantial percentage of Christians among Chinese Indonesians. The distribution of religious followers among Indian Indonesians is the most equitable. Less than half the Indian Indonesians were Hindus, and there were relatively large percentages of Muslims, Buddhists, and Christian Indian Indonesians.

In this chapter, we have also examined the province of the Riau Archipelago as a case study so as to go deeper into the statistics on Chinese Indonesians, but we should always remember that the situation in the Riau Archipelago may not necessarily be the same as that in other provinces in Indonesia.

We have found out that Chinese Indonesians are not a small minority in the province. The Chinese was the third largest ethnic group, after the Malays — who was often said to be the "stakeholder" of the province of the Riau Archipelago and the neighbouring province of the Riau — and the Javanese, the largest ethnic group in Indonesia with Central Java, East Java, and Yogyakarta as their home provinces. The concentration of Chinese Indonesians was even higher in urban areas.

Furthermore, like for the Malays, Chinese Indonesians also had a high percentage of non-migrants. Most of them were born in the province of the Riau Archipelago or already lived in the province five years earlier. With migration as the criterion, Chinese Indonesians, like the Malays, may not be regarded as *pendatang* either in the province.

Chinese Indonesians in this province had a relatively low level of education. However, as the economy advances, the percentage of Chinese Indonesians, as well as Malays, may shrink. On the other hand, Chinese Indonesian migrants from other provinces may be and will be more educated although their numbers will not be large. As a result, the educational composition of Chinese Indonesians will change too. Chinese Indonesians in the province of the Riau Archipelago may become smaller in percentage, but may be higher in educational attainment as economic development progresses.

Finally, it can be noted in general that their low fertility rate — one of the lowest among all ethnic groups in Indonesia — may reflect a demographic trend of the general population in the world, where low fertility seems to be an irreversible process. This low fertility has endowed them with the opportunity to provide higher education to their children. Higher income, better transportation, and communication in the era of globalization and regionalization may have further resulted in the rising mobility of younger Chinese Indonesians around the world, enabling them to pursue advanced education and/or compete in the world market. Therefore, it will not be a surprise if future statistics show an increasing percentage of Chinese Indonesians living abroad, while maintaining their Indonesian citizenship and network. Can the government of Indonesia and the Indonesian society as a whole utilize this overseas Chinese Indonesian network for the benefit of developing Indonesia as a whole?

Notes

[1]   This is a revision of a paper presented at the seminar on "Ethnic Chinese in Indonesia in an Era of Globalisation", jointly organized by the Institute of Southeast Asian Studies, Chinese Heritage Centre, and NABIL Foundation, in Singapore on 19 July 2007. The authors would like to acknowledge the generous permission from Statistics Indonesia to work with the raw data of both the 2000 Indonesian Population Census and 2005 Intercensal Population Survey. The authors would also like to convey their appreciation to Leo Suryadinata, who had made the authors interested in the study of Chinese Indonesians. The authors also appreciate the Institute of Southeast Asian Studies, Singapore, and Statistics Indonesia, Indonesia, for providing the authors with a conducive academic environment to carry out this study. Special thanks goes to Hui Yew-Foong for his insightful comments on the draft of this paper. However, the authors have sole responsibility on all findings and any errors in this paper.

[2]   Some of them marry "indigenous people" and their children formed a confused generation in defining their own identity. Yet, this is a common phenomenon in mixed marriages. In many literatures on ethnic Chinese, there were two groups: the *peranakan* Chinese and the *totok* Chinese. Many ethnic Chinese who were born and grew up during Indonesia's New Order are Indonesian citizens having "Indonesian" names and speaking Bahasa Indonesia and even local languages. However, as argued by Chua 2004, it becomes irrelevant for most Chinese Indonesians to classify themselves as either *peranakan* or *totok*. Many of them

cannot define themselves in one of these categories as there is no strong basis to be either of these.

3   Some key elements of the new citizenship law in ending discriminatory elements include the revision of the definition of "indigenous Indonesian" to mean all citizens who have never assumed foreign citizenship, thus enabling Indonesian women to pass on their citizenship to their children born from mixed marriages (having foreign spouses) and allowing children of mixed marriages to hold dual citizenship until they reach age twenty-one. When the child turns eighteen, he or she has three years to choose one nationality. The law also enables foreign spouses to seek Indonesian citizenship after living in Indonesia for five consecutive years or ten accumulated years and entitles the spouse to permanent residency under the same conditions.

4   Chinese Indonesians refer to those Chinese with Indonesian citizenship. The term "ethnic Chinese in Indonesia" includes Chinese foreigners, Chinese Indonesians, and those China-born who grew up in Indonesia without a proper identity (stateless).

5   Cited and calculated from the Department van Economische Zaken 1936, Table 1.

6   The total number of the population of Indonesia successfully enumerated in the 2000 Population Census was 201,241,999 (Badan Pusat Statistik 2001). Due to internal conflicts in several areas such as Central Sulawesi, Maluku, North Maluku, and Papua, the census could not cover all areas in these provinces. In Aceh, an extremely difficult area, the census only covered 44.15 per cent of the population. Taking into account the unenumerated population, the Indonesia's population in 2000 was estimated to be about 205.8 million. The newest estimate of Indonesia's population, based on the 2005 Intercensal Population Survey, was 218,086,288 for the year 2005. <http://www.datastatistik-indonesia. com/component/option,com_tabel/task,/Itemid,165>.

7   "Ethnic Chinese Celebrate New Year Throughout Indonesia", *Xinhua Online*, *18 February 2007* <http://news.xinhuanet.com/english/2007-02/18/content_ 5753883.htm>.

8   There were thirty volumes, one for each province, and one volume for Indonesia.

9   This study was part of a larger project on "Ethnicity and Fertility in Southeast Asia" in five ASEAN countries: Indonesia, Malaysia, the Philippines, Singapore, and Thailand. Among other things, the study gathered important information such as religion, ethnic identification, and the relative importance of ethnic versus national identification among various ethnic groups. The study on Indonesia, cited in this paper, covered five ethnic groups (ethnic Chinese, Javanese, Sundanese, Bataks, and Minangkabaus) and five provinces (Jakarta, West Java, East Java, North Sumatra, and West Sumatra). As Chinese Indonesians typically lived in urban areas, the information on Chinese Indonesians was collected in four cities (Jakarta, Bandung, Surabaya, and Medan).

[10] They are Indonesian citizens. They may have lived in Indonesia for many generations and may even have considered Indonesia as their home. Yet, they are often called "foreign" simply because they do not have their "home territories", such as North Sumatra for the Bataks and West Sumatra for the Minangs. Furthermore, some of them may no longer identify themselves as Chinese, Indian, or Arab, but consider themselves as belonging to the local ethnic groups. Generally, however, there are four "foreign minorities" in Indonesia: the Chinese, Arabs, Indians, and Europeans (Bachtiar 1993).

[11] Calculated from the raw data of the 2000 Indonesian Population Census and 2005 Intercensal Population Survey. As is the case with Chinese Indonesians, the number and percentage of Indian and Arab Indonesians in 2005 may be slightly underestimated. The data for the year 2005 were collected in a sample, rather than in a census as was the case for the 2000 data. The statistics were also based on the concept of self-identification.

[12] Statistics Indonesia 2006*a*, Table 126.

[13] Statistics Indonesia 2006*b*, Table 76. The statistics for Indonesia as a whole are cited from Statistics Indonesia 2006*c*, Table 15.

[14] Cited and calculated from Statistics Indonesia 2006*c*, Table 5.

[15] The U.S. dollar equivalent is calculated assuming an exchange rate of 9,500 rupiah per U.S. dollar.

[16] See Ananta and Bakhtiar 2005 for some discussion on fertility and mortality in the districts in the province of the Riau Archipelago.

[17] See Ananta, Arifin, and Suryadinata 2004 for more discussion on the role of migrants in the districts in the Riau Archipelago and other provinces in Indonesia.

[18] Suryadinata, Arifin, and Ananta 2003.

Selected References

Ananta, Aris. "Changing Ethnic Composition Potential Violent Conflict in Riau Archipelago, Indonesia: An Early Warning Signal". *Population Review*, vol. 45, no. 1, 2006.

Ananta, Aris and Bakhtiar. "Who are 'the Lower Class' in Riau Archipelago, Indonesia?" Presented at the 6th Annual Population Researcher Conference on "Linkage between Population and Millennium Development Goals: The Asian Perspective". Conducted by the Population Association of Pakistan, Islamabad, Pakistan, 29 November 2005 to 1 December 2005.

Ananta, Aris and Evi Nurvidya Arifin. "Riau Archipelago (Kepri): How to Produce the Most with "Indonesia", the Region, and the World?" Presented at "Riau Roundtable 2007: Opportunities and Challenges in the Riau Archipelago and Riau Province", organized by S. Rajaratnam School of International Studies, Nanyang Technological University, Singapore, 27 June 2007.

Ananta, Aris, Evi Nurvidya Arifin, and Leo Suryadinata. *Indonesian Electoral Behaviour: A Statistical Perspective*. Singapore: Institute of Southeast Asian Studies, 2004.

————. *Indonesia's Population: Ethnicity and Religion in a Changing Political Landscape*. Singapore: Institute of Southeast Asian Studies, 2003.

Bachtiar, Harsja W. "Indians in Indonesia: A Component of Indonesian National Integration". In *Indian Communities in Southeast Asia*, edited by K.S. Sandhu and A. Mani. Singapore: Institute of Southeast Asian Studies and Times Academic Press, 1993.

Chua, Christian. "Defining Indonesian Chineseness Under the New Order". *Journal of Contemporary Asia*, vol. 34, 2004.

Coppel, Charles A. "Studying Ethnic Chinese in Indonesia". *Asian Studies Monograph Series* no. 7. Singapore: Singapore Society of Asian Studies, 2002.

Cribb, Robert and Colin Brown. *Modern Indonesia: A History since 1945*. London, United Kingdom: Longman Group Limited, 1995.

Department van Economische Zaken. *Census of the 1930 in the Netherlands Indies, Volume VIII. Summary of the Volumes I – VII*. Batavia, 1936.

Esmara, Hendra. "An Economic Survey of Riau". *Bulletin of Indonesian Economics Studies*, vol. 11, no. 3 (1975): 25–49.

Gunawan, Apriadi. "Kampung Keling: Economic Symbiosis in Medan's Chinese-Indian Enclave". *Jakarta Post* (no date) <http://www.thejakartapost.com/community/ina9.asp> (accessed 28 September 2007).

Hull, Terence H. "First Results from the 2000 Population Census". *Bulletin of Indonesian Economics Studies*, vol. 37, no. 1 (2001): 103–11.

Koning, Juliette. "On Being 'Chinese Overseas': The Case of Chinese Indonesian Entrepreneurs". Asia Research Centre, Copenhagen Discussion Papers 2006–5 <http://chinaworld.cbs.dk/cdp/paper/juliette.pdf>.

Mackie, Jackie. "How Many Chinese Indonesians". *Bulletin of Indonesian Economics Studies*, vol. 41, no. 1 (2005): 97–101.

Malik, Adam. *Yin-tu-ni-his-ya jih-pao*, 26 April 1973, as cited in Suryadinata, Arifin, and Ananta 2003, p. 73.

Mani, A. "Indians in North Sumatra". In *Indian Communities in Southeast Asia*, edited by K.S. Sandhu and A. Mani. Singapore: Institute of Southeast Asian Studies, 1st reprint, 2006.

Statistics Indonesia. *Gross Regional Domestic Product of Provinces in Indonesia by Expenditure 2001–2005*. Jakarta, 2006a.

————. *Gross Regional Domestic Product Regencies/Municipalities in Indonesia, 2001–2005*. Jakarta, 2006b.

————. *Gross Regional Domestic Product of Provinces in Indonesia, 2001–2005*. Jakarta, 2006c.

Surbakti, Sudarti, R. Lukito Praptoprijoko, and Satwiko Darmesto. "Indonesia's 2000 Population Census: A Recent National Statistics Activity". Presented at the Economics and Social Commission for Asia and the Pacific Committee on Statistics, Bangkok, 29 November to 1 December 2000.

Suryadinata, Leo. *Pribumi Indonesians, the Chinese Minority and China: A Study of Perceptions and Policies*. Singapore: Heinemann Asia, 1978.

Tan, Mely G. and Budy Soeradji. *Ethnicity and Fertility in Indonesia*. Singapore: Institute of Southeast Asian Studies, 1986.

Turner, Sarah. "Speaking Out: Chinese Indonesians After Suharto". *Asian Ethnicity*, vol. 4, no. 3 (2003): 337–52.

Turner, Sarah and Pamela Allen. "Chinese Indonesians in a Rapidly Changing Nation: Pressures of Ethnicity and Identity". *Asia Pacific Viewpoint*, vol. 48, no. 1 (2007): 112–27.

Volkstelling 1930. Census of 1930 in the Netherlands Indies. Published in 1936. Call number: SCRfhA4601.5 D97

3

INDONESIAN GOVERNMENT POLICIES AND THE ETHNIC CHINESE: SOME RECENT DEVELOPMENTS

Eddie Lembong

This chapter aims to examine Indonesian government policies towards ethnic Chinese with special reference to recent and new developments. However, as Wang Gungwu has noted in one of his books, "[I]t is not really possible to understand what seems to be new, without reference to the past."[1] I shall thus present a historical background before discussing the various government policies.

PRE-COLONIAL AND COLONIAL PERIODS: THE ORIGINS OF THE ETHNIC TENSION

The Chinese had arrived in Southeast Asia in general and in Indonesia in particular long before the coming of the Western powers. Some of them were Muslims, and their numbers began to increase in the fifteenth century, coinciding with the seven voyages (1405–32) of Admiral Zheng He. These Chinese Muslims posed no problems for the Indonesian population as they were able to assimilate into the local communities.[2]

However, the position of the Chinese began to change after the coming of the West, especially after the Dutch had established their colonial rule.

The Dutch divided the inhabitants in the Dutch East Indies (colonial Indonesia) into at least three racial groups: Europeans (particularly Dutch), foreign orientals (particularly Chinese), and the indigenous people. These different racial groups played different economic roles. The Dutch were in the wholesale business, the Chinese in intermediary trade (acting as middlemen), while members of the indigenous population were farmers and small traders.[3]

In fact, the Dutch introduced this "*Divide et Imperia*" (divide and rule) policy to bolster their colonial rule. They feared that if there was racial unity between the indigenous people and the Chinese, it would threaten and even put an end to their colonial rule.

The separateness of the Chinese from other racial/ethnic groups in colonial Indonesia was a fact of life.[4] However, the Chinese themselves were divided into at least the *singkeh* (*totok*) and *peranakan* (local-born with mixed blood). The rise of Chinese nationalism in the early twentieth century also resulted in the reorientation of the Chinese in Indonesia towards China. Modern Chinese schools were set up and many ethnic Chinese children began to learn the Chinese language and Chinese culture. The Tiong Hoa Hwee Koan (THHK) movement, often known as a pan-Chinese movement, broke out in the Dutch East Indies.[5] The Dutch authorities attempted to suppress this "overseas Chinese nationalism" by introducing the Dutch citizenship law and establishing Dutch and native schools for Chinese children.[6] Politically and culturally, the Chinese in colonial Indonesia were divided.

Under the Japanese Occupation of Indonesia (1942–45), new policies impacted the Chinese when the new rulers treated them as one population. No Dutch schools were allowed and all Chinese children were forced to learn Japanese and Chinese.[7] As such, *peranakan* Chinese children were put through a "resinicization" process.

In August 1945, Japan surrendered. The Dutch returned intending to reinstate colonial rule to the whole of Dutch East Indies. However, Indonesian nationalists refused to accept the Dutch. When clashes took place between the indigenous Indonesians and the Dutch, the Chinese were caught in the middle.

Under colonial rule, the Chinese gradually developed into a trading minority placed between the Dutch and the indigenous population. They were often perceived by the indigenous population as "economic creatures" and politically closer to the Dutch than to the indigenous population. During the Indonesian revolution (1945–50), the Dutch authorities purposely created the impression that the Chinese were on their side and against Indonesia's independence, thus inciting hatred among the indigenous people towards the ethnic Chinese. A series of anti-Chinese incidents erupted. In fact, the situation was much more complicated. The Chinese were not a homogeneous group, and many sided with the indigenous population.

INDEPENDENT INDONESIA: GOVERNMENT POLICIES AND ANTI-CHINESE VIOLENCE

The Soekarno Period (1950–65): Early Discriminatory Policies

If the ethnic Chinese were heterogeneous prior to Indonesia's independence, they were equally divided culturally and economically after Indonesia became independent. Nevertheless, it appears that, in general, the economic strength of the Chinese minority remained strong, if not stronger. As the young republic gradually focused on nation building, it was undecided on its policy towards the Chinese. On one hand, the new government intended to include ethnic Chinese in the nation building process. On the other hand, it introduced discriminatory measures, especially in the economic field, against the ethnic Chinese minority. The most conspicuous were two government regulations which brought about a major impact on Indonesia's political economy. One was the so-called *Benteng* (Castle) System introduced in the early 1950s, which prohibited Chinese Indonesians from engaging in the import-export business. This resulted in the emergence of the "Ali Baba" system in which Chinese Indonesians used indigenous Indonesians as "front men" or "sleeping partners". The other was the Presidential Decree no. 10 passed in 1959 which prohibited Chinese Indonesians from engaging in retail trade in rural areas. The regulations led to an exodus of the Chinese from the country, crippling the Indonesian economy. These two measures were, however, not successful in undermining the economic strength of the ethnic Chinese.[8]

Many indigenous leaders who envied the economic status of the ethnic Chinese also organized campaigns against the latter. One of the most well known was led by Assaat, a former republican leader turned businessman.[9] The circumstances were complicated by the Cold War situation in which the Western and the Communist camps were at odds with each other. The Chinese Indonesians were often perceived as and accused of being the "proxy" of Communist China. Indeed much anti-Chinese violence (including riots) during this period was politically motivated; they were also a manifestation of discontent with this minority group.

The Soeharto Period (1966–98)

In 1966, General Soeharto became the new leader of Indonesia and went on to rule the country for the next thirty-two years. Soekarno, who was anti-colonialist, was eventually overthrown by the pro-Western Indonesian military. The PKI was also eliminated in the struggle for hegemony in Indonesian politics.

There were two dimensions in Soekarno's policy towards ethnic Chinese: cultural and politico-economic. Culturally, he introduced the total assimilation policy by eliminating the three pillars of Chinese culture, that is, Chinese schools, Chinese organizations, and the Chinese media. Economically, he tolerated Chinese economic activities. This was related to his overall strategy of promoting economic growth and development in Indonesia in order to legitimize his rule. Accordingly, he opened up Indonesia and implemented a pro-business policy. Chinese Indonesians were deemed useful in the economic field and were confined to this field as Soekarno was suspicious of the ethnic Chinese politically. Thus, Chinese Indonesians were discriminated against politically while they enjoyed economic freedom. The unintended result of this policy was that the economic strength of Chinese Indonesians increased. At the same time, they were politically very vulnerable and their security was in the hands of the indigenous rulers. Anti-Chinese incidents occasionally occurred, but most of them were on a small scale.

The economic crisis of 1997 led to turmoil the following year. Large scale — some of which were engineered — anti-Chinese violence erupted in Jakarta, Solo, and other major Indonesian cities.[10] The difference between the May 1998 violence and other anti-Chinese riots is that this time there was not only looting, killing, and arson, but also the systematic raping of Chinese women. The violence was politically motivated and in some ways linked to power struggle; it left a dark page in the history of Indonesia.

The situation deteriorated after the May 1998 riots and Soeharto was eventually forced to step down, leaving his position to his deputy, Habibie, who led the first government in the post-Soeharto period.

The Reform Era: Changing Policies and Improved Position of the Ethnic Chinese (1998–Present)

The post-Soeharto era has coincided with changes in the international arena. Globalization and democratization have taken place affecting Indonesia and much of the rest of the world. The image of China has also changed. It is no longer seen as a country which exports "revolution", but one which favours the *status quo*.

It should be noted that the Cold War ended around 1989 and 1990, and the Communist ideology has not been a problem in Indonesia-China relations since. Even during the latter part of the Soeharto era, Sino-Indonesian relations began to improve, but his fall from power has speeded up the process of good relations.

The rise of China as an economic power has also had an impact not only on Southeast Asia, but also the world at large. The economic power of China can no longer be ignored while Chinese "soft power" has been welcomed by and large.

In Indonesia, democratization has taken place. There has also been the gradual and fundamental improvement in the legal and political status of Chinese Indonesians. Such improvements are related to the changing domestic and international situations as stated earlier. The new governments have realized that in order to bring about improvement in economic conditions in Indonesia, the participation of ethnic Chinese is crucial.

Post-Soeharto Indonesian governments have introduced many policies that favour Chinese Indonesians. It will be useful if we take a look at these policies.

Habibie Presidency

President Habibie issued the Presidential Instruction no. 26/1998, which revoked the use of *pribumi* (indigenous people) and *non-pribumi* (non-indigenous people) terminology. During the Soeharto period, the terms were used freely in the press to refer to "indigenous Indonesians" and "Chinese Indonesians" respectively, at a time when government regulations favoured the indigenous population.

Abdurrahman Wahid (GUS DUR) Presidency

Habibie was replaced by Abdurrahman Wahid (Gus Dur) in the 1999 general election. During his administration, Gus Dur issued the Presidential Decree no. 6/2000, which abrogated the notorious Presidential Instruction no. 14/1967 issued by the Soeharto administration. The 1967 Act prohibited the practice of Chinese religions and customs in public places. The abolition of this decree paved the way for Chinese Indonesians to revive their traditional cultures.

In 2000, Gus Dur also declared Lunar New Year an optional public holiday. During the Soeharto era, the Lunar New Year was not celebrated.

The Chinese were prohibited from celebrating it publicly. Chinese shops were not permitted to close for the Lunar New Year.

Megawati Presidency

Gus Dur did not finish his term and was replaced by his deputy, Megawati Sukarnoputri. Megawati declared Lunar New Year a national public holiday, effective from 2 February 2003. This policy has not been changed in the following administration.

SBY Presidency

In 2004, Susilo Bambang Yudhoyono (SBY) was elected the new president. During his administration, two important laws have been promulgated. One is Law no. 12/2006 on Indonesian citizenship; the other is Law no. 23/2006 regarding civil registration. Dr Frans Hendra Winarta has discussed these laws in detail in his chapter which is included in this book. Here I would like to mention briefly that the new citizenship law has adopted the democratic principle, while the civil registration law has introduced the concept of using a national, rather than ethnic, basis for the registration of Indonesian citizens.

The developments during the Reform Era have been very encouraging. Various governments have adopted a democratic and multicultural approach in addressing the ethnic Chinese issue with a view to making Indonesia more prosperous. I personally believe that multiculturalism will benefit Indonesia through cross-cultural fertilization.

Indeed, Chinese culture in Indonesia has begun to revive in the post-Soeharto era as evidenced by the restoration of the three pillars of Chinese culture. Let us look at these pillars briefly…

RESTORATION OF THE THREE PILLARS OF CHINESE CULTURE

Media

The Reform Era has brought about a new beginning for the Chinese media. There has been a re-emergence of no fewer than eight Chinese-language newspapers such as *Guoji Ribao*, *Shang Bao*, etc. However, almost half have closed down due to a lack of advertisement and readership. For a detailed description of the Chinese media, see Dr Aimee Dawis' chapter in this book.

It is also worth noting that there has been a revival of Chinese-language radio, and an emergence of TV broadcast in Mandarin such as *Metro Xinwen* in Jakarta.

Chinese Education

Pre-New Order Chinese schools have not been re-established, but new bilingual and trilingual schools have been set up. The teaching of Mandarin in various schools is permitted, giving the impression that there is a renaissance of Chinese culture. For a detailed discussion on Chinese education, see Aimee Dawis' chapter.

Ethnic Chinese Organizations[11]

Chinese communities have also made use of the democratic environment to form ethnic Chinese political parties such as Partai Reformasi Tionghoa Indonesia (Parti) and Partai Bhinneka Tunggal Ika Indonesi (PBI), although they are currently dormant.

It appears that Chinese Indonesians prefer to join the indigenous Indonesian-dominated political parties to ethnic Chinese parties. They are much more forthcoming in joining Chinese social and cultural organizations, however. Some believe that there are at least 400 such organizations, including those based on province/district (either in China or Indonesia), clan/kinship/surnames, Chinese religions, hobbies, and alumni. Nevertheless, most of these organizations are local in nature, except for two which are national, viz. Paguyuban Sosial Marga Tionghoa Indonesia (PSMTI) and Perhimpunan Indonesia Tionghoa (INTI, initially known as Perhimpunan Indonesia Keturunan Tionghoa).

Business Organizations

Chinese businessmen have also formed their own organizations after the fall of Soeharto. There are at least four business organizations which are either dominated by Chinese Indonesians or have strong participation of Chinese Indonesians. These are: (1) Institute of Indonesia-China Economic Social and Cultural Cooperation (LIC); (2) Indonesian Chamber of Commerce and Industry: China Committee (KIKT); (3) Chinese Indonesian Entrepreneurs Association (PERPIT); and (4) Indonesia-China Business Council (ICBC).

The emergence of these business organizations coincided with the end of the Cold War and the advent of globalization. Both the domestic situation and international environment have made such developments possible. Unlike during the Soeharto period when building economic relations with, and investing in, China were often considered to be detrimental to the interests of Jakarta, doing business in China is now perceived as beneficial to both sides. These business organizations have indeed contributed to the rapid development of economic relations between Indonesia and China.

Concluding Remarks

It is clear that Indonesian government policies towards the ethnic Chinese have seen much change since the attainment of independence.

In the past, many laws and regulations did not favour Chinese Indonesians. However, the fall of Soeharto and the period of *reformasi* have brought many reforms — political, cultural, and legal — which have benefited Chinese Indonesians.

Chinese Indonesians are no longer forced to be assimilated; they are able to retain their ethnic culture and identity, but are expected to integrate into a larger Indonesian society. Such an improved environment will continue to be an incentive for Chinese Indonesians to work towards a better Indonesia.

Notes

[1]   Wang Gungwu, *China and the Chinese Overseas* (Singapore: Times Academic Press, 1991), p. vii.
[2]   Chen Dasheng (Tan Ta Sen), "Zheng He, Dongnanya De Huijiao Yu 'San Bao Long Ji Jing Li Wen Biannianshi'" (Zheng He, Southeast Asian Muslims, and 'Semarang and Cirebon Malay Annals'), in *Zheng He yu Dongnanya* (Zheng He and Southeast Asia), edited by Liao Jianyu (Leo Suryadinata), (Singapore International Zheng He Society, 2005), pp. 52–83; Sumanto Al Qurtuby, *Arus Cina-Islam-Jawa: Bongkar Sejarah atas Peranan Tionghoa dalam Penyebaran Agama Islam di Nusantara abad XV and XVI* (Yogyakarta: Inspeal Ahimsakarya Press, 2003).
[3]   W.F. Wertheim, "Social Change in Java, 1900–1930", in *East-West Parallels* (The Hague: W. Van Hoeve Ltd., 1964), pp. 211–37.
[4]   Lea E. Williams, *Overseas Chinese Nationalism: The Genesis of the Pan-Chinese Movement in Indonesia, 1900–1916* (Glencoe: Free Press, 1960), pp. 13–16.
[5]   Ibid., pp. 54–113.
[6]   William Skinner, "Java's Chinese Minority: Continuity and Change", *Journal of Asian Studies* 20, no. 3 (1961): 353–62.

[7] Li Quanshou (Lie Tjwan Sioe), "Yindunixiya Huaqiao Jiaoyu Shi" (History of Overseas Chinese Education in Indonesia), *Nanyang Xuebao* 15, no. 1–2, 1959.

[8] For a brief discussion on these two regulations, see Leo Suryadinata, *Indigenous Indonesians, the Chinese Minority and China: A Study of Perceptions and Policies* (Kuala Lumpur and London: Heinemann Asia, 1978), pp. 129–53.

[9] For the Assaat movement, see Leo Suryadinata, *Pribumi Indonesians, the Chinese Minority and China: A Study of Perceptions and Policies* (Kuala Lumpur, Singapore and London: Heinamann Asia, 1978), pp. 25–28.

[10] There are many publications on the May 1998 anti-Chinese violence, e.g. Jemma Purdey, *Anti-Chinese Violence in Indonesia 1996–1999* (National University Press of Singapore, 2006); *Kerusuhan Mei 1998: Fakta, Data and Analisa: Mengungkap Kerusuhan Mei 1998 Sebagai Kejahatan Terhadap Kemanusiaan* (Jakarta: Solidaritas Nusa Bangsa (SNB) dan Asosiasi Penasehat Hukum dan Hak Asasi Manusia Indonesia, 2007).

[11] For a brief discussion on ethnic Chinese organizations after the fall of Soeharto, see Leo Suryadinata, "Resurgence of Ethnic Chinese Identity in Post-Suharto's Indonesia: Some Reflections", *Asian Culture* 31, June 2007.

4

NO MORE DISCRIMINATION AGAINST THE CHINESE

Frans H. Winarta

THE HISTORY OF DISCRIMINATION AGAINST THE CHINESE

The Dutch Government Era

Indonesia did not have regulations of citizenship during the Dutch colonization period that started with the establishment of the old Dutch Association of East Indies Company (*Vereenigde Oostindische Compagnie or VOC*) in 1815. The population then was not classified into "indigenous people" and "foreigners", but according to physical appearances and other criteria such as, for example, a VOC official (*compagniesdienaren*), a freeman, or a slave. Another classification was based on religion such as "Christian" (*christenen*) or "non-Christian" (*onchristenen blinde heidenen*). The race or ethnicity of a person was acknowledged, but without distinctions made, for example, a Chinese was entitled to declare himself a Chinese at that time.

This segregation policy started when the government of the Netherlands-Indies took over the colony from the VOC. The segregation problem and its negative consequences which are being seen nowadays are due to the "divide and conquer" policy inherited from the Netherlands-Indies that was effected through the issuance of the 163 Netherlands-Indies State Regulation (*Indische Staatsregelling*), dated 2 September 1854, Ned. S. 154–2, S. 1855–2 jo. 1, which segregated the population into three groups: (1) Europeans; (2) Foreign Orientals such as the Chinese, Indians, Arabs; and (3) the indigenous.[1] The segregation policy was also found in Civil Registration, such as State Regulation 1849–25 of year 1849, regarding Civil Registration for Europeans; State Regulation 1917–130 of year 1917, regarding Civil Registration for Chinese Foreign Easterners; State Regulation 1920–751 of year 1920 concerning Civil Registration for Muslim Indigenous People; and State Regulation 1933–75 of year 1933 on Civil Registration for Christian Indigenous People.

This segregation policy was introduced by the Netherlands-Indies Government, which gave the Europeans the highest status and distinguished rights to the best facilities in society. The Chinese were recognized at that time as Foreign Orientals (*vreemde oosterlingen*) who were inferior to the Europeans. The Indigenous People (*inlander*) were given the lowest status, with the exception of the royal family who shared the same status as the Europeans. Such segregation aligned with the "divide and conquer" policy of the Netherlands-Indies Government.[2]

The Netherlands-Indies Government believed that they would be threatened if the indigenous people joined the Chinese to oppose the government.[3] Thus, the population was segregated into three groups, each differing in role and economic conditions. The government was then able to apply the "divide and conquer" principle to the indigenous people and the Chinese, causing distrust which generated constant hatred between them.

The indigenous people considered this unjust and were jealous and angry. Not only did the segregation policy make them suspicious, but the process of segregation and the growing prejudice were intentionally created by the Netherlands-Indies Government. This condition has persisted until now.

During this period, the *peranakan* Chinese were segregated into two political groups: the first group was the *Chung Hwa Hui* (CHH), which supported the Dutch Colonial Government;[4] the second group was the Partai Tionghoa Indonesia (PTI), which supported the Indonesian Independence Movement.[5] Some of their prominent figures fought together with other non-Indonesian Chinese leaders for the independence of Indonesia. However, this fact has been ignored by Indonesian society and historians.[6]

The Japanese Government Era

The "divide and rule" policy against the Chinese continued into the Japanese Occupation during the Second World War (WWII). The Japanese had deliberately forced and segregated the Chinese, forcing them to study in a particular school established for them which used the Chinese language in the classroom.[7] Furthermore, they were forced to speak Chinese outside school. Some of them were recruited by the Japanese for espionage, which worsened the image of Chinese Indonesians because they were accused of collaborating with the vicious Japanese against the indigenous people.

The Chinese were having difficulties and hesitated to determine their future as citizens. Some of them believed they were foreigners although they had settled in Indonesia as they had experienced segregation during the Dutch and Japanese colonial periods. Although, they had settled in Indonesia, their status was unclear. They also had emotional ties with what they considered their motherland, China. Liem Koen Hian, the founder of PTI, said that although they were physically Chinese, their culture was Indonesian, and their position would always remain unclear so long as the situation did not change.[8] The uncertainty is particularly obvious in politics.

Post-Independence

The proclamation of the Republic of Indonesia was considered a watershed in the pillar of the Indonesian history and an important moment for the people of the Republic of Indonesia because it states that the people of Indonesia have common ground and the same fate. It is the declaration of a nation state,[9] expressed by the symbol of the state, with the motto of Unity in Diversity (*Bhinneka Tunggal Ika*), in which the various attributes of the people of Indonesia, such as ethnicity, race, descent, religion, sociocultural and economic backgrounds are acknowledged.

The ramifications of the "divide and rule" policy have been deeply rooted in society and inadvertently strengthened by a bilateral agreement signed on 22 April 1955 with the People's Republic of China (PRC) during the Soekarno period. In this agreement, Indonesia was represented by Foreign Minister Soenaryo and the PRC was represented by Foreign Minister Chou En Lai (Zhou Enlai). This bilateral agreement was followed up with Law no. 2 of year 1958, which dealt with the agreement between the Republic of Indonesia and the PRC on dual citizenship. The most important result of this bilateral agreement was that all local-born Chinese Indonesias must declare whether they wanted to become an Indonesian citizen or a PRC citizen. The option was provided by the Government of the Republic of Indonesia because Indonesia adopted a single-citizenship principle.

The Chinese Indonesians were divided into two groups: those who selected to become Indonesian citizens and those who wanted to be PRC citizens. Those who selected Indonesian citizenship were mostly *peranakan*

Chinese and those who selected the PRC citizenship were mostly *totok* Chinese. However, the *totok* Chinese were divided into pro-Communist/PRC and pro-Kuomintang/Republic of China Taiwan (ROC) groups. Those who were pro-Kuomintang usually became stateless.

Nevertheless, under the Soekarno government, a number of Indonesian Chinese ministers were present in the cabinet. Among them were Tan Kim Liong (Minister of Revenue, Expenditure, and Supervision), Oei Tjoe Tat (Minister of State), and David G. Cheng (Minister of Housing, Planning, and Urban Development).

During this era, there were also two prominent Indonesian Chinese figures, Siauw Giok Tjan ("Siauw") and Yap Thiam Hien ("Yap").[10] Both of them joined the Indonesian Citizenship Consultative Body (also known as "Baperki"). Baperki was established in 1954 with the objective of gaining equality for Chinese Indonesians throughout Indonesia. However, Siauw refused to acknowledge that Baperki only fought for the survival of the Chinese Indonesians.[11]

Baperki participated in the 1955 election to vote for members of parliament (29 September 1955) and members of *konstituante* (15 December 1955). In those two elections, Baperki gained 178,887 votes for the Member of Parliament and 160,456 votes for the member of *konstituante*, or 70 per cent votes from all Chinese Indonesians in Java. With those votes, Baperki managed to gain one seat in parliament and appointed Siauw as its representative. In *konstituante*, Baperki was represented by Siauw, Oei Tjoe Tat, Yap, Go Gien Tjwan, Liem Koen Seng, Oei Poo Djiang, Jan Ave, and C.S. Richter. The last two were representatives of Baperki representing the Eurasians.[12]

Despite the struggle for minorities' rights by Siauw and Yap from the same organization, they had different visions on how best to represent the *peranakan* Tionghoa minority, according to the political principles of the Indonesian state. Siauw chose to support President Soekarno, and for that he consistently brought Baperki along to support the president and the Indonesian Communist Party (PKI). Yap, however, worked on the basis of the jurisdicial assumption that people are less promising than sound institutions and legal processes. He insisted that the best hope for the security Indonesia and its Chinese minority rested in effective laws, which required the constitution to be taken more seriously than political figures.[13]

Yap resigned as Vice-Chairman of Baperki after the Baperki Congress in Semarang in December 1960. Yap's resignation generated the debate on the differences between Yap and Siauw, one of which was the debate over Article 6 of the 1945 Constitution (1945 Constitution before amendment).

Yap argued that it was very discriminatory, but Siauw and the others in the organization tried to defuse the issue by pushing it aside. The other debate between the two was about how integration should be done. Yap disagreed with the pro-assimilationist idea that recommended the *peranakans* to change their names into "Indonesian" names. Yap argued that while the name-changing issue was sound and enforceable, it would not achieve the assimilation goal. Assimilation of a minority into a "dominant group" could not possibly be achieved if only the minority wished it to happen and when its objective was rejected by the "dominant group". Yap argued that it was the right of every person from every tribe to be acknowledged and respected for his/her identity (amalgamation). People or group should not be erased (literally) due to a dislike for the group for any reason at all. Integration was the answer for getting rid of the differences between the majority and minority groups — and all groups in Indonesia are given equal treatment as human beings and citizens, without regard to their race, culture, and religion.[14]

After the 30 September 1965 tragedy, Baperki was banned by the New Order regime because it was accused of being involved as the *onderbouw* of the Indonesian Communist Party. Many Baperki's leaders such as Siauw Giok Tjan and Oei Tjoe Tat were sent to prison without any court trial.

The Era of The New Order

The "divide and rule" policy introduced by the Netherlands-Indies colonial government was also applied by the New Order to segregate Indonesian people such as Javanese and non-Javanese, Muslims and non-Muslims, the military and civilians, the majority group and minorities, the indigenous and non-indigenous, West and East Indonesians, and so forth. Such a segregation method reflects the practice of racial, cultural, economic, and political discrimination against various ethnic groups in Indonesia, that fits with the definition of racial discrimination according to the International Convention on the Elimination of All Forms of Racial Discrimination[15] as stated below:

> ... shall mean any distinction, exclusion, restriction, or preference based on race, color, descent, or national or ethnic origin which has the purpose or effect of nullifying or impairing the recognition, enjoyment, or exercise, on an equal footing, of human rights and fundamental freedoms in the political, economic, social, cultural or any other field of public life.

The New Order used the regulations as an instrument to discriminate against ethnic Chinese in Indonesia. The New Order regime systematically and consistently limited, pressed, and crushed the political rights of ethnic Chinese by promulgating discriminative policies in order to expel ethnic Chinese from Indonesia or turn them into an apolitical community with no effective representation in the government or in parliament. This policy was supported by the military who were anti-communist and regarded ethnic Chinese as a group prone to sympathizing with the Communists.

Charles Coppel, in his book titled, *Indonesian Chinese in Crisis*, has argued that the Chinese Indonesians are in a dilemma in the area of politics. If they get involved in opposition politics, they will be branded subversive; if they support the power holder, they will be branded opportunists; and if they stay away from politics, they will equally be branded opportunists because they will be accused of looking only to gain profit.[16]

Besides that, in the New Order era, violence against Chinese Indonesians was widespread, starting from Medan to Makassar. The violence in Java had been increasing both in number of cases and intensity, and culminated in the 13–14 May 1998 incident in Jakarta. Although the New Order applied an anti-Chinese/PRC policy, in their efforts to build a crucial sector in the economy, the ethnic Chinese were given significant roles and opportunities. Furthermore, many became cronies of the authorities who were engaged in *KKN* (Corruption, Collusion, and Nepotism) in order to build their businesses. This has resulted in ethnic Chinese being seen as *"srigala ekonomi"* (economic wolves) and criminals.

Under the New Order, at least sixty-four discriminating regulations against ethnic Chinese were still enforced or newly issued. The following shows some of them:

1. Government Regulation no. 10, Year 1959, on foreign small businessmen and retailers in region of Level I and Level II and prefectures, which prevents ethnic Chinese from doing business in the regions;
2. Presidential Instruction no. 14, Year 1967, on Religion, Faith, and Chinese Culture;
3. Cabinet Presidium Decree no. 127/U/Kep/12/1966 on the regulation to change the names of Indonesian citizens with Chinese names;
4. Decree of The People's Consultative Assembly no. XXVII/MPRS/1966 on religion, education, and culture, which prohibits Chinese Tao worshipping in public, and bans Chinese education and characters;
5. Cabinet Presidium Instruction no. 49/U/8/1967 on the utilization of the Chinese language in Mass Media.

These regulations clearly suppressed the sociocultural life of ethnic Chinese by prohibiting the usage of Chinese characters and the Chinese language and banning Chinese newspapers, closing Chinese schools, changing Chinese names, limiting the celebration of the Lunar New Year, restricting Tao worship to the temples and Capgome festival (15th day of first lunar month), and promoting the use of the derogatory term "Cina" to humiliate ethnic Chinese. Everything related to ethnic Chinese and the Chinese culture was considered bad and had to be avoided. This policy also aimed at eliminating the affinity of the Chinese towards recognizing China as their homeland.* The question is how Chinese cultural elements could be avoided, when the acculturation of the Chinese had started a long time before the Dutch arrived in Indonesia? Local Betawi, Cirebon, and Balinese cultures have been influenced by the Chinese culture.

Besides, under the New Order, marriages of *Kong Hu Cu* (Confucian) believers were not recognized by the state because officially only five religions were admitted by the state: Islam, Catholicism, Christianity, Hinduism, and Buddhism. The prohibition of the learning and use of the Chinese language, Tao worship, and the "compulsory" change of Chinese names into Indonesian names, and other restrictions imposed on the expression of the Chinese culture were clearly a violation of human rights by the state against individuals, particularly with respect to their cultural rights. It can be considered cultural genocide[17] against the Chinese and their culture. Concurrently, the same was true in reverse when ethnic Chinese businessmen were given privileges to form business conglomerates in various sectors without regard to the fact that they had been accused of being the cause of poverty in Indonesia.[18] The Chinese were and are just regarded as opportunists who only want to gain profit and be close to the power holder in order to obtain privileges.

The institutionalization of SBKRI (Certificate for Citizenship), which is discriminative in nature, happened during the New Order government. The certificate was originally meant for naturalizing foreigners, but was manipulated to discriminate against the Chinese Indonesians. Regardless of the background of the policy, Soeharto, at the beginning of the New Order era, issued a Presidential Decree no. 240, Year 1967, followed by a more discriminative new policy on SBKRI, that was regulated in the Minister for Justice Decree no. JB3/4/12, Year 1978, in conjunction with Joint Decree of the Minister for Justice and Minister for Home Affairs

---

* The meaning is slightly changed here because not all Chinese saw China as their homeland but the non-Chinese perceived this to be the case.

no. M.01-UM.09.03.80 and no. 42, Year 1980. The purpose of the Ministerial Decree and the Joint Decree was to implement the Presidential Decree no. 52, Year 1977, for the Registration of Citizens.

The agreement between Soenaryo and Chou En Lai on double citizenship in 1958 was revoked on 10 April 1969, through Law no. 4, Year 1969, on Agreement between Republic of Indonesia and PRC on dual citizenship, which stipulates that children of Chinese Indonesians born before 20 January 1962 cannot elect any other citizenship except Indonesian citizenship. As such, Chinese Indonesians born after 20 January 1962 did not need to prove their citizenship with SBKRI. The SBKRI was only valid for the naturalization of Indonesian citizens of Chinese decent who had not become Indonesian citizens, or did not possess dual citizenship. This again strengthens the reason ethnic Chinese now do not need SBKRI to prove that they are Indonesian citizens. Meanwhile, the SBKRI in practice remains the same, but it is still needed by immigration authorities.

The SBKRI has been an ongoing problem for Chinese Indonesians. In reality, it has been misinterpreted and applied only for Chinese Indonesians. It is important to note that if the New Order government at that time had the right understanding about citizenship, there would be no problem in applying SBKRI, which to this day, is only targeted at Chinese Indonesians. Many aspects of life, such as legal interests, economical interests, and the application of citizenship, have been hampered because of the SBKRI. This regulation has clearly violated the 1945 Constitution which guarantees equality before the law, such as equal treatment, rights, and obligations. Every citizen, without exception, is equal before the law. In other words, SBKRI is another form of apartheid (segregation) or state racial discrimination, expressed in legal products and customs that are legally executed.[19] On top of that, SBKRI is also a target of blackmail and corruption. Bureaucrats and civil servants constantly, shamelessly, and openly ask for bribes from Chinese Indonesians who cannot present their SBKRI. The SBKRI has become a means for profiting for every government department and especially the department that issues the document.[20] This is detrimental to the reputation of Indonesia.

Reformation Era

At the beginning of the Reformation era, the government acknowledged that the paradigm to corner the Chinese Indonesians from time to time must be abolished from the mindset of all Indonesian people. This was evident in the revocation of various policies which were discriminative against ethnic Chinese in Indonesia, some of which are shown:

1. Presidential Decree no. 56, Year 1996, on the Certificate of Citizenship of Indonesia (in fact this decree was issued at the end of Soeharto era, but was not implemented);

2. Presidential Decree no. 6, Year 2000, on the Revocation of Presidential Instruction no. 14, Year 1967, on Chinese religion, Chinese beliefs, and Chinese customs;

3. Presidential Instruction no. 26, Year 1998, on Revocation of the termination of *Pribumi* and Non-*Pribumi*;

4. Circulation Letter of the Minister of Home Affairs no. 471.2/1265/SJ dated 18 June 2002 on the Certificate of Citizenship of Indonesia;

5. Circulation Letter of the Directorate-General of Immigration of the Department of Justice and Human Rights no. P.U.M. 01.10.0626, dated 14 April 2004 on SBKRI for the Application of a Passport of the Republic of Indonesia;

6. Presidential Decree no. 19, Year 2002, on the Decision about Lunar New Year as a National Day.

It is not an easy task for the government in the Reformation era to strengthen the integrity of the nation and uphold democracy and human rights. Although the government has issued policies to revoke the discriminative decrees against the Chinese in Indonesia, discrimination still exists in practice. The prerequisites to present SBKRI in applying for passports and identity cards and the discriminating treatment of marriages of Confucian followers are some examples.

Besides, some of the discriminative regulations are still valid and have not been revoked by the government. One of the regulations regarding citizenship and population affairs, such as the regulation on civil registration enacted during the Netherlands-Indies era, that is, State Gazette 1849–25, Year 1849, on Civil Registration for Europeans; State Gazette 1917–130, Year 1917, on Civil Registration for Foreign Orientals of Chinese Decent; State Gazette 1920–751, Year 1920, on Civil Registration for Muslim Indigenous Indonesians; and State Gazette 1933–75, Year 1933, on Civil Registration for Christian Indigenous Indonesians, are still valid and applied by the Civil Registration Office all over Indonesia in issuing birth and death certificates, and marriage and divorce certificates. That is why the efforts to eliminate discriminatory treatment will not be sufficient only by revoking the discriminative regulations of the SBKRI, but also by reviewing other regulations such as civil registration, application of passports, and other formal documents in the administration of the population.

A REVOLUTIONARY LAW ON INDONESIAN CITIZENSHIP TO ELIMINATE ALL FORMS OF DISCRIMINATION AGAINST ETHNIC CHINESE

Since the Independence of the Republic of Indonesia, all matters concerning citizenship are provisioned in Law no. 3, Year 1946, on Citizenship and Population of Indonesia. This particular law was replaced by Law no. 6, Year 1947. In the same year, Law no. 6 was again replaced by Law no. 8, Year 1947, on the extension of time in submitting the declaration concerning the citizenship of Indonesia. In the following year, Law no. 8 was replaced by Law no. 11, Year 1948, on the extension of time in submitting the declaration concerning the citizenship of Indonesia.

Furthermore, citizenship matters were provided for under Law no. 62, Year 1958, on Citizenship of the Republic of Indonesia. This law was partially amended in the Law no. 3, Year 1976, on the revision of article no. 18 of Law no. 62, Year 1958, on Citizenship of the Republic of Indonesia.

Law no. 62, Year 1958, is philosophically, juridically, and sociologically not suitable anymore with the progress and structure of the Indonesian state.

Philosophically, this particular law retains provisions that are not in line with the Pancasila philosophy. Among other things, they are discriminative in nature and do not respect human rights, equality before the law, or women and children's rights.

Juridically, the constitutional base of the drafting of that law is the 1950 Provisional Constitution, which has not been valid since the Presidential Decree of 5 July 1959, which declared the reinstatement of the 1945 Constitution. In its development, the 1945 Constitution has been amended to protect human rights and citizen rights.

Sociologically, the law is not suitable anymore with the development and demand of Indonesian society as part of the international community in an era of globalization, which stipulates the equal treatment of, and foundation for, citizens before the law, as well as gender equality.[21]

Based on these considerations, Law no. 12, Year 2006, on Citizenship of the Republic of Indonesia as the implementation of Article 26 verse (3) of the 1945 Constitution, stated that with the promulgation of this law, Law no. 62, Year 1958, on Citizenship of Republic of Indonesia, and Law no. 3, Year 1976, are repealed and declared invalid.

THE 2006 CITIZENSHIP LAW:
NEW BREAKTHROUGH IN COUNTERING
MASS DISCRIMINATION
AGAINST ETHNIC CHINESE

According to Yap Thiam Hien, the problem of an ethnic minority facing discrimination can be solved in the following ways:[22]

1. By enforcing law, which deprives and punishes with imprisonment every act that provides privileges to an ethnic group or race; or punishes an individual or individuals who has/have committed or provoked discrimination against a certain ethnic group or race.
2. By offering general education on human rights, that is general education on the essence of nationality, on human rights and the principles of democracy, on the crime of discrimination, on the truth or fact that national unity and loyalty are not threatened by a minority.
3. By implementing policies, which create and maintain good relationship among various ethnic and racial groups.

In a move that is relevant to Yap Thiam Hien's comments, the government of Indonesia on 11 July 2006, promulgated Law no. 12, Year 2006, on Citizenship of Republic of Indonesia (**"Law on Citizenship of Indonesia 2006"**). This was considered "revolutionary" for certain groups in society, particularly ethnic Chinese, who experienced discrimination in a state which is based on law and democracy. Tan Joe Hok and Hendrawan, both of them prominent badminton athletes, are probably two out of hundreds, or maybe thousands, of discrimination cases against Indonesian citizens of Chinese descent who are considered "foreigners" or "stepson of the soil" by the state. This is based on the "divide and rule" doctrine.

The Law on Citizenship of Indonesia 2006 reflects many important breakthroughs which minimize problems relating to citizenship. The breakthroughs deal with the following issues:

1. The concept of Indonesian citizenship;
2. The revision of single citizenship to become limited double citizenship (Bipatride);
3. The acceptance of foreigners as Indonesian citizens based on their contributions to the development of the country;
4. Criminal sanction against discriminatory treatment provided in the Law on Citizenship of Indonesia 2006.

The following discusses these issues in greater detail:

1. The Concept of Indonesian Citizenship

Article 2 of the Law on Citizenship of Indonesia 2006, makes the following provisions:

> "*Those who become Indonesia citizens are <u>indigenous Indonesians</u> and other persons of non-indigenous acknowledged by law as citizens.*"

The term "indigenous Indonesians" in this article provokes public debate, considering that the term is sometimes considered to segregate the indigenous from the non-indigenous. However, the term "indigenous Indonesians" in the Law on Citizenship of Indonesia 2006 has been clarified in the interpretation of Article 2 of the Law on Citizenship of Indonesia 2006, which defines "indigenous Indonesians" as follows:

> 'The 'indigenous Indonesians' are those who have become citizens of Indonesia since their birth and have never become other citizens on (sic) their own free will."

The legislators of the Law on Citizenship of Indonesia 2006 have accommodated the problem by making a breakthrough in creating a new terminology for Indonesian citizens. In general, Article 4 and Article 5 of the Law on Citizenship of Indonesia 2006 describe the meaning of an Indonesian citizen as:

- **All persons,** whether before or after the Law on Citizenship of 2006 is enacted, have been legally admitted as Indonesian citizens;
- **Children born to Indonesian-citizen parents** are Indonesian citizens, if their parents are Indonesians, or at least, one of the parents is an Indonesian citizen (mixed marriage);
- **Children born in the territory of the Republic of Indonesia,** but the citizenship of their parents is not known, or the whereabouts of their parents is not known;
- **Children born outside the territory of the Republic of Indonesia,** and have obtained their citizenship from the state where they are born (dual citizenship);
- **Children born outside the legal marriage of their Indonesian mothers,** or foreign mothers, but have obtained the affidavit of their Indonesian

fathers before they are eighteen years old or are acknowledged by their foreign fathers (dual citizenship);

– **Indonesian children adopted** by foreign parents before they are five years old.

Based on the abovementioned terminology, ethnic Chinese born in the territory of the Republic of Indonesia are automatically Indonesian citizens and no longer require the SBKRI. The SBKRI has been revoked by Presidential Decree no. 56, Year 1996, on SBKRI, and Presidential Instruction no. 4, Year 1999. However, in practice, government authorities within the bureaucracy consistently demand SBKRI from ethnic Chinese in their application for identity cards, birth certificates, passports, *kartu keluarga* (family registration cards), and other official documents. The recent issuance of the Law on Citizenship of Indonesia 2006 has at least strengthened the revocation of SBKRI. What we need now is to eliminate the SBKRI.

With new definitions for the term "Indonesian citizen", no ethnic Chinese is stateless (apatride) now because every child born in the territory of Republic of Indonesia is an Indonesian citizen.

2. Revision of Single Citizenship to Limited Dual Citizenship (Bipatride)

A few terminologies of citizenship in Article 4 on Law on Citizenship of Indonesia 2006 make it impossible to obtain dual citizenship for a child. This is an innovation in the history of citizenship in Indonesia.

Has the new Law on Citizenship of Indonesia 2006 changed the principle of citizenship, which had been adopted by Indonesia for many years? Article 6 of Law on Citizenship of Indonesia 2006 has the answer. That article mentioned dual citizenship (bipatride) which is not permanent, but only limited to a child who has not reached the age of eighteen.

The Law on Citizenship of Indonesia 2006 basically does not recognize dual citizenship (bipatride) or the stateless status (apatride). The dual citizenship offered to a child as provisioned in Article 4 and Article 5 of the Law on Citizenship of Indonesia 2006 is basically considered an exception.

Article 6 of the Law on Citizenship of Indonesia 2006 carries the following provisions:

(1) In case the status of Indonesian citizenship of a child mentioned in articles 4 c, d, h, and I, and article 5 resulted in the child having double citizenship

after 18 years of age or after marriage, the child must choose either one of the citizenships, between either the Indonesian or the foreign citizenship.

The declaration to elect a citizenship as provisioned in Article 6 should be done in writing within three years after the child has reached the age of 18 years or is married.

3. Granting Foreigners Indonesian Citizenship Because of Their Contribution to the Development and Honour of the Country

Discrimination is not targeted only at ethnic Chinese in general but also ethnic Chinese athletes who have contributed to the honour of Indonesia. When some ethnic Chinese badminton athletes applied for Indonesian citizenships, they became the targets of discrimination and were asked to submit their SBKRI.

Ironically, this happened to great athletes such as Ivana Lie, Hendrawan, and Tang Hsien Hu. Although they have succefully won international badminton tournaments and become champions, it was not easy for them to obtain Indonesian citizenships. In the case of Hendrawan, he finally managed to obtain his Indonesian citizenship after President Megawati intervened in the matter.

The bad experiences of these badminton athletes were considered by lawmakers in legislating the Law on Citizenship of Indonesia 2006. The result was that foreigners who have contributed to the country may now be granted Indonesian citizenship, as regulated by Article 20 of the Law on Citizenship of Indonesia 2006:

> *"… foreigners who have contributed to Indonesia or to the interest of the state may be granted the Indonesian citizenship by the president of the Republic of Indonesia after obtaining the approval of the parliament, except in cases whereby the granting of the Indonesian citizenship will result in the person concerned having dual citizenship".*

The interpretation of Article 20 is that a foreigner who because of his/her remarkable performance in the areas of humanities, science and technology, culture, environment, and sports, has contributed to the development and honour of Indonesia. By having this article, it is expected that discrimination against badminton and other athletes will not occur again. Besides, the government is trying to minimize discriminative treatment against foreigners who have lived in Indonesia, especially those who have contributed to Indonesia.

4. Criminal Sanctions Against Discriminatory Treatment Provisioned in the Law on Citizenship of Indonesia 2006

In the Law on Citizenship of Indonesia 2006, the government of Indonesia is trying hard to eliminate the discrimination against those who are considered "foreigners" from becoming Indonesian citizens. This time, lawmakers are trying to avoid discrimination by bureaucrats. Among other things, they will be punished if they make a person lose his citizenship.

This is provisioned in Article 36 of the Law on Citizenship of Indonesia 2006:

> "(1) A bureaucrat because of his negligence to perform his duty and obligation as provisioned in this Law causes a person to lose his chance of obtaining or regaining and/or losing his Indonesian citizenship will be punished for a maximum of 1 (one) year by imprisonment;
> (2) In the case of the criminal offence mentioned in sub 1 being intentionally commited, the act will be punishable by a maximum of 3 (three) years' imprisonment."

Some parties doubt the "efficiency" of this Article in eliminating discriminative acts commited by the bureaucracy. Past experiences explain the pessimistic attitudes of various groups in society. For example, the problem of SBKRI still exists and becomes an "obligation" in the administration of the population, although SBKRI has been revoked since the government of President Abdurrachman Wahid (popularly known as Gus Dur). This shows the ineffectiveness of law enforcement in Indonesia.

The Law on Citizenship of Indonesia, dated 20 July 2006, was promulgated by the Minister for Law and Human Rights, Hamid Awalludin. He promised that he will instruct the Secretary General of the Department of Justice and Human Rights to conduct a briefing on the Law on Citizenship of Indonesia 2006 in the regional offices of the department so that illegal payment and discrimination can be avoided for ethnic Chinese applicants of Indonesian citizenship.

Nevertheless, the efforts to eliminate and minimize discrimination against ethnic Chinese are not easy owing to the fact that SBKRI is still required in practice. The department conducted a yearly evaluation which yielded the following results:

EVALUATION OF THE FINDINGS OF THE DEPARTMENT OF JUSTICE AND HUMAN RIGHTS IN 2006

The Province of DKI Jakarta

27 respondents or 90 per cent of 30 ethnic Chinese respondents admitted that they had to submit SBKRI to apply for a passport. Most of them were applying for a renewal of an existing, rather than a new, passport. This means that they do not have to submit SBKRI as they had done so in the first application.

Based on the Circulation Letter of the Immigration Director General no. F-UM.01.06–845, Year 2002, and the Circulation Letter of the Immigration Director General no. F-UM.01.10.6626, Year 2004, only applicants who are suspected of being non-Indonesians, for example, because of their inability to speak Indonesian, are requested to show their documents.

The Province of East Java

25 or 83.3 per cent of 30 ethnic Chinese respondents admitted that they had to submit SBKRI to apply for a passport. This means that almost 100 per cent of the respondents had to submit SBKRI, contrary to the statement made by the Circulation Letter of the Immigration Director General no. F-UM.01.06-845, Year 2002, and the Circulation Letter of the Immigration Director General no. F-UM.01.10.6626, Year 2004.

No matter how the Law on Citizenship of Indonesia 2006 was enacted, if the root of discrimination is not properly tackled, the practice of discrimination remains. The policy of "divide and conquer" introduced by the Dutch Colonialists is implemented through State Gazette 1917 no. 130 (State Gazette 1917, p. 130) entitled, "Peraturan Penyelenggaraan Daftar-Daftar Catatan Sipil Untuk Golongan China" (Regulation on the Registration of Ethnic Chinese at the Civil Registration Office). If that particular State Gazette is not repealed by Law no. 23, Year 2006, on the Administration of Population (UU Administrasi Penduduk), the situation remains the same.

Concluding Remarks

As a state based on law (*rechtsstaat*), Indonesia should respect and protect the human rights of every individual, including the right of being equally treated before the law. Equality before the law as a postulate should be applied in every legislation and in everyday life in order to guarantee social justice for every individual.

The government is expected to provide equal opportunities for every member of society, including ethnic Chinese, so that there are equal opportunities for everyone in all areas, such as employment, bureaucracy, law enforcement, politics, economy, and culture, without the loss of any individual identity for any person. As such, ethnic Chinese are expected to contribute to the development of the country not only in trade and industry, but also in other areas of life. The acknowledgment of equality before the law should be accompanied by equal treatment.[23] Equality before the law should be intrepreted dynamically and not statically. At the end of the day, the ethnic Chinese must be prepared to develop Indonesia into a democratic and modern state.

Notes

[1] See Stuart W. Greif, *WNI: Problematik Orang Indonesia Asal Cina* (Jakarta: Pustaka Utama Grafiti, 1991), p. xi.

[2] See M. Ocorandi, *An Analysis of the Implication of Soeharto's Resignation for Chinese Indonesians*, Worldwide Huaren Peace Mission, 1998.

[3] See Leo Suryadinata, *Negara dan Etnis Tionghoa: Kasus Indonesia* (Jakarta: Pustaka LP3ES Indoenesia, 2002), p. 8.

[4] See Leo Suryadinata, *Pribumi Indonesians, The Chinese Minority and China: A Study of Perceptions and Policies* (Kuala Lumpur, Singapore, and London: Heinemann Educational Books, 1978), p. 54.

[5] Ibid., p. 56.

[6] Leo Suryadinata 2002, op. cit., pp. 21–23.

[7] Leo Suryadinata 1978, op. cit., p. 147.

[8] Ibid., p. 59.

[9] In fact, Indonesia adopted the concept of the nation state as proposed by French philosopher Ernest Renan.

[10] Yap Thiem Hien was an Indonesian Chinese lawyer. He spent his entire life empowering Justice and Human Rights. Yap Thiem Hien was imprisoned in 1968 because of his determination to fight corruption in the government, Wikipidia <http://id.wikipedia.org/wiki/Yap_Thiam_Hien>.

[11] See Indonesia Wikipedia, *Baperki's Goal* <http://id.wikipedia.org/wiki/Baperki#Tujuan>.

[12] Ibid.

[13] See Daniel S. Lev, *Becoming An Orang Indonesia Sejati: The Political Journey of Yap Thiam Hien* <http://cip.cornell.edu/DPubS/Repository/1.0/Disseminate/seap.indo/1106972023/body/pdf>, pp. 104–06.

[14] See T. Mulya Lubis and Aristides Katoppo, *Yap Thiam Hien: Pahlawan Hak Azazi Manusia* (Jakarta: Pustaka Sinar Harapan, 1990).

¹⁵ The International Convention on the Elimination of All Forms of Racial Discrimination was adopted and opened for signature and ratification by General Assembly Resolution 2106 (XX) of 21 December 1965, and came into force on 4 January 1968.

¹⁶ See Bambang Setiawan, "Mendung Politik di Balik Imlek", *Kompas*, 12 February 2002.

¹⁷ Cultural genocide, according to Geoffrey Robertson, is "by prohibiting the use of a group's language, rewriting or obliterating its history or destroying its icon" (Geoffrey Robertson Q.C., *Crimes Against Humanity, The Struggle for Global Justice* [Australia: Penguin Books, 1999], p. 229).

¹⁸ Bambang Setiawan, op. cit.

¹⁹ "The crime of Apartheid means inhumane acts of a character committed in the context of an institutionalized regime of systematic oppression and domination by one racial group over any other racial group or groups and committed with intention of maintaining that regime." (Article 7, point 2.h. the Rome Statue of the International Criminal Court.)

²⁰ Tang Hsien Hu is a national badminton coach who spent fifty million rupiah in early 1999 to earn the SBKRI and had to wait for ten years for that.

²¹ General Justification of Law no. 12, Year 2006, concerning Law of Republic of Indonesia Citizenship.

²² See Yap Thiam Hien, "Therapi Kelompok 10 (II)", *Star Weekly*, 30 April 1960.

²³ "In a formal and general sense, equality is a postulate justice. Aristotle's 'distributive justice' demands the equal treatment of those equal before the Law." (W. Friedmann, *Legal Theory* [London: Steven & Son Limited, 1960], p. 385).

5

CHINESE EDUCATION IN INDONESIA: DEVELOPMENTS IN THE POST-1998 ERA

Aimee Dawis

Introduction

The history of Chinese education in Indonesia is inextricably tied with the political, cultural, and social dimensions of the country. Like their neighbours in Malaysia and Singapore, members of the Chinese community in Indonesia have tried to establish their own educational systems for their youth upon their settlement in Indonesia. Due to shifts and fluctuations in the Indonesian political history, from Dutch colonial administration (1600–1942), and the Japanese Occupation (1942–45), to the Soekarno and Soeharto eras (1945–65 and 1965–98 respectively) and *Reformasi*[1] (1998–present), the Chinese in Indonesia have encountered many different situations that have dictated the conditions of their education in Indonesia.

Recent literature on *Reformasi* has focused on the cultural, political, socio-economic, and cultural developments that have occurred since the fall of Soeharto (for example, Budianta 2000 & 2003; Lane 1999; Lubis and Santosa 1999). Many of these works have also centred on the changing role and identity of the Chinese in Indonesia (for example, Tan 1999 and Budiman 2005). One area that scholars have not specifically touched on is the development of Chinese education in post-1998 Indonesia. This chapter presents a preliminary overview of this development. However, because the current situation of Chinese education in Indonesia cannot be fully grasped without an understanding of the political and sociocultural factors that precede it, this chapter will begin with a summary of the history of Chinese education in Indonesia. Data for this chapter have been obtained from newspaper articles, books, and in-depth interviews with current and past leaders in Chinese education. The section on the present situation of Chinese education in Indonesia is supplemented with interviews with parents who choose to send their children to schools offering Mandarin, as well as those who have opted not to do so. The chapter concludes with projections on the future of Chinese education in Indonesia.

HISTORICAL OVERVIEW

According to Ming Govaars' (2005) *Dutch Colonial Education: The Chinese Experience in Indonesia, 1900–1942*, the formal development of Chinese education by the Dutch colonial administration in Indonesia did not start until the beginning of the twentieth century. Before 1900, the Dutch East India Company laid the foundations for the education of European and indigenous communities. Attendance of Chinese students at the schools was minimal due to the high school fees and the segregated society whereby the Dutch and other Europeans were placed on the highest rungs of the society while Foreign Orientals (that is, the Chinese) and Natives (that is, the indigenous community) were on the lowest rungs.

Although nothing was established especially for the Chinese under the auspices of the Dutch East India Company, the Chinese set up their own schools to educate their young. The classical education system in mainland China, based on the teachings of Confucius (551–479 B.C.), became the model in these early schools. For 2000 years, the teachings of Confucius, based on virtue and respect for authority in all social relationships, were the state doctrine in China. Virtue was achieved through study and education. A thorough knowledge of the Confucian classics was necessary for all government positions in the Chinese empire. An imperial examination system, in which all future public servants were required to exhibit this knowledge, was developed and executed. Earning a degree in the examination system and an appointment to an official post paved the way to wealth and influence. It also brought immense honour to the family. Although there was no possibility of a career in the civil service in the Dutch East Indies,[2] the system of Confucianism was maintained until 1900. The maintenance of Confucianism indicates the strong Chinese literary tradition and the great reverence of the Chinese people for education.

In China, the imperial examination system was abolished in 1905 under the pressure of modern developments. In 1912, the Chinese Empire became a Republic. The founders of the new Republic witnessed the rise of Western powers and Japan and credited their success in part to the introduction of modern education (Yen 2005). In order to move Chinese education away from the centuries-old ideals of the preservation of the dynasty and loyalty to the emperor, they called for extensive restructuring, which set education as the instrument for nation building and the key to wealth and power for a new China. Accordingly, Qing textbooks were replaced by new Republican textbooks; the study of Confucian classics was banished from the curriculum; the link between education and bureaucracy was eradicated; co-education at the primary level was introduced; and high school education was set as general education (Peake 1970). Yen (2005) observed that the replacement of Qing textbooks with new ones was designed to free Chinese children from the old frame of mind that encouraged students to look back to the past rather than to the future. Moreover, the introduction of co-education was meant to remove gender barriers and ease traditional discrimination against females in the Chinese society, while setting high school education as general education aimed to lift China's education and literacy standards to realize the Republicans' belief that literacy was the key to national strength and democracy.

The above circumstances precipitated sweeping educational reforms not only across China, but also overseas Chinese communities. After the founding of the Republic, the Chinese government, both central and provincial, was interested in promoting ethnic Chinese education outside China (Yen 1976). The governments in Fujian and Guangdong, the two provinces that provided most of the ethnic Chinese migrants to Southeast Asia, sent officials to tour the region for that purpose. In 1929, an "Ethnic Chinese Education Planning Committee" was established within the Ministry of Education. The committee was responsible for the planning and consultation with the Ministry of Education over ethnic Chinese education (Yen 2005). It was this committee that sent various officers to monitor the progress of Chinese education in Indonesia, maintaining especially close ties with the Tiong Hoa Hwee Koan.

In Indonesia, the Tiong Hoa Hwee Koan (THHK) association was formed on 17 March 1900 "to serve as the centre of the whole [Chinese] movement for the reform of Chinese customs and traditions" (Kwee 1969, p. 11). The THHK established schools that were quintessentially Chinese and unquestionably modern. The first of these schools were opened in Jakarta in 1901. They broke with tradition in three ways: first, within a few years, the language of instruction was Mandarin[3] and not Hokkien or another southern Chinese dialect; second, they derived their curriculum from modern Western education as was taught in modern Chinese and Japanese schools, and not the classics; third, classes for girls soon opened and, in 1928, the school in Batavia (as Jakarta was formerly called) went co-educational (Heidhues 2006). A few years later, they also broke with Confucianism when Chinese secular nationalism condemned the teachings and influence of the sage. Beginning in 1906, a Chinese school inspector visited the THHK schools in the Dutch East Indies almost every year. By 1908, there were seventy-five modern Chinese schools in the Dutch East Indies (not all of them officially affiliated with the THHK), with an estimated 5,500 students (Heidhues 2006). From 1912, when the Republic was established, the Chinese Ministry of Education continued to provide educational methods, books, and teachers for the THHK schools (Govaars 2005). The THHK, along with the *Siang Hwee* (a Chinese business association or Chamber of Commerce) and the *Soe Po Sia* (reading clubs focused on politics and revolution), strove to improve the position of the Chinese community as a whole and to strengthen the feeling of affiliation with China (Govaars 2005). They formed the nationalistic Chinese Movement that unified the Chinese community.

The growth of Chinese schools and the increased nationalistic fervour among the Chinese community alarmed the Dutch authorities. In order to curb Chinese nationalism, the Dutch established the HCS (Hollands-Chinese School) or the Dutch-Chinese Schools, which were modelled on European schools (Suryadinata 1997). Neither the Chinese language nor Chinese culture was taught at these schools. These schools drew many *peranakans* (Indies-born Chinese), whose numbers continued to increase over the years. Although the Dutch established the HCS, which became popular among the Chinese because a command of the Dutch language meant higher stature in the colonial society, they did not interfere in Chinese-medium schools (Govaars 2005). These schools were given freedom to determine their own curricula and textbooks. They could even invite teachers from China, except when particular school teachers were regarded as "subversive" and dangerous to "public security" (Suryadinata 1992).

When Japanese forces occupied the East Indies from 1942 to 1945, all Dutch and Western-influenced schools were closed. Only Indonesian and Chinese-medium schools were allowed to operate beginning from 1 August 1942. *Peranakan* children found that they had to learn to read and write in Chinese because they now had to attend Chinese schools (Heidhues 2006). This led to the *peranakans'* heavy immersion in Chinese culture and language and a rapid increase in the number of Chinese schools. After Indonesia proclaimed its independence in 1945, the number of Chinese schools continued to rise. Between 1952–53, 1,371 Chinese schools with 254,730 students were registered with the Ministry of Education (Suryadinata 1992).

Suryadinata (1992) attributed the significant surge in Chinese-medium schools to several factors. First, the closure of Dutch schools and the limited number of Indonesian schools meant that there was a shortage of schools for the growing number of Chinese children after the war. Second, there was a lack of confidence among the Chinese in the newly opened Indonesian schools. Third, the emergence of the People's Republic of China stirred up strong Chinese nationalistic feelings. The Chinese community, indeed, closely followed the political struggles in China. Chinese schools in Indonesia were divided into pro-Kuomintang (pro-Taiwan) and pro-Peking (pro-China) groups. The pro-Peking group became more influential because Indonesia recognized the Chinese government. However, because of the 1958 regional rebellions that occurred in Sumatra and Sulawesi, the Indonesian government drastically reduced the number of Chinese-medium schools. The Ministry of Education closely controlled the remaining schools, some of which were run by Baperki (Badan Permusyawaratan Kewarganegaraan Indonesia), a mass organization with an overwhelmingly Chinese membership. The teachers were required to take tests, including an Indonesian-language proficiency test, sponsored by the Ministry. Only those who passed the test were allowed to teach. The curriculum of these schools was also altered to include more subjects on Indonesia. The Ministry mandated Indonesian language, history, and geography as compulsory subjects at both the primary and secondary levels. However, these subjects could be taught in either Indonesian or Chinese.

When Indonesia entered a period of political turbulence and crisis in 1965, all Baperki schools were closed. In 1965, Soeharto came to power following the failed attempted coup[4] by the PKI (Partai Komunis Indonesia or The Indonesian Communist Party). Following the coup, Soeharto led a campaign against all traces of Communism, which Soekarno, the first president of Indonesia, allegedly supported. Since the Chinese Indonesians were suspected of maintaining close ties to Communist China, Soeharto implemented an assimilationist policy[5] that resulted in an erosion of Chinese language and culture. The closure of the schools was in accordance with this assimilationist policy. Charles Coppel (1983), in his book, *Indonesian Chinese in Crisis*, wrote that the Special Staff on Chinese Affairs (SCUT) attached to the cabinet presidium recognized that the closure of the schools had created social problems. Although some of the students whose schooling had been interrupted had been able to find a place in the national (and particularly in the private, Christian) schools, there were many who had not. Some of these were receiving tutoring at home, which was uncontrolled and thus could lead to the spread of undesirable or subversive ideas, while those children who were not receiving any education were susceptible to delinquency and other anti-social behaviour. Therefore, the SCUT recommended the creation of Special Project National Schools (SNPC) which were to follow the Indonesian national curriculum, with Indonesia as the language of instruction and in which teachers must be Indonesian citizens. The schools were to be private, but under government supervision. To encourage the Chinese to fund the new schools, the Indonesian government made special provisions for the teaching of the Chinese language for a specified number of hours each week. The SCUT proposal was adopted by the government in early 1968, and the first SNPC was established in 1969. By early 1971, there were eight such schools. By the end of 1973, there were thirty-five SNPC in Sumatra alone. The authorities were greatly concerned about the rapid growth of these schools because they did not want to awaken feelings of nationalism among the Chinese. Hence, the Ministry of Education and Culture announced their abolition in 1975.

From 1975–98, all children of Chinese descent had to enrol in Indonesian-language schools. In these schools, Chinese children were to learn Indonesian history, politics, and social practices alongside their Indonesian peers. Coppel (1983) noted that most Chinese school children attended private, particularly Christian, schools. Although the Christian schools were attracting a much higher proportion of Chinese among their students than was to be found in the community at large, they also enrolled many indigenous children who came not only from Christian families, but not infrequently, also from non-Christian ones who valued the high standard of education and discipline found there. At the tertiary level, there were no exclusively Chinese institutions. Trisakti University, like its predecessor, the Baperki-run Res Publica University, attracted a much higher percentage of Chinese students than the state universities. The Christian universities, such as Atma Jaya University, had also accepted a fairly substantial number of Chinese students. A number of Chinese parents had been moved to sending their children abroad for higher education, choosing Western countries such as the United States and Australia as the places where their children could attain the advantages of an overseas qualification.

THE PRESENT SITUATION

The current environment in Indonesia is radically different from the suppressive atmosphere of the Soeharto era when Chinese culture and language were not allowed to be taught and practised. The situation of the Chinese Indonesians has improved remarkably after the downfall of the Soeharto regime following the May 1998 riots. When Abdurrahman Wahid came into power as the president of Indonesia from November 1999 to August 2001, he led efforts to end discriminatory regulations against the Indonesian Chinese population. The first step he took was to abolish the Presidential Instruction Number 14, signed in 1967 by Soeharto, which restricted the practice of Chinese customs and religions to the private domain. He formalized this act by signing the Presidential Instruction no. 6, stipulated in the year 2000, which allows the public celebration of the Chinese New Year. Under Megawati, who headed Indonesia's government from August 2001 to September 2004,[6] Chinese New Year has been made into a national holiday, starting from 1 February 2003.[7]

Other than the official celebration of Chinese New Year, the revival of Chinese culture can be seen in the establishment of private schools offering Mandarin as a mode of instruction, along with Bahasa Indonesia and English. Numerous language centres have also opened to cater to the growing needs of Mandarin students and their parents. The Ministry of Education has also collaborated with the Chinese government and the Indonesian Chinese community to introduce Mandarin education in national schools. The Indonesian Chinese community is represented by the National Coordinating Association for Mandarin Education (Badan Koordinasi Pendidikan Bahasa Mandarin) or the BKPBM. The following sections of this chapter will first discuss the establishment and growth of private trilingual schools and language centres before presenting the recent activities of the BKPBM, the Ministry of Education, and the Chinese government, with respect to Mandarin education in Indonesia's national schools.

National Plus and International Curriculum Schools

Since 1998, many private trilingual schools have sprung up all over Indonesia,[8] most notably in the capital city of Jakarta. There are two types of trilingual schools — the National Plus schools and International Curriculum schools. The National Plus schools offer the national curriculum that is sanctioned by the Ministry of Education, along with the teaching of languages such as Bahasa Indonesia, English, and Mandarin. There are at least fifty[9] trilingual schools in Jakarta by 2007. According to Mala Holland, who runs a National Plus school called *Chandra Kusuma* in Medan, there are no official figures regarding the number of schools in Medan. However, according to her observations, there are at least seven National Plus schools in the city. Lim Wenchu (the Vice-President of the Fuqing Association in Surabaya) and Hadi Koesmanto (the head of the Coordinating Body of Mandarin Education in Surabaya) also said that there are no official figures regarding trilingual schools in Surabaya. Based on their experience and observations, they estimate the number of National Plus schools in Surabaya to be close to twenty. They note that there is one National Plus school with an international curriculum that is run by Lim Wenkuang or Alim Markus, the tycoon who is at the helm of the Maspion group.

In Jakarta, where this preliminary assessment on the recent developments on Chinese education was implemented, National Plus schools include institutions such as Tunas Muda and Global Nusantara which enroll students from pre-school level up to secondary school.[10] These schools employ mostly local teachers who are guided by one or two Chinese-language teachers who have been hired directly from Taiwan or Mainland China. Unlike national schools which require their students to sit for national exams such as the EBTANAS[11] (primary, secondary, and high school national examinations), schools such as Tunas Muda provide their students with the option of sitting for International Baccelaurate (IB) examinations. These internationally recognized examinations allow students to continue their studies at overseas institutions in countries such as Singapore, Australia, the United Kingdom, and the United States.

Parents who decide to send their children to National Plus schools believe that the availability of options such as the IB examinations give their children more flexibility for their higher education abroad. Roger Brumby,[12] the Vice-Principal of Academic Affairs at the Jakarta International School, affirms that the overall acceptance rate for students applying to North American colleges with an IB diploma is higher than with any other qualification. As far as universities in Europe, Australia, and many other parts of the world are concerned, the IB diploma is almost a must for university entrance. Moreover, the advanced credit and advanced placement at North American colleges that can result from having an IB diploma may mean significant savings in terms of money and time. It also gives students the opportunity to pursue other courses.

Other than taking advantage of the IB system, parents who send their children to National Plus Schools reason that their children would be able to learn Chinese in National Plus rather than national schools, which mostly teach their students only Bahasa Indonesia and English as a second language. Although some national schools offer Mandarin as an extra-curricular activity, these parents believe that more intensive academic instruction in Mandarin is a necessity. To them, not being able to speak and write in Chinese is a tremendous disadvantage in today's world, where China is fast becoming an economic superpower. In his book, *The Chinese Century: The Rising Chinese Economy and its Impact on the Global Economy, The Balance of Power, and Your Job*, Oded Shenkar (2006), a professor of management and human resources at Ohio State University's Fisher College of Business, argued that China is on course to surpass the United States as the world's largest economy within twenty years. China-based factories already make up seventy per cent of the world's toys, sixty per cent of its bicycles, half its shoes and one-third of its luggage. China already has an impressive amount of technological know-how and manufacturing capability, thanks in part to American companies that have set up operations there. Companies from the United States, Japan, and Europe have been eager to share their technology, with the hope that they can penetrate the huge Chinese market. Along with evidence that China is growing at a faster clip than any other nation,[13] parents of children born in the post-Soeharto era believe that by learning the Chinese language, especially from mainland Chinese teachers, their children will have the necessary tools to enter China's lucrative economic realm. In the words of Jenny, a parent who sent her two sons to a National Plus school:

> Well, we now have the option of sending our children to National Plus schools … instead of having to send them to Singapore or Malaysia. I don't want my sons to grow up not knowing their culture and heritage, like me, who cannot speak Chinese. I know these schools are expensive, but I don't want my sons to lag behind their friends. I mean … what if we need to conduct business with China in the future? Wouldn't those who know the language be at an advantageous position? Besides, we live in Indonesia, so my sons still need to learn Bahasa Indonesia and know how to live the 'Indonesian way'. I've seen too many children who grew up in Singapore or Malaysia who got a culture shock when they returned to Indonesia. They'll still get to learn Bahasa Indonesia and live in Indonesia when they attend National Plus schools.

The emphasis on conducting business with China is a common sentiment among parents who send their children to National Plus schools. This is because many of them operate their own businesses and hope their children may help them expand their businesses in the future. Moreover, because National Plus schools offer Bahasa Indonesia, and are located in Indonesia, their children would be trained to deal with the Indonesian culture and way of living, instead of growing up in a foreign country such as Singapore or Malaysia.

The second type of trilingual schools, the International Curriculum schools, generally charge higher fees than National Plus schools because they are often direct franchisees from Singapore and Australia. Schools such as the Nasional High Junior and Senior School (also known as Nasional High) are affiliated with The Chinese High school in Singapore. This affiliation gives the school credibility and prestige because The Chinese High School is a highly-ranked secondary school in Singapore, which admits only the top two per cent of students who sat for their PSLE (Primary School Leaving Examination). The Chinese High School also happens to be the first secondary school that was established in Singapore on 21 March 1919 for Chinese-educated students (Yen 2005). Being closely linked with The Chinese High School means that Nasional High looks to the Singapore education system to form the foundation for their teaching methods, standards, and curriculum. Therefore, it has to send its teachers to Singapore for frequent training sessions to maintain the high standards it promises. The school also employs Singaporean teachers to teach its students.

Although many National Plus schools and International Curriculum schools have been embraced by parents who belong to the middle to upper middle classes that can afford the high school fees, they have met with criticisms because they tend to be elitist. Consequently, there are other National Plus schools such as the Budi Agung school, located on Terusan Bandengan, in the Chinatown area of Jakarta, which charge reasonable fees (up to eighty per cent less than the fees charged by Bina Bangsa and Nasional High). According to Sidharta Wirahadi Kusuma (Xu Jingneng), the deputy chairman of the Advisory Board of BKPBM, who is also the Vice-President and the Culture and Education Division Head of the Hakka Association, the Budi Agung school, which was established by the Hakka Association in 2001, offers instruction from kindergarten to high-school levels for students who come from the lower middle class. Rather than relying on expatriate teachers, the school employs local teachers who teach Mandarin for up to eight hours a week. The subsidies from the Hakka Association also help to lower the school fees for the 1,000 students who are currently enrolled at the school.

Another criticism of National Plus and International Curriculum schools lies in the difficulty of checking the standard of the schools. This is because the schools are all relatively new (most were established between the years 2000–07) and, for the most part, are not controlled by the Ministry of Education. In my research, parents whom I have spoken to agree that the

Nasional High school seems to offer the highest standard of learning so far. However, these parents also say that the high standard of Mandarin education at the school is actually a double-edged sword. They are pleased that their children are learning Mandarin of the same standard as the one in Singapore's schools. However, they also realize that their children are not living in the same environment as Singaporeans, where Mandarin is spoken much more widely in the society. As a consequence, some of Nasional High's students struggle in their Mandarin classes. It is common for these students to attend remedial Mandarin lessons at school or seek the help of personal tutors and language centres.

Language Centres

One prevailing problem that has plagued parents who send their children to National Plus and other Chinese-language schools is their inability to reinforce at home what their children have learned at school. Many of these parents are concerned that they may not be able to help their children with their schoolwork, despite the availability of remedial classes at their children's schools. As a response to these concerns, a large number of language centres have been established throughout Indonesia. These centres not only provide classes to help young children with their schoolwork, but also offer intensive Mandarin classes for their parents and professionals who want to sharpen their language skills. In Jakarta, there are more than a hundred of such centres, which are located mainly in housing areas occupied predominantly by Chinese Indonesians.

In fact, one of the most popular language centres in Jakarta which specifically caters to children, Berri, is located in the Kelapa Gading area in East Jakarta, where many Chinese Indonesians live. Berri imports its books from Singapore and enforces the Singapore curriculum. Correspondingly, it employs instructors from Singapore who also hold story-telling sessions at bookstores such as the Kinokuniya bookstore in Plaza Senayan, Plaza Indonesia, and Senayan City shopping centres. Like Berri, Inlingua Education Center in the Puri Indah area of West Jakarta also offers Mandarin classes to children. Established in 1996, Inlingua Education Center occupied a small room at Puri Indah Mall before moving to its present location on a main road in the Puri Indah area in 2005. Its new building contains twenty classrooms and boasts state-of-the-art computers which allow students to take qualifying Mandarin examinations. It is also equipped with play areas, language laboratories, and a library that encourages students to simulate conversations and develop reading skills in Mandarin. It currently employs a teacher from Beijing, who is assisted by local teachers. Unlike Berri, Inlingua Education Center also enrols adults, mostly professionals who would like to learn Mandarin to further their career. While a few of the adult students are mothers who are learning or relearning the language to help their children with their schoolwork, Inlingua Education Center does not offer specific classes for these mothers.

These classes are, however, available at the Fuqing Association's Wise Language Center in Ancol, North Jakarta. According to Yau Thungjung (Yao Zhongcong), Secretary General of the Fuqing Association (Jakarta division) and the Executive Vice-President of the World Fuqing Association, Wise Language Center occupies a 1000-square metre house that has been converted into a language school for children as young as three years old, professionals, and housewives. It also functions as a meeting venue for the Fuqing Association. Like the Budi Agung National Plus school, the subsidies that the school receives from the organization allows it to charge low fees for its Mandarin classes. Other than the Wise Language Center, Yau said that the Fuqing Association also subsidizes a language school in Bandung with an enrolment figure of 1,400. He stressed that not all of the 1,400 students at the school are ethnic Chinese. Some are *pribumi*[14] students who come all the way to Bandung from places such as Purwakarta.

The fact that not all students who attend language and National Plus schools are ethnic Chinese is significant to the notion of national-identity formation for the Chinese Indonesians. Whereas Chinese schools were banned during the Soeharto era, National Plus and language schools now thrive as places where both Chinese and *pribumi* may learn Bahasa Indonesia, English, and Mandarin of their own free will. It is also important to note that not all Indonesian Chinese parents have selected National Plus or International Curriculum schools for their children. A mother of two children, Maria, told me that the discipline at the National Plus and International Curriculum schools cannot compare to the discipline that she had at national schools such as Santa Ursula, Canisius College, or Sekolah Menengah Atas Kristen (The Christian High School), which are consistently ranked as the best schools in the nation. Even though they may not get as much Mandarin (Mandarin is taught at these national schools as an extra-curricular activity) as their peers at National Plus schools, Maria said that she preferred her children to be nurtured in a purely Indonesian environment, with Bahasa Indonesia as the main language in the curriculum. Coming from a family that hardly spoke Mandarin and rarely celebrated Chinese festivals when she was growing up, Maria does not see the importance of learning Mandarin. She said that it is more essential for her children to know what it means to be Indonesians because they live in Indonesia. Learning and excelling in Bahasa Indonesia is thus a priority for them instead of learning Chinese. Maria's comments illustrate Ien Ang's assertion that:

> Chineseness is not a category with a fixed content — be it racial, cultural or geographical — but operates as an open indeterminate signifier whose meanings are constantly renegotiated and rearticulated in different sections of the Chinese diaspora. Being Chinese outside China cannot possibly mean the same thing as [being] inside. It varies from place to place, moulded by the local circumstances in different parts of the world where people of Chinese ancestry have settled and constructed new ways of living (2001, p. 38).

Maria's choice not to take up the option of enrolling her children in National Plus or International Curriculum schools shows how "the local circumstances" of living in Indonesia have influenced the way in which she perceives her own sense of Chineseness. Other than the fact that they are Chinese by ethnicity, Maria and many others like her believe that their sense of Chineseness has been diluted because their families no longer practise Chinese customs or culture in their homes.

INTRODUCING MANDARIN IN NATIONAL SCHOOLS: FORMAL COLLABORATION BETWEEN THE CHINESE COMMUNITY, INDONESIA, AND CHINA

In 2000, the National Coordinating Association for Chinese Language (that is, Mandarin) Education (Badan Koordinasi Pendidikan Bahasa Mandarin) or the BKPBM was formed. The president of the association is Kakan Sukandadinata, a successful businessman who has numerous property holdings, financial firms, and factories dealing with paper products. He is also the current leader of the Nanan[15] association. BKPBM is the formal organization which is recognized and supported by both the Indonesian and Chinese governments. In my interview with Arifin Zain (Chai Changjie), the coordinating leader of the BKPBM, I learned that, other than primarily acting as a bridge between the two governments, it actively monitors the progress of Chinese language (that is, Mandarin) education in Indonesia's national schools.

The association also regularly organizes various seminars for Mandarin teachers to come together and learn about the most current teaching techniques from one another, as well as from teachers from Mainland China and Malaysia. In fact, the first activity when BKPBM was formally established was to organize a joint seminar with the East Java Department of Education on Mandarin education in August 2000. The seminar — the first of its kind ever since Abdurrahman Wahid eradicated the Presidential Instruction no. 14, signed in 1967 by Soeharto, which restricted the practice of Chinese customs and religions to the private domain — attracted 300 participants from all over East Java. As a follow-up to this seminar, a national seminar on Mandarin education was implemented at the end of 2001 in Jakarta. The organizers' target of 100 participants was surpassed when 500 teachers and others interested in Mandarin education turned up. The tremendous success of this seminar exerted a huge influence throughout Indonesia. From 2001 to 2003, many Mandarin courses were established all over the country and teachers asked for more definite instructions to teach the language. At the end of 2001, a team of teachers dedicated to the teaching of Mandarin was formed and the BKPBM held a formal ceremony where the Indonesian government officially appointed the association as the coordinating body for Mandarin education in the nation. In order to support the formal appointment of the BKPBM, the Chinese and Malaysian governments sent their representatives to attend the ceremony. The Malaysian government even sent the president and the vice-president of the Chinese language division of the Department of Education. Following the ceremony, the Malaysian government continued its support for the BKPBM by implementing a joint seminar in early 2004 centring on the exchange of Mandarin teaching experiences between Indonesian and Malaysian teachers.

By the end of 2002 and in early 2003, the Indonesian government and the BKPBM held intensive discussions regarding the government's serious intention to introduce Mandarin as an extra-curricular subject in national schools. In early 2002, the government organized a one-day seminar that focused on the feasibility of Chinese-language education in national schools. The conference, held in Jakarta, was attended by the Director-General of Youth and Extra-Curricular Affairs, the Director of National Education, and the Cultural Attaché from the Chinese embassy. The discussions, held in private or public forums such as the 2002 seminar, reached fruition when the Department of Education mandated the official introduction of Mandarin as an extra-curricular subject in national schools, with governmental aid. According to this mandate, Mandarin may be taken in lieu of Japanese or German as a third language (in addition to Bahasa Indonesia and English — which are required subjects in the national curriculum). The announcement was formalized by the Ministry of Education in June 2004.

From the very beginning of the discussions, it was clear that there would be a shortage of qualified teachers who could teach students proper

Mandarin. Both the Indonesian and Chinese governments were aware of this problem and often collaborated to come up with solutions. In mid-2001, the Director-General of the Department of Education signed an agreement with the Chinese government's Hanban, a consortium of eleven departments, including the Department of Education, the Department of Culture, and the Departments of Internal and Foreign Affairs. The agreement mobilizes the implementation of HSK examination in Indonesia. The HSK[16] is an internationally recognized examination that tests proficiency in Mandarin. In countries and regions such as the United States, Australia, Canada, and Europe, one must pass Grade 8 in the examination in order to attain certified status to teach Mandarin. The highest grade for the examination is 11. In Indonesia, however, the BKPBM and the Ministry of Education concur that a minimum of Grade 6 would be sufficient to attain qualification to teach Mandarin because the restrictions on Chinese culture and language during the Soeharto era had caused profound difficulties for those who were interested in learning the Chinese language. In October 2001, when the HSK examination was first offered in Indonesia, 1200 examinees sat for it — the highest number of examinees in Southeast Asia that year.

Apart from the HSK, the Indonesian and Chinese governments also worked together in the area of teacher training. Shortly after the official announcement that allows Mandarin to be taught at national schools was made, the Indonesian government sent fifty-one teachers from Indonesia (Jakarta, Medan, Pontianak, Surabaya, and several other cities) to participate in teacher training courses for one month at the Fujian Normal University in Fuzhou, China. Expenses for the courses were shared by the two governments. The Indonesian government paid the fiscal and visa fees for the teachers. They also supplied the domestic tickets for those coming from cities outside of Jakarta and a stipend for all the teachers. Once the delegation arrived in China, Hanban took care of all costs and living expenses. The return plane tickets for the teachers to and from China were also provided by Hanban. The cooperation between the two governments came as a welcome surprise for the Chinese community and the educational sector in Indonesia. It also indicated the serious intention of both governments to promote Mandarin education in Indonesia. Before the training in Fuzhou, many schools and teachers were sceptical about the feasibility and actual manifestation of Mandarin programmes in Indonesia. After the trip to Fuzhou, however, more national schools were emboldened to move forward with Mandarin language courses.

Although the training programme succeeded in moulding existing teachers in China, the Indonesian government, along with BKPBM, believed that more qualified and experienced teachers were needed to teach Mandarin courses in Indonesia's national schools. Acting on this need, Hanban agreed to send twenty teachers from China. Again, the costs for bringing in the teachers were shared by Hanban and the Indonesian government; Hanban paid for the return airfare to and from China and the teachers' salaries, while the Indonesian government was responsible for the living costs of the teachers while they were in Indonesia. On 21 July 2004, Lu Shumin, the Chinese ambassador to Indonesia, was present at a reception held by the Department of Education to welcome the twenty teachers from China. In the one year when they were in Indonesia, the twenty teachers did not only teach at their assigned national schools, but they also offered guidance in seminars conducted by BKPBM on Mandarin curriculum development, examination questions, as well as grading standards for the next academic year (2005–06). By the end of the teachers' tenure in Indonesia on 22 June 2005, both the Indonesian and Chinese governments proclaimed their continued support for Mandarin education in Indonesia. In the following year, in August 2006, the number of teachers from China doubled to forty. Prior to their arrival in Indonesia, the Department of Education, BKPBM and Hanban printed 7,000 sets of textbooks to be distributed to the national high schools (Sekolah Menengah Atas or SMA) offering Mandarin courses. According to the Ministry of Education, there are a hundred national high schools that have started offering Mandarin courses. However, Zain said that this number is under-reported because there are many other national high schools offering Mandarin education that have not registered with the Ministry of Education. These schools are mainly in Jakarta, but there are also those in Surabaya, Medan, Bandung, Sumatra, Kalimantan, and other areas of Indonesia.

The efforts of the Indonesian government, the Chinese community (as represented by the BKPBM), and the Chinese government continue to this day as they endeavour to increase the number of teachers and national schools offering Mandarin courses. Their most recent joint effort was a seminar on the teaching of Mandarin and syllabus arrangement on 1 June 2007. The seminar featured teachers from China and was attended by 300 participants.

Concluding Remarks

In mid-2007, the time when this chapter was written, the future of Chinese education in Indonesia looks bright. Some scholars such as Lee Guan Kin (2005) have even referred to the burgeoning number of Chinese schools as a "fever of Chinese school establishment" (p. 247). As mentioned, the Chinese and Indonesian governments, together with the BKPBM, are actively engaged in promoting Mandarin education in Indonesia. The current leaders in Chinese education (e.g. Chinese community leaders such as Kakan Sukandadinata and Yau Thungjung) are also positive that more members of the next generation of Indonesian Chinese will be able to read and write in the Chinese language as opposed to their parents, who grew up in the Soeharto era. They also point out that National Plus and International Curriculum schools, as well as language centres and national schools offering Mandarin as part of their curriculum, are not the only places where the next generation of Indonesian Chinese may learn the Chinese language. The media also play an important educational function for members of this generation. In the post-Soeharto era, they may choose from a growing number of Chinese-language newspapers, whereas between 1965–98, only one Chinese-language newspaper was allowed to circulate (that is, *Harian Indonesia*,[17] which was heavily controlled by the government). Unlike in the Soeharto era, the Chinese-language newspapers that are currently in circulation have little or no government control. These newspapers include *Yindunixiya Shang Bao* or *Shang Bao*, a business-oriented newspaper, and *Guoji Ribao* (The International Daily News), which is distributed together with *Wen Wei Po* (a Hong Kong based newspaper), and the *People's Daily* Overseas Edition (the overseas edition of People's Republic of China's official newspaper). Of these publications, *Guoji Ribao* is the most successful, with circulation figures that have jumped from 20,000 in 2002 to 50,000 in 2007.[18] It obtains most of its revenues from congratulatory notices and advertisements for various events in the Chinese community, ranging from weddings to large-scale public events.

Other than newspapers, the next generation of Indonesian Chinese and others who are interested in the Chinese language and culture may also turn to television and radio. Since 1999, Metro TV has begun broadcasting news in Chinese. The cable providers such as *Cable Vision* and *Indovision* widen the options of Chinese-language television channels by transmitting programmes and shows directly from China and Taiwan. There are also channels such as the *Celestial Channel* on *Cable Vision* that feature Hong Kong serials and films throughout the day. These television and cable channels are further complemented by Mandarin programmes and songs that are broadcast from a radio station called *Cakrawala*. All of these media offerings would thus encourage Mandarin students to practise what they have learned at school.

If members of this generation are interested in pursuing higher education in the Chinese language, leaders of Chinese education point out that provisions, such as scholarships from the Chinese government and various Chinese community organizations, are available. As Arifin Zain of BKPBM mentioned, in July 2005, Hanban offered twenty full scholarships for

Indonesian students to study at Guangzhou's Jin Nan University. Furthermore, a college catering to tertiary Chinese education,[19] Xin Ya College, was established in 2005. Hartono (Lie Pe Chiau), the head coordinator of Xin Ya College, said that high school graduates spend two years at the Jakarta campus and complete their final two years either at Fujian University in Fuzhou or Quanzhou Huaqiao University. Upon graduation, they can either work as Mandarin teachers or as professionals in companies that need people skilled in Mandarin. There is also a scholarship committee at Xin Ya College, supported by prominent members of the Indonesian Chinese community, such as The Ning King, Prajogo Pangestu, and Anthony Salim. This committee provides scholarships to exceptional students at Xin Ya College and offers no-interest loans to students.

In light of the above opportunities, Chinese education in Indonesia does have a bright future. The main difference between recent developments in Chinese education compared with those in the Soeharto era is the fact that everyone in the country, the ethnic Chinese notwithstanding, has the freedom to learn the Chinese language and culture. Depending on their various personal and social needs, all Indonesians can now decide, without any restrictions, whether they should take advantage of the myriad opportunities to learn Mandarin.

Notes

[1]   According to Arief Budiman, Barbara Hatley, and Damien Kingsbury in their introduction to *Reformasi: Crisis and Change in Indonesia* (Monash: Monash Asia Institute, 1999), *Reformasi* reflects its ubiquitous yet complex usage in contemporary Indonesia to designate an ideal state, a process, a cliched slogan, and a state of mind. In the political field, *Reformasi* implies the aspiration of democracy, however that ideal might be measured and interpreted (p. ii).

[2]   Indonesia was known as the Dutch East Indies before it proclaimed its independence on 17 August 1945.

[3]   Kwee 1969 asserted that Mandarin is the language that could express the aspirations of the entire nation (that is, China). The idea of employing Mandarin came from Phoa Keng Hek who led a debate on the curriculum of the schools in which he argued for a dialect then alien to Java. Such thinking had been a basis for the founding of THHK by the Chinese of various groups, namely, Hokkien, Cantonese, Hakka, and *peranakan*. If Hokkien were used in the schools, the Cantonese would surely feel mistreated. On the other hand, Mandarin was the official language used by officials and by a large number of scholars in all the provinces. Natives of North and Central China who spoke Mandarin almost never came to Java, thus Mandarin could be said to be a neutral language.

Based on these reasons, it was finally agreed to use Mandarin, although many Hokkien people felt threatened and would have preferred to see the school use the language of their own group. However, their objections were gradually overcome and all THHK schools taught Mandarin (pp. 18–19).

[4]   For a more comprehensive discussion on the 1965 coup, see George Kahin 1966, *Nationalism and Revolution in Indonesia* (Ithaca, NY: Cornell UP).

[5]   One of the most comprehensive of the Soeharto regime's assimilationist regulations is *The Basic Policy for the Solution of the Chinese Problem*. For more information on this policy, the policy restricting religion, beliefs and Chinese customs, and the basic policy concerning Indonesian citizens of foreign descent, see Mely G. Tan 1991, "The Social and Cultural Dimensions of the Role of Ethnic Chinese in Indonesian History", paper presented during a symposium, *The Role of the Indonesian Chinese in Shaping Modern Indonesia Life*, held at Cornell University in conjunction with the Southeast Asian Studies Summer Institute from 13–15 July 1990.

[6]   Susilo Bambang Yudhoyono became the sixth president of Indonesia following his success in a national election held in September 2004.

[7]   Megawati's government declared Chinese New Year an elective holiday (which means that the Chinese may take that day off to celebrate it) for the Chinese in 2002, but formally declared it a national holiday in 2003.

[8]   I asked the BPS (Biro Pusat Statistik or the Central Board of Statistics) and Dinas Pendidikan Dasar Jakarta (Jakarta Basic Education Agency) regarding data on trilingual schools in Indonesia but they said that they do not have data on these schools. Therefore, I asked Arifin Zain of BKPBM about the registered number of National Plus and International Curriculum Schools at the Ministry of Education, and he said that the numbers are under-reported (only twenty-eight schools were officially registered by 2006).

[9]   There are no official data for trilingual schools. For parts of Jakarta that have a large population of Chinese, such as Jakarta Barat (West Jakarta — Puri Indah, Kebon Jeruk, Permata Buana), Jakarta Timur (East Jakarta — Kelapa Gading, Pulomas), and Jakarta Utara (North Jakarta — Pluit, Pantai Indah Kapuk), I personally recorded about thirty-six trilingual schools (National Plus and International Curriculum schools) from my own observations and from the yellow pages in the phone directory. Leaders in Chinese education such as Arifin Zain of BKPBM, Hartono of Xin Ya College, and Sidharta Wirahadi Kusuma of the Hakka Association and BKPBM, all estimated the number to be about fifty.

[10] Since the National Plus schools are fairly new (most were established between 2000–03), they are mainly kindergarten and primary schools. Moreover, most of the students have not yet graduated to move on to secondary schools. Tunas Muda, Global Nusantara, Nasional High, and Bina Bangsa, however, do offer secondary school education to their students.

¹¹ The EBTANAS, or National Examinations, have come under intense scrutiny and criticisms in recent months. There have been controversies over the administration of the tests because teachers were found guilty of providing answers to students (see *Jakarta Post* article on "The National Exam and Indonesia's Education Woes", published on 30 May 2007, p. 7). These teachers were pressured to do so because schools needed to boost the passing numbers of EBTANAS. Although this practice incurred the wrath of parents, it is still widely practised in many schools across Indonesia, and reveals the general problem of poor infrastructure, teaching methods, and staff training. Moreover, violence and vandalism erupted on 16 June 2007 when students at a senior vocational high school in East Nusa Tenggara rioted after they discovered that none of them had passed the National Examinations (see related articles in *Kompas*, 18 June 2007, p. 1 and *Jakarta Post*, 18 June 2007, p. 1).

¹² Roger Brumby, "Advantages of IB Diploma Program for Students", *Jakarta Post*, 6 May 2007, p. 22.

¹³ According to recent United States National Bureau of Statistics estimates conducted in early 2007, the GDP (Gross Domestic Product) growth of China is expected to exceed ten per cent once again. Four consecutive years of growth at over ten per cent have seen China surpass Britain to become the world's fourth largest economy. In 2006, China also surpassed Japan as the world's greatest saver, amassing foreign exchange reserves of over US$850 billion. Despite accounting for only five per cent of the world's GDP, the world's fastest growing economy is set to continue on its recent trajectory of development.

¹⁴ *Pribumi* literally means "sons of the soil" in Bahasa Indonesia. It reflects the Indonesian nationalist spirit that instills pride in the indigenous population of their motherland. For instance, during the struggle for Indonesia's independence in the 1940s, nationalists called upon their fellow *pribumi* to fight against the Dutch for their motherland's freedom. In Soeharto's New Order, several economic policies favouring *pribumi* capitalists served to buttress the expansion of indigenous industries and corporations. For a more complete discussion on these policies, refer to Richard Robison, *Indonesia: The Rise of Capital* (Sydney, Australia: Allen & Unwin, 1988), especially the chapter on "Indigenous Capitalists Under the New Order", pp. 323–72.

¹⁵ Nanan is part of the Fujian province in China.

¹⁶ The HSK may also be used to enter tertiary institutions in China. Although the HSK certificate has a lifetime validity, the scores are only valid for two years. That is, Chinese universities will not accept scores that are more than two years old.

¹⁷ Since 2006, *Harian Indonesia* has been taken over by the Malaysian Sin Chew Group. The Chinese name has been changed from *Yindunixia Ribao* to *Yinni Xing Zhou Ribao*. The Indonesian name has remained unchanged.

¹⁸ These figures were released by the marketing department of *Guoji Ribao*.

19   Although Ma Chung University in Malang, East Java, which was established in early July 2007, does not cater specifically to Chinese education, it is noteworthy because its founders and sponsors are former students of Ma Chung Chinese High School (Sekolah Menengah Tiong Hwa Ma Chung). These former students, led by Mochtar Riady, the founder of Lippo Group, are well-known and successful members of the Indonesian society. The university's student guide states that Ma Chung University is an institution which aspires to create "future business leaders" who are conversant in Mandarin and skilled in Bahasa Indonesia and English. The guide also mentions that the modern, 40,000-square metre campus and its collaboration with University of Glascow in Scotland would provide an excellent opportunity for Indonesian students to "compete globally".

References

Ang, I. *On Not Speaking Chinese: Living Between Asia and the West.* New York: Routledge, 2001.

Budianta, Melani. Women's Activism during the *"Reformasi."* Years. In *Challenging Authoritarianism in Southeast Asia: Comparing Indonesia and Malaysia*, edited by Ariel Heryanto and Sumit K. Mandal, pp. 145–77. New York, NY: Routledge, 2003.

———. *Discourse of Cultural Identity in Indonesia During the 1997–1998 Monetary Crisis.* Inter-Asia Cultural Studies, vol 1, no. 1 (2000): 109–28.

Budiman, Arief. "Portrait of the Chinese in Post-Soeharto Indonesia". In *Chinese Indonesians: Remembering, Distorting, Forgetting*, edited by Tim Lindsey and Helen Pausacker, pp. 95–104. Singapore: Institute of Southeast Asian Studies, 2005.

Coppel, Charles. *Indonesian Chinese in Crisis.* New York: Oxford University Press, 1983.

Govaars, Ming. *Dutch Colonial Education: The Chinese Experience in Indonesia, 1900–1942.* Singapore: Chinese Heritage Centre, 2005.

Heidhues, Mary S. "Indonesia". In *The Encyclopedia of the Chinese Overseas*, edited by Lynn Pan, pp. 151–68. Singapore: Chinese Heritage Centre, 2006.

Kwee, Tek Hoay. *The Origins of the Modern Chinese Movement in Indonesia*, translated and edited by Lea E. Williams. Ithaca, NY: Cornell University Press, 1969.

Lane, Max. "Mass Politics and Political Change in Indonesia". In *Reformasi*, edited by Arief Budiman, Barbara Hatley, and Damien Kingsbury, pp. 239–51. Clayton, Australia: Monash Asia Institute, 1999.

Lee, Guan Kin. "Singapore Chinese Society in Transition: Reflections on the Cultural Implications of Modern Education". In *Chinese Migrants Abroad: Cultural, Educational and Social Dimensions of the Chinese Diaspora*, edited by Michael W. Charney, Brenda S.A. Yeoh, and Chee Kiong Tong, pp. 229–51. Singapore: Singapore University Press, 2005.

Lubis, T. Mulya and Santosa, Mas A. "Economic Regulation, Good Governance and the Environment: An Agenda for Law Reform in Indonesia". In *Reformasi*, edited by Arief Budiman, Barbara Hatley, and Damien Kingsbury, pp. 343–61. Clayton, Australia: Monash Asia Institute, 1999.

Peake, Cyrus H. *Nationalism and Education in Modern China*. New York: Howard Fertig, 1970.

Shenkar, Oded. *The Chinese Century: The Rising Chinese Economy and its Impact on the Global Economy, The Balance of Power, and Your Job*. The Wharton Press Paperback Series, 2006.

Suryadinata, Leo. *The Culture of the Chinese Minority in Indonesia*. Singapore: Times Books International, 1997.

———. *Pribumi Indonesians, the Chinese Minority and China*, 3rd ed. Singapore: Heinemann Asia, 1992.

Tan, Mely G. "The Ethnic Chinese in Indonesia: Trials and Tribulations". In *Struggling in Hope: A Tribute to the Rev. Dr Eka Darmaputera*, edited by Ferdinand Suleeman, Adji A. Sutama, and A. Rajendra, pp. 683–703. Jakarta: Gunung Mulia, 1999.

Yen, Ching-Hwang. "Hokkien Immigrant Society and Modern Chinese Education in British Malaya". In *Chinese Migrants Abroad: Cultural, Educational and Social Dimensions of the Chinese Diaspora*, edited by Michael W. Charney, Brenda S.A. Yeoh, and Chee Kiong Tong, pp. 114–44. Singapore: Singapore University Press, 2005.

Yen, Ching-Hwang. *The Overseas Chinese and the 1911 Revolution: With Special Reference to Singapore and Malaya*. Kuala Lumpur: Oxford University Press, 1976.

6

ETHNIC CHINESE RELIGIONS: SOME RECENT DEVELOPMENTS

Susy Ong

When looking into recent developments of ethnic Chinese religions in Indonesia, we should bear in mind the domestic and external factors which have contributed to the religious scene of the local Chinese community.

It is well acknowledged that during three decades of the Soeharto regime, the public discourse in this country was dominated by Communist-phobia and China-phobia. In order to survive and thrive, all Indonesians had to state clearly their affiliation to a certain state-sanctioned religious group; and this is especially necessary for the ethnic Chinese, who are vulnerable to accusations of being pro-Communist or Communists. The assumption here is that Communists are atheists. To be accepted as non-communist, Chinese Indonesians are expected to have a religion. Understandably ethnic Chinese religious groups such as Buddhist and Christian groups in Indonesia flourished.

The other domestic factor that should not be overlooked is that, as a consequence of the delegitimization of cultural practices associated with "Chineseness", some religious practices (for example, those relating to the Confucian religion) were viewed as a pretext for Chinese cultural practices and were hence discouraged. Nevertheless, the Soeharto regime did not ban the Confucian religion as it claimed that Indonesia had religious freedom. But the New Order derecognized Confucianism, thus making its development difficult. This encouraged the rise of certain religions which are perceived to be "less Chinese". Buddhism was considered to be such a religion at that time.[1] But in reality, Buddhism has been quite divided and there is Sinicized Buddhism, which is strongly embedded in Chinese culture. Through Buddhism, Chinese cultural/ethnic identity can be preserved.

The flourishing of Buddhism and Christianity among ethnic Chinese Indonesians has also been encouraged by international (but mostly dominated by Chinese-speaking groups) Buddhist and Christian organizations. These international organizations provided their co-religious groups in Indonesia with both material and spiritual support, making it possible for the Chinese Indonesians to retain their ethnic/cultural identities. The fall of Soeharto and the advent of the era of globalization gave further impetus to the development of Chinese religious groups. This chapter attempts to examine recent developments of ethnic Chinese religions such as Buddhism, Confucianism, and Protestant Christianity. Islam and Catholicism will not be discussed here due to lack of data and time to do further research.

BUDDHISM: THE RELIGION AND "CULTURE" OF ETHNIC CHINESE

Studies on the history of ethnic Chinese Buddhist groups from early till the end of the twentieth century have been conducted extensively by Leo Suryadinata.[2] However, for this chapter, I would like to focus on the intra-ethnic contention between Buddhist and Confucian groups for hegemony. Young-generation ethnic Chinese have affiliated themselves with Buddhist groups, both to satisfy their longing for association with fellow ethnic Chinese, and assert their legitimacy as being non-exclusive. This is due to the general belief that religious belief is universal, thus non-ethnic in nature. Finally, I would like to examine the external factors, which are Chinese factors, that have exerted hegemony over ethnic Chinese Buddhist groups, empowering them domestically, and assess the possible consequences of those in the future.

External "Hegemony" and the Establishment of Buddhist Power

As Suryadinata stated, at the beginning of the twentieth century, the religion of ethnic Chinese in Indonesia was basically a form of syncretism, consisting of Buddhism, Confucian teachings (which was originally the philosophy of the Chinese political elites, and hence not well-understood by the uneducated masses), and Taoism, a kind of folk belief.[3] It is, like most of ancient religions, a polytheistic religion.

Nevertheless, soon after the birth of modern Indonesia, ethnic Chinese were, with regard to religion, divided into followers of Buddhism or Agama Konghucu, the so-called Confucian religion.[4]

When Soeharto came to power at the height of the Cold War, Indonesia entered an era of anti-Chinese hysteria and China-phobia. However, the regime also needed support from religious groups, particularly the large and financially strong ones. Among them were Buddhist groups supported by wealthy ethnic Chinese.

The beginning of the Soeharto era was also marked by the severance of diplomatic relations with Communist China, while cultural and economic ties with the Chinese regime in Taiwan were maintained and even strengthened. In 1971, it was reported that a local Buddhist organization invited a prominent China-born (but who then resided in Taiwan) Buddhist monk, Shi Dongchu (释东初), to visit Jakarta and several other cities in Indonesia. He was warmly received by ethnic Chinese Buddhists. It appears that international Buddhist organizations paid much attention to the development of Indonesian Buddhism and, finally, in 1983, the Indonesia government sanctioned the *Waisak* as a national holiday.[5] *Waisak* day simultaneously celebrates the birth, enlightenment, and death of Buddha.

The success of those Buddhist groups had understandably been achieved through forming alliances with the national political, and as it was the era of military rule — also the military elites. However, when allied with political power, something religious tends to turn political, which stresses dominance over tolerance. This is obvious when the government declared that Agama Konghucu was not a religion, but a philosophy, and thus ordered its adherents to proclaim themselves Buddhist. The Buddhist group, with its mostly ethnic Chinese members, welcomed this policy, since it would result in an increase in its membership. In 1984, the Buddhist community supported the government officials' proposal to convert *kelenteng*, which accommodates a number of Chinese legendary demi-gods, to *vihara*, in Buddhist temples.[6] This confirmed the truism that ethnic Chinese religious groups must approach and ally themselves to the political power in order to survive. In other words, they cannot confine themselves to the religious or spiritual sphere.

Ethnic Chinese Buddhists and Buddhist Temples

How many ethnic Chinese Buddhists are there in Indonesia? There is no data available, partly because the persons in charge of the Buddhist groups are of the opinion that such surveys might cause distrust among non-ethnic Chinese

Buddhists and make ethnic Chinese Buddhists vulnerable to discrimination and social alienation.

An alternative way to estimate the size of the ethnic Chinese Buddhist population in Indonesia is by grasping the distribution of Buddhist temples nationwide. According to a survey published by a Buddhist group in Jakarta,[7] there are 1,627 *vihara* or *kelenteng* in Indonesia. A large number of them still retain Chinese-sounding names; therefore, they are supposed to be the places of worship for ethnic Chinese Buddhists.

Table 6.1 shows the provinces with significant ethnic Chinese populations. It does present exhaustive results, but we can estimate that in the areas with higher percentages of ethnic Chinese (Java island [including Jakarta], North

Table 6.1
Chinese Temples/Buddhist Temples in Indonesia

Province	Number of *Kelenteng* or *Vihara*
Bali	3
Aceh	12
North Sumatra	401
West Sumatra	5
Bengkulu	7
Jambi	7
Riau (including the present Kepulauan Riau Province)	85
Lampung	242
South Sumatra	77
West Java (including the present Banten Province)	114
Jakarta	246
Central Java	146
DIY Yogyakarta	5
East java	206
West Kalimantan	37
South Kalimantan	6
North Sulawesi	8
Central Sulawesi	6
Southeast Sulawesi	6
Nusa Tenggara Barat (West Nusa Tenggara)	1
Maluku	1
Irian Jaya (now changed into Papua and Papua Barat)	6

Source: <www.infobuddhis.com>.

Sumatra, Riau, Lampung, South Sumatra, and West Kalimantan), local ethnic Chinese still maintain their Buddhist traditions and beliefs.

Recent Developments

There are two national Buddhist groups, KASI (Konferensi Agung Sangha Indonesia, or Indonesian Great Sangha Conference) and WALUBI (Perwakilan Umat Buddha Indonesia, or Indonesian Buddhist Council), which are contending for supremacy. Alliance with political power and recognition from national leaders are often more important than internal religious affairs. However, in recent years, from 1990s, a number of young and well-educated ethnic Chinese Buddhists, organized themselves into a number of Youth Buddhist Groups which are more religious and idealistic. They aim at self-enhancement through better understanding of Buddhist scriptures and discussions with fellow Buddhists, and fulfilling their social obligations by getting involved in charity activities. The following outlines these youth Buddhist groups.

Youth Buddhist Groups
Hikmahbudhi

The Hikmahbudhi (Himpunan Mahasiswa Buddhis Indonesia, or Association of Indonesia Buddhist College Student), according to its website, was founded "in 1988, but did not became significant until the middle 1990s, when Buddhist student activists tried to revive this organization as a medium to build sensitivity for Indonesian society problems". Its activities include offering language courses, meditation, discussions, sports, leadership training, Dhamma Comprehension Week (Retreat), Commemoration of Buddhist Days, song composition contests, pop singer contests, national Buddhist Choir Contests, magazines, books, and bulletin publications.[8]

It is impossible to ask explicitly whether it is exclusively an ethnic Chinese organization, but judging from its advisory board, which is chaired by Kwik Kian Gie (郭建义), a former minister in President Megawati's cabinet and a prominent national figure, it would appear so. Of the seven members of its advisory board, at least one can be clearly identified as ethnic Chinese, namely Prajnavira Mahastavira (慧雄法师), who also serves as Assistant Secretary General of World Buddhist Sangha Council (with its headquarters in Taipeh, Taiwan). One other member is Eddy Sadeli (李祥胜), an ethnic Chinese lawyer who has been actively participating in social movements since 1998.

We might assume that the expansion of higher education in the 1980s and 1990s has resulted in the birth of a generation of well-educated ethnic Chinese with higher social awareness and idealism. During the tumultuous years of the 1990s, when social awareness among the young generation, including young-generation ethnic Chinese, was heightening and when association with something "Chinese" remained a taboo, those young and idealistic ethnic Chinese organized themselves under the banner of Buddhism.

Patria: Theravadin Youth Buddhist Group

Another young ethnic Chinese Buddhist Group is Patria (Pemuda Theravada Indonesia, or Theravadin Buddhist Youth of Indonesia), established in December 1995, with headquarters in Jakarta. It is clearly stated that its objectives are to strengthen faith towards Buddhist teachings among young Buddhists, strive for self-improvement, strengthen solidarity among fellow Buddhists, and enhance the social well-being of its members and society in general.

Presently, the size of its membership is unavailable, but it has set up branches in fifteen provinces (North Sumatra, Jambi, Lampung, Jakarta, Banten, West Java, Cenral Java, Yogyakarta, East Java, Bali, West Kalimantan, South Kalimantan, East Kalimantan, West Nusa Tenggara, and South Sulawesi) and more than fifty cities nationwide, most of them places with significant ethnic Chinese populations. Patria is affiliated with the World Fellowship of Buddhist Youth, headquartered in Bangkok, Thailand.[9]

According to my source, a member of Patria's Tangerang city (Banten Province) branch, Patria is indeed an ethnic Chinese organization, although no one would state this openly. Its activities include leadership training, national sports and art competitions, teaching Dhamma to teenagers, and outdoor and charity activities, such as helping the funding of the education of impoverished children.

Judging from its stated objectives and daily activities, Patria is both a religious and social organization. Its members, young ethnic Chinese, are fully aware that they need to understand Buddhist teachings well in order to nourish a sound mind, and to strive to improve their material well-being; since impoverishment may lead to degradation of the mind.

Campus Student Groups

As a result of the expansion of higher education since the 1980s, more and more young ethnic Chinese have enrolled in institutions of higher learning in big cities, and among them are ethnic Chinese Buddhists. In some of these institutions, they took the initiatives to set up Buddhist organizations, which might serve as a forum for communication, and to build solidarity and mutual help among fellow ethnic Chinese. As religious organizations, they are supposed to be trans-ethnic, but since most of their members are ethnic Chinese, they turn out to be ethnic-based.

We will take two organizations as examples: one is from the Universitas Bina Nusantara, a private university located in Jakarta with Chinese students as a majority, and the other is from Universitas Indonesia in Depok, with ethnic Chinese students as a minority.

KMBD at Binus University

Universitas Bina Nusantara, or Binus University, was originally a computer academy set up in the 1970s. In 1987, it changed its name to Institute of Management and Computer Science as a result of its expansion, and started to offer a Bachelor's course in computer science. In 1996, it acquired full-fledge university status;[10] presently, it is one of the fastest growing institutions of higher learning in Indonesia.

The majority of its students are ethnic Chinese from Outer Islands (Sumatra and Kalimantan), where ethnic Chinese still largely preserve Chinese traditions, using Chinese dialects for communication within the family or community, and Buddhism is more or less regarded as part of the Chinese traditional culture. Now that they are in Jakarta, a "foreign land" for studies, cut off from their Chinese cultural roots, they need to rebuild their cultural communities here. One of them is the campus Buddhist organization, Keluarga Mahasiswa Buddhist Dhammavaddhana, or Dhammavaddhana Buddhism Students Family, abbreviated as KMBD (Dhammavaddhana means growth in Dhamma; Dhamma means the teachings of Buddha).

According to their website <http://www.kmbd.info/tentangkmbdinfo. php>, KMBD was set up in 1989 by Buddhist students studying here. Its objectives were to serve as a religious, cultural, and social organization for the students.

By stressing the words "cultural" and "social", KMBD is indeed not intended solely as a religious organization. During my interview with a certain Buddhist monk at the Ekayana Buddhist Centre, which is situated adjacent to Binus University, and where many Binus students come regularly to pray, I was informed that quite a few of those students are very pious, even fanatical, Buddhists, although they do not actually know or understand much of Buddha's teachings.

This might help to explain the demand for "social" and "cultural" accommodation among young urban ethnic Chinese, and it turns out that such a religious organization is to accommodate those demands.

KMBUI at University of Indonesia

The University of Indonesia (UI) is the most prestigious public university in Indonesia. Because of the legacy there of racial prejudice and discriminatory policies against ethnic Chinese during the Soeharto era, the percentage of ethnic Chinese students enrolled there has been extremely low.

There is a Buddhist student organization at UI called Keluarga Mahasiswa Buddhis Universitas Indonesia (abbreviated as KMBUI), or Family of Buddhist Students of University of Indonesia. According to its website,[11] the KMBUI was founded in the late 1960s, but it was not until the end of the 1980s that it gathered momentum. We are unable to know exactly whether the "founding persons" are ethnic Chinese, since raising this question is a political taboo.

I sent a questionnaire to the person in charge, enquiring about the present ethnic composition of the KMBUI. The reply was, as predicted, that statistical data was not available; the explanation was that they did not collect such data in order to avoid being accused of being exclusive.

We can imagine how embarrassing it must be, in such a non-ethnic Chinese dominated environment, to ask a person whether he or she is an ethnic Chinese.

However, I am also informed that the majority of its members are indeed ethnic Chinese students.

To my next question on whether ethnic Chinese students regard KMBUI as a forum for communication and building solidarity among fellow ethnic Chinese, the answer was that KMBUI does serve as such a forum for its ethnic Chinese members, but they try to avoid such a development to avoid creating ethnic segregation.

I am also told that KMBUI members actively socialize with members of other religious groups within the campus.

These attitudes might help to explain the self-image and aspiration of those ethnic Chinese youth. They need an "ethnic" organization wherein they feel culturally comfortable. However, they do not intend to confine themselves to their ethnic circle, and wish to participate actively in the larger multi-cultural community, in order to avoid being labelled "exclusive".

External Influence

As I mentioned earlier, ethnic Chinese Buddhist organizations in modern Indonesia are largely empowered by foreign influences, especially influences from Taiwan. These influences, I would like to argue, are like a double-edged sword; they serve to empower tiny Buddhist-cum-ethnic Chinese groups in Indonesia, and while doing so, further make it self-evident that ethnic Chinese are indeed "foreign" in this country.

Vihara Mahavira Graha Pusat and its External Connection

The biggest Buddhist temple with the most modern facilities in Jakarta is Vihara Mahavira Graha Pusat (大丛山西禅寺), located in the northern part of Jakarta, the ethnic Chinese residence quarters in Jakarta. It was built in 1986 on the initiative of Prajnavira Mahasthavira (慧雄法师). Presently, he is still serving as chief monk (住持) of the temple and of another temple in Medan, as well as that of two Buddhist temples in Singapore.[12]

According to the website of Kai Yuan temple in Fuzhou, China, Prajnavira Mahasthavira is a prominent figure well known in Buddhist communities in Southeast Asia, as well as in China and Taiwan. He has been recruiting Buddhist monks from China to serve at his Buddhist temple in Singapore.

The Vihara Mahavira Graha Pusat in Jakarta is reported to have all its regular Dhamma (Buddha's teaching) assemblies conducted in Mandarin.[13] One will easily notice that the temple intends to serve ethnic Chinese in Indonesia exclusively, with no less an emphasis on "culture" than "religion".

A further look at this "international connection" may confirm the external influence, even 'hegemony' on ethnic Chinese Buddhism in Indonesia. In May 1966, the World Buddhist Sangha Council (世界佛教僧伽会) was established, with its headquarters in Taipei, Taiwan. Its main objective was to preach Buddhism worldwide, especially among ethnic Chinese communities. We may assume that the visit by Buddhist monks from Taiwan to Indonesia since 1970s is part of its activities.

Presently, among its executive committee members, six are prominent Buddhist figures in Indonesia, out of whom five have Chinese-sounding Buddhist names. Its Indonesian members are as follows:

(1) Prajnavira Mahasthavira (慧雄法师), Assistant Secretary-General (中文副秘书长) and chief monk at Vihara Mahavira Graha Pusat in Jakarta. He serves as a member of the Elderly Board of KASI (Indonesian Great Sangha Conference).

(2) Dharmasagoro (定海法师), Vice-president; a member of the Elderly Board of KASI
(3) Sukhemo, a Dhamma Committee member and a member of the Elderly Board of KASI
(4) Ven. Hung Fei (宏慧法师), a Rituals Committee member
(5) Aryamaitri (定盛法师), a Cultural Committee member and member of the Elderly Board of KASI
(6) Dhyana Vira (定雄法师), a Liaison Committee member.[14]

The rise of Buddhism among ethnic Chinese in Indonesia has been linked to external support. Buddhism is indeed flourishing among ethnic Chinese in Indonesia nowadays. But it is also evident that it is sometimes more "cultural" and "ethnic" than "religious".

Indonesia's Branch of the Tzu Chi Foundation

The Tzu Chi Foundation is a Taiwan-based Buddhist organization founded in 1966, which focuses on charity activities such as disaster relief, medical aid, free housing, and free education. Its Indonesian branch, Yayasan Budha Tzu Chi Indonesia, was founded in 1994[15] by Taiwanese business persons residing in Jakarta, and local ethnic Chinese entrepreneurs. Presently, the executive director for its Indonesia branch is still a Taiwanese expatriate, Liu Su Mei.[16]

This religious organization, a collaboration between Taiwanese expatriates in Indonesia and local ethnic Chinese, has indeed ethnic characteristics. However, unlike Western religious charity groups which encourage conversion, this group stresses universal human solidarity and brotherhood, without much dogmatic preaching. Through its generous charity work, which aims especially to help impoverished non-ethnic Chinese, it is generally well-received by the Indonesian lower class and government authorities.

Domestic branches are set up in Jakarta, Medan, Makassar, Surabaya, Bandung, Batam, Pekanbaru, and Tangerang.[17] All these are cities with relatively large numbers of ethnic Chinese residents. This organization also operates two housing facilities in Jakarta, and a TV station, named *Da-ai*, or great love.

The Indonesian Branch of Tzu Chi Foundation is a social rather than religious organization for the middle and upper classes of ethnic Chinese. But the banner is still religious, not ethnic. It thus enables its members to claim universality, instead of ethnicity. By showing its charitable nature, it is apparently allowing its ethnic Chinese members to gain moral legitimacy.

RELIGIONS WITH DISTINCTIVE
CHINESE CULTURAL LEGACIES

Konghucuisme as a Religion: Its Historical and Political Dimension

The history of Agama Konghucu (Confucian religion) in Indonesia from the early twentieth century has been elaborated by Leo Suryadinata.[18] In this chapter, I would like to discuss three points hitherto taken for granted: first, the historical and political context that "religionized" Confucianism in the early twentieth century, which, in the Indonesian case, must be interpreted as part of this universal trend; second, the consequence of the Indonesian government's dereligionization of Agama Konghucu in the late 1970s; and third, the political economy rationale that gave rise to "Confucian Renaissance" in the late twentieth century.

Historical Context of the "Religionization" of Confucianism

In "'Is Confucianism a Religion?' A 1923 Debate in Java",[19] Coppel drew our attention to a debate in *peranakan* Chinese society in Java concerning the problem of how to define their "Chineseness", or identity. The Khong Kauw (Confucian) group, which argues that "Confucian teaching" is the quintessence of Chinese people, cited the argument by Tan Hwan Tjiang (Chen Huanzhang; 陈焕章). Chen's paper has been translated into Malay by Lim Hok Gan and appeared in a newspaper in Surabaya earlier. Chen was a disciple of Kang Youwei (康有为), the royalist. While studying at Columbia University in the United States, he established Kung Jiao Hui (The Society of Confucianism) in New York in 1907. After the Xinhai Revolution in 1911 that gave birth to the young republic, toppled the Manchu Dynasty, and thus put an end to the history of several thousand years of dynasty rule, a group of royalists sought to restore the monarchy system and make Confucianism the official state religion of China. Under the leadership of Kang You Wei, they rallied under the banner of Kong Jiao Hui.

The movement to install Confucianism as an official state religion in China failed. As a consequence, Chen Huanzhang retreated to Hong Kong — then a British colony serving as an asylum for Chinese political activists who failed — and established the Hong Kong Confucian Institute (香港孔教学院). This Confucian group endeavoured to spread Confucian teaching in Hong Kong first, before expanding back in China and other ethnic Chinese communities worldwide.[20] This may help to explain why Indonesian Confucianists insist that Confucianism should be recognized by the government as a religion.

Agama Konghucu Derecognized, Confucianists Martyrized

As Suryadinata elaborated in his essay on Indonesian Buddhism and Confucianism,[21] in 1978, at the height of the Cold War, the Soeharto regime issued a circular declaring that Confucianism was excluded from the list of stated-sanction religions. This, indeed, was an assault on its followers. And as mentioned above, local Buddhist groups, including the ethnic Chinese dominated ones, welcomed this by encouraging the conversion of *kelentengs* to *viharas*, thus eradicating the folk-belief and non-Buddhist elements within those ethnic Chinese religious compounds.

The political rationale for this government decision is still unclear. And unfortunately, it seems that no effort has been made to explain it; not even by the victims, the Confucianist groups. Thus, it remains a pathetic episode in the modern history of ethnic Chinese in this country.

However, the consequences of this government decision are clear. First, it drew a divisive line separating ethnic Chinese previously practising a syncretistic form of religious belief — where Buddhism teachings coexisted well with demigods in Chinese folklore — into two self-assertive groups, the Buddhists and the Confucianists, with deep mutual distrust. Second, since the decision was, and still is, widely regarded as an ethnic/cultural, rather than a religious persecution, the rehabilitation of the Confucian group in the post-Soeharto era has come to be regarded as a state recognition of ethnic Chinese culture. Therefore, Confucian teachings have gained authority as the essence of ethnic Chinese culture.

The Rationale for the Rise of Confucianism in the Late Twentieth Century and Its Implications

After decades of persecution under the Soeharto regime, the ethnic Chinese Confucian group, Matakin, The Supreme Council for Confucian Religion (Kong Jiao), has now become one of the most prominent religious groups in Indonesia. Its top leaders cultivate good relationship with top national politicians and prominent leaders of other religious groups, especially powerful Muslim groups. In recent years, the president himself attended the *Imlek* (Chinese Lunar New Year) celebration, organized by Matakin.

This change of official attitude towards Matakin is often hailed as the triumph of democracy and pluralism, and respect for the religious and cultural rights of minorities. One tends to neglect, or is reluctant to mention, the China factor, and the post-Cold War conflict-stricken world that turned to Confucian teaching in search of "harmony".

The Rise of East Asian Newly Industrialized Countries (NICs) and China as the Legitimacy for Confucianism

With the rise of Confucianism as a religion in the late nineteeth and early twentieth century as a reaction against the assault from the Christian West, it is again the reappraisal of Confucianism by Western Scholars at the end of the twentieth century that brought Confucianism into prominence.

In 1989, two Australians, Reg Little, a diplomat from 1963 to 1989 in Japan, Laos, Bangladesh, Ireland, China, and the Caribbean, and Warren Reed, a former intelligence officer with the Australian Secret Intelligence Service who had spent many years living in Asia and the Middle East, published a book of far-reaching influence, *The Confucian Renaissance* (Australia: Federation Press, February 1989), based on the observation of the rapid economic growth of East Asia NICs, Hong Kong, Singapore, Taiwan, and South Korea or the so-called "four little dragons of Asia". While Western scholars in the past tended to dismiss non-Christian culture as incompatible with capitalism and progress, the performance of those four economies, which were all, coincidentally, considered "within the Confucian cultural influence", surprised those Westerners. It was their appreciation that Confucianism is compatible with capitalism and progress that served as the starting point for the global reappraisal of Confucianism at the turn of this century.

Meanwhile, as mentioned above, the Confucian group led by the disciple of Kang Youwei, lost its ground in China and retreated to Hong Kong. They established the Hong Kong Confucian Academy and worked to promote Confucian teachings in Hong Kong, with the long term strategy of rehabilitating Confucianism in mainland China and in ethnic Chinese communities worldwide.

The global expansion of Confucianism has made China, home to the sage Confucius, a "holy land" which unifies the power of Confucianists worldwide. In 1994, the Chinese government sanctioned the founding of the International Confucian Association (ICA, or 国际儒学联合会) whose members consist of prominent politicians, scholars, and entrepreneurs all around the world. Presently, there are ten prominent ethnic Chinese entrepreneurs from Indonesia who have joined this organization.[22]

Entering the new millennium, with social conflicts resulting from rapid but uneven economic growth, the Chinese government has a new national motto, which is to build a harmonious society. The Confucian idea of social harmony thus fits into this national development goal.

The present director of the above-mentioned Hong Kong Confucian Institute, Dr Tang Enjia (汤恩佳), clearly stated the objectives of the Institute as, among other things, persuading the (China) government to promulgate Confucianism as a religion, and to make the birthday of Confucius a national holiday. Since assuming the directorship in the early 1990s, he has been actively making contact with Kong Jiao Hui (Confucian Society) members in Indonesia and other countries to further spread Confucian teachings. The global influence on Matakin is thus significant.

From 20 to 23 November 2007, the 4th Confucianism International Conference was held in Jakarta. The theme for the conference was "Reinventing Kongzi's Value to Strengthen the Peaceful and Harmonious World". Indonesian Minister of Religious Affairs, Muhammad M. Basyuni, attended the conference. In his welcoming speech, Basyuni praised the principles of universal brotherhood and social harmony in Confucianism and thus confirmed the universality (trans-border and trans-religious characteristics) of Confucian teachings and the legitimacy for the domestic Confucian group. However, one cannot help but point out that it is indeed not unhistorical. It is highly appreciated today precisely because of its usefulness in the contemporary global context.

ETHNIC CHINESE CHRISTIANS: INDONESIANIZED VS CHINESE SPEAKING CHURCHES

The history of ethnic Chinese Christians in Indonesia has been elaborated by Dr Natan Setiabudi in his doctoral dissertation, "The Christian Chinese Minority in Indonesia, with Special Reference to the Gereja Kristen Indonesia: A Sociological and Theological Analysis" (Boston College 1994). According to his research, at the end of the nineteeth century, Dutch Christian missions came to Java to preach the gospel, and Christianization was quite successful in the ethnic Chinese community. However, the so-called traditionalist group within the same society struck back by claiming that Christianity was not compatible with Chinese culture. It was the visit to Java by Christian figures directly from China such as Dr John Sung (宋尚节) that confirmed for them the legitimacy of being both Chinese and Christian. They first organized themselves into Tiong Hoa Kie Tok Kauw Hwee (Chinese Christian Church). After Indonesia's independence in the 1950s, they changed its name to Gereja Kristen Indonesia (GKI, Indonesian Christian Church). The language used has been Malay, which after independence, was renamed Bahasa Indonesia. Though it was originally racially exclusive, its usage of Bahasa Indonesia encouraged Christians of non-ethnic Chinese to join, thus making it less and less ethnic.

GKI should be categorized as an indigenized, or Indonesianized ethnic Chinese church, as opposed to the Chinese-oriented churches, which preserve the tradition of preaching in the Chinese language and keeping in touch with churches in Chinese-speaking areas, such as Taiwan and Hong Kong. The typical ones of those Chinese-oriented churches are Gereja Kristus Yesus, Communion of Chinese churches in Indonesia, and Gereja Reformed Injil Indonesia, which will be discussed further here.

Gereja Kristus Yesus, or Indonesian Christian Mandarin Church (印尼基督教国语堂)

Gereja Kristus Yesus (GKY, or Church of Jesus Christ) was founded in 2002, from its precedent, Gereja Kristus Jemaat Mangga Besar (GKJMB, or Mangga Besar District Church of Christ), founded in 1945. Mangga Besar is a district in West Jakarta with a large number of ethnic Chinese residents. GKJMB was formerly called Chung Hua Chi Tuh Chiao Hui (CHCTCH) Kuo Yu Thangg (Guo Yu Tang, 中华基督教会国语堂, or the Mandarin section of Chinese Christian Church.[23]

The term "guo yu", also known as *putonghua*, or common language of the Chinese population, is used by Chinese people to refer to their "national language". It became evident that this was an exclusively ethnic Chinese church. In 1963, it took the name of GKJMB, the church of Mangga Besar, after the name of the district where it was located. Since the church kept expanding to other residential areas with large numbers of ethnic Chinese Christians, it has become irrelevant to retain the name "Mangga Besar". Therefore, in June 2002, it changed its name to Gereja Kristus Yesus. On its pamphlets, the church still retains its Chinese name, 基督耶稣教会国语堂, or the Mandarin Church of Jesus Christ.

Presently, GKY churches hold services in twenty-eight places nationwide[24] with considerable ethnic Chinese presence. The services are, however, mostly conducted in Bahasa Indonesia since the younger generation has barely mastered the Chinese language. Services for the elderly, who were educated in Chinese-language schools prior to 1966, are conducted in the Chinese language. In my interview with Rev. Hendra Mulia at GKY Green Ville (in West Jakarta), I was told that for those talented youth who wish to serve the church, there are scholarships available for them to study in Taiwan. Since learning the Chinese language has become a global trend, it is hoped that in the future, when those proficient in Chinese grow up, the church will be able to conduct services in Chinese again.

Gereja Reformed Injili Indonesia (GRII, or Indonesian Reformed Evangelical Church)

This church is led by the charismatic spiritual leader, Stephen Tong (唐崇荣), a China-born ethnic Chinese, and heir to the global Chinese evangelical movement in the twentieth century initiated by Andrew Gih (计志文).

Gih founded the "Evangelize China Fellowship" in 1947, with the goal of the Christianization of China and ethnic Chinese worldwide, especially in Asia. It set up branches in Hong Kong, Macau, Taiwan, Singapore, Malaysia, Indonesia, and Thailand. In 1952, he founded the Southeast Bible Seminary in Malang, East Java, to train young ethnic Chinese for future evangelical movement. Among the prominent alumni of this seminary is Stephen Tong, who graduated in 1961.[25]

In 1978, Stephen Tong founded "Stephen Tong Evangelistic Ministries International", with its areas of evangelization covering Hong Kong, Singapore, Taiwan, and North America.[26] These are areas outside mainland China with large Chinese population. He also taught at the theological colleges in those areas, such as China Graduate School of Theology in Hongkong (1975, 1979), China Evangelical Seminary in Taiwan (1976), and Trinity College in Singapore (1980) <http://www.grii.org/grii-profil.htm>.

In 1989, he founded Gereja Reformed Injili Indonesia (GRII, or Indonesian Reformed Evangelical Church). Presently, GRII has set up branches in Jakarta and the suburban areas (Depok, Karawaci, Bintaro), cities in Java and Sumatra with large populations of ethnic Chinese, such as Bandung, Semarang, Yogyakarta, Malang, Pasuruan, Surabaya, Batam, Medan, and Palembang, and Denpasar in Bali.

The term "Indonesian" in GRII indicates its national or non-ethnic characteristics; however, with its strong links to Chinese Christian groups abroad, and the initial goal of "the Christianization of Chinese (regardless of political affiliation)", it turns out to be less national (Indonesian) and more ethnic (Chinese).

Persekutuan Gereja-gereja Tionghoa di Indonesia (PGTI, or Communion of Chinese Churches in Indonesia; 印尼华人基督教会联会)

This exclusively ethnic Chinese Christian organization was founded in August 1998, during a chaotic era of social turmoil and economic hardship. It was a time when spiritual consolation was badly needed. A number of Chinese-speaking ethnic Chinese entrepreneurs, together with prominent ethnic Chinese evangelists, decided to establish this Christian organization. One of its affiliates is the Terang dan Garam (Light and Salt) working group, which specializes in social and charity works.

The headquarters is set up in Jakarta, with nationwide branches in areas concentrated with ethnic Chinese, such as Medan, Palembang, Pontianak, Batam, Semarang, Malang, Denpasar, Pangkal Pinang (on Bangka island), Makassar, Bandung, Surabaya, Jambi, Samarinda, and Manado. The source of funding are domestic and foreign churches, individuals, foundations and organizations.[27]

Since all its personnel are ethnic Chinese who are mainly Chinese-speaking, it is probable that this organization has links to ethnic Chinese churches or Christian organizations abroad, such as the Chinese Coordination Centre of World Evangelism in Hong Kong, and the Chinese Christian Evangelistic Association and Chinese Christian Relief Association in Taiwan, as shown on its website.[28]

Taiwanese Christian Evangelical Works in Sumatra

Sumatra has a large percentage of ethnic Chinese. Due to its characteristics ethnic Chinese settlements (culturally and linguistically bound Chinese communities), most ethnic Chinese here speak one or more Chinese dialects, or even *putonghua*, and mainly go to temples which accommodate Buddhist gods and Chinese legendary demigods (see Table 6.1). The largest number of temples is found in North Sumatra.

The situation has changed in recent years. An evangelical group in Taiwan, Taiwan Christ Ching Ping (TCCP, or Association of Elite Troop for Christ), in cooperation with local ethnic Chinese churches and evangelists, has launched its evangelical work in Sumatra.[29]

We are unable to know the exact number of ethnic Chinese converts in Sumatra. But according to information provided by a Buddhist monk at Ekayana Buddhist Centre in Jakarta, the pattern of religious demography in Sumatra has changed, especially in North Sumatra. Previously, ethnicity coincided with religion, with local ethnic Batak being Protestants, ethnic Chinese, Buddhists, and Malays, Muslims; now, a large number of ethnic Chinese in North Sumatra has converted to Christianity.

Concluding Remarks

The decolonization and birth of modern states posed a dilemma for minority groups within the new political entities because the line of demarcation between the so-called indigenous and the foreign are forcibly drawn. This also applies to ethnic Chinese in Indonesia.

Furthermore, at the height of the Cold War, and with the consolidation of a regime hostile to everything Chinese, their situation became much more dilemmatic. Their cultural practices were denied because of the nationwide anti-China hysteria, and they were regarded as being less legitimate for social participation.

To overcome these dilemmas, many ethnic Chinese strengthened their ties to existing religious groups, or even established new religious groups. By joining one among these religious groups, it was possible for ethnic Chinese here to assert their moral legitimacy, as opposed to conveying the image of "the cruel communist China supporting the 1965 coup d'etat".

Socially, when ethnic-based social organizations were banned, religious organizations became almost the only path for ethnic Chinese to social participation, social exposure, and self-fulfillment (though for those purposes, a few among them were also able to join professional organizations).

Special mention should be made of Buddhist and Confucianist groups. These religious groups were designated the function of serving as cultural haven for ethnic Chinese eager to guard their cultural identity. In the case of the Confucianist group, the boundary line between culture and religious beliefs is unclear. For example, the self-proclaimed Confucianists demanded that the government sanction the public celebration of *Imlek* (Lunar New Year, or often incorrectly called Chinese New Year) and that *Imlek* be made a national holiday, the reason given being that it is a religious celebration. But now that it has become a national celebration and holiday, ethnic Chinese of all religious beliefs welcome and celebrate it, making it appear less religious than ethnic/cultural.

Another distinctive point concerning the recent development of ethnic Chinese religious life in Indonesia, is the "support" from religious groups in Chinese-speaking areas, such as Hong Kong and Taiwan, and from the ethnic Chinese groups in Malaysia. Such "international" support, while appearing "religious", and thus "trans-ethnic", undeniably exerts influence over ethnic

Chinese in Indonesia and strengthens ethnic (Chinese) identity and ethnic solidarity with ethnic Chinese outside Indonesia.

This might pose a new problem of legitimacy for ethnic Chinese here in the future. Strengthening solidarity with such foreign religious groups might result in their further segregation domestically, and make them appear a more foreign (and hence less legitimate) element in this country; thus hindering the natural process of their integration into mainstream Indonesian society.

Notes

[1] Leo Suryadinata, "Buddism and Confucianism in Contemporary Indonesia: Recent Development", in *Chinese Indonesians: Remembering, Distorting, Forgetting*, edited by Tim Lindsey and Helen Pausacker (Singapore: Institute of Southeast Asian Studies, 2005), pp. 77–94.

[2] Leo Suryadinata, *The Culture of the Chinese Minority in Indonesia* (Singapore: Times Books International, 1997).

[3] Ibid.

[4] Ibid.

[5] <http://www.globalbuddhist.net/shijiefojiao/Indo/Indo.asp>.

[6] Leo Suryadinata, op. cit.

[7] <www.infobuddhis.com>.

[8] <http://www.hikmahbudhi.org/aboutus.php>.

[9] <http://www.patria.or.id/networks.html#ntt>.

[10] <http://www.binus.ac.id/about/history>.

[11] <http://www.kmbui.net/kmbui.php?screen=sejarah_kmbui>.

[12] <http://www.jcedu.org/edu/ddfs/pt/17.htm>.

[13] <http://www.buddhanet.net/wbd/region.php?region_id=7&offset=1100>.

[14] <http://www.wbsc886.org/C-index.html>.

[15] <http://www.sinarharapan.co.id/berita/0612/30/jab05.html>.

[16] <http://gb.newdaai.tv/?view=detail&id=17541>.

[17] <http://www.tzuchi.or.id/Penhubung.html>.

[18] Leo Suryadinata, *The Chinese of Chinese Minority*, pp. 79–85.

[19] Archipel 38.

[20] <http://www.confucianism.com.cn/html/jiaoyu/842217.html>.

[21] Leo Suryadinata, op. cit, pp. 77–94.

[22] <http://www.ica.org.cn/content/view_content.asp?id=1224>.

[23] <http://www.gky.or.id/>.

[24] <http://www.gky.or.id/>.

[25] <http://www.ebaomonthly.com/ebao/readebao.php?eID=e00618>.

[26] <http://www.stemi.org/>.

[27] <http://www.indocms.net/pgti/index.html?m=text&a=12>.

[28] <http://www.indocms.net/pgti/index.html?m=news&p=0>.

29   See Wei-min Tsai (蔡维民), "A Preliminary Research to the Chinese Protestant
      Church in Indonesia: Focus on Sumatra", <http://wwws.au.edu.tw/~tsaiwm/3–
      16.htm>; for descriptions of their evangelical work in Sumatra, see <http://www.
      gospelherald.com/template/view.htm?code=gen&id=1981&c_lang=GB> and
      <http://www.tccp.org.tw/p1-1.htm>.

7

ANTI-CHINESE VIOLENCE IN INDONESIA AFTER SOEHARTO

Charles A. Coppel

The notion of "anti-Chinese violence" has become a cliché in writing about Indonesia. Any journalistic account of an outbreak of anti-Chinese violence is likely to have the following ingredients: a rough estimate of the number of ethnic Chinese in Indonesia; a statement that they are disproportionately wealthy; a reference to anti-Chinese prejudice and discrimination (especially under the Soeharto regime); and an assertion that anti-Chinese violence has deep historical roots in Indonesia. Stated in this way, the propositions seem unexceptionable. But the ingredients are frequently distorted and exaggerated to such an extent that they colour the reporting and the understanding of the violence under consideration.

DISTORTIONS AND EXAGGERATIONS OF EARLIER ANTI-CHINESE VIOLENCE

The fact that anti-Chinese prejudice and discrimination has existed in Indonesia and that it has underpinned outbreaks of anti-Chinese violence over a long period is undeniable. This undoubted fact has, however, been distorted into a fantasy approaching Holocaust proportions. Take, for example, the *Wikipedia* entry for "Chinese Indonesian" (as of 22 June 2007) which speaks of the "slaughter of millions of Chinese Indonesians" in 1965 and of "the two genocidal riots … in 1965 and 1998" (Wikipedia 2007). This absurdity echoes the nonsense in Jack Pizzey's 1988 film *Slow Boat from Surabaya* in which he says that "hundreds of thousands of [Chinese], perhaps millions, were butchered by Indonesians" in 1965 (Pizzey 1988).

The representation of the Indonesian massacres of 1965–66 as an anti-Chinese genocide has even infected supposedly academic writing. According to the report of the Minority Rights Group on the Southeast Asian Chinese published in 2000:

> "There are still no precise figures on the number of Chinese killed, but the figure is likely to be in the hundreds of thousands (Chin 2000, p. 14)."

The author added in an endnote:

> "Some commentators put the number of casualties among the Chinese at tens of thousands rather than hundreds of thousands (Chin 2000, p. 33, endnote 10)."

but he gave no source for either of these estimates, or even a hint that hundreds of thousands of *non-Chinese* Indonesians were massacred.

The entry by Mary Heidhues on "Indonesia" in *The Encyclopedia of the Chinese Overseas* (edited by Lynn Pan) presents a more sober and accurate picture (Heidhues 1999, p. 166):

> This harassment has led some commentators to perceive the violence and killings of hundreds and thousands of people as an anti-Chinese pogrom. While it is true that some thousands of Chinese lost their lives, the number killed was proportionately less than the number of ethnic Indonesians. The violence of 1965–67 was directed against Communists or suspected Communists, not against ethnic Chinese.

This judgment conforms with my own research and that of Robert Cribb, who is the leading authority on the Indonesian killings of 1965. The precise number of those killed in the Indonesian massacres of 1965 will never be known. But the victims were overwhelmingly Javanese and Balinese, not Chinese; and the slaughter was politicide rather than genocide (Coppel 1983, pp. 58–61; Cribb 1990).

A similar distortion and exaggeration has occurred in the case of the May 1998 rioting. To describe it — and the 1965 violence — as "genocidal", as in the *Wikipedia* entry referred to earlier, is to debase the meaning of the word "genocide". In both cases there is a lack of certainty about the precise number of those killed, but in the 1998 case there were several, albeit conflicting, attempts to establish the facts within a few months of the events (Purdey 2002). None of them supports the view that the killings were genocidal either in scale or in composition of the victims. In its final report on 23 October 1998 about the 13–15 May 1998 Riot, the Joint Fact-Finding Team (TGPF) listed the number of deaths in the Jakarta area identified by various sources as either 1,190 (Volunteer Team for Humanity [TRuK]), 451 (Police), 463 (Jakarta Military Command), or 288 (Jakarta Government) (TGPF 2001, p. 345). Most of the victims were burned to death in Jakarta shopping complexes. The shopping complexes were owned by ethnic Chinese, but the victims were overwhelmingly non-Chinese looters, who according to a member of the Volunteer Team for Humanity "came from the families of petty civil servants, casual labourers, clothes washers and domestic servants" (Farid 2006, p. 273).

The point needs to be laboured because the lenses through which we view future, as well as past, violence that has Chinese victims will otherwise be tinted and seriously out of focus. The genocidal image is so powerful that even well-informed and authoritative commentators can succumb to it. For example, in a widely syndicated newspaper article in July 2002, Professor Wang Gungwu wrote (Wang 2002):

> "Despite memories of the slaughter of Chinese during the anti-communist purges of the 1960s, Indonesia's Chinese were unprepared for the intense hatred shown in the riots of May 1998 ..."

Sometimes, as in this presumably unintentional example, the suggestion of genocide is implied rather than explicit, but in my opinion that only makes it the more insidious.

A related trope is the image of the Chinese in countries like Indonesia as "essential outsiders" analogous to the Jews in Central Europe before the Holocaust (Chirot and Reid 1997). The prevalence of the notion that Southeast Asian Chinese are the "Jews of the East" may, in fact, be more than just an analogy, as Hillel Kieval suggested:

> [Walter Zenner] wonders ... whether one can adequately assess Southeast Asian attitudes toward ethnic Chinese without taking into account the importation by European colonialists of classical Western, anti-Jewish stereotypes. Such attitudes conveyed crucial cultural information about

an ethnic group that did not exist so far as Javanese or Thais were concerned, but they learned from European colonial administrators and scholars to assign the specific moral evaluations of anti-Semitism to the local ethnic context. Early Thai nationalists, then, were able to see the Chinese in their midst as the "Jews of the East" by first learning to visualize Jews (Kieval 1997, pp. 215–16).

Whatever the merits of that argument (and I believe it to be plausible), the notion of a Chinese Indonesian minority surrounded by an anti-Sinicist majority itching for another pogrom is never far from popular literature. The same *Wikipedia* entry speaks of "the enmity of centuries" between ethnic Chinese and Indonesians and Jack Pizzey in *Slow Boat from Surabaya* intones in a voice-over, "There's a saying here that it is necessary to cull the Chinese every fifty years."

CONTRARY EVIDENCE

How would those who propagate so deep-rooted and pervasive a hostility to ethnic Chinese in Indonesia explain the following five recent phenomena?

- Chinese New Year is now an Indonesian national festival and holiday. In 2007, President Susilo Bambang Yudhoyono attended the *Imlek* celebrations at the Jakarta Fairground and the event was broadcast live on national television.
- Since October 2004, Dr Mari Pangestu, a Chinese Indonesian, has been the Indonesian Minister for Trade under President Susilo Bambang Yudhoyono. Kwik Kian Gie was State Minister/Head of the National Planning Board from July 2001 to October 2004 under President Megawati Soekarnoputri, and was Coordinating Minister for the Economy, Finance and Industry under President Abdurrahman Wahid from October 1999 to August 2000.
- On 1 August 2006, a new Indonesian Citizenship Law came into effect (Undang-Undang 12/2006) in which the term *orang-orang bangsa Indonesia asli* (indigenous Indonesians) was redefined to mean those who became Indonesian citizens at the time of their birth and have not voluntarily accepted any other citizenship. This change removes the key legal rationale for discrimination against Chinese Indonesians.
- On 3 April 2007, the Secretary General of the Indonesian Defence Ministry and the General Chief of Staff of the People's Liberation Army signed a memorandum of understanding on defence and security matters

in Beijing. A few weeks later the Chinese ambassador to Indonesia, Lan Lijun, said that "since 2005 the two countries had established a strategic partnership ... in the political, economics, cultural, educational, scientific, technological and military sectors" and that the Chinese government would welcome any proposal from Indonesia [to] purchase Chinese military hardware without any political strings (*Jakarta Post* website 20 April 2007 as reported by the *BBC Worldwide Monitoring Service*; see also *Jakarta Post* 2007*b*).

• China and Indonesia have recently agreed to strengthen their cultural ties with a view to increasing tourism between the two countries. The Indonesian Minister for Culture and Tourism, Jero Wacik, said that Indonesia is hoping to receive at least 300,000 Chinese tourists in 2007 as compared to 80,000 in 2006. Indonesian tourists to China in 2006 numbered 200,000. Jero announced that the two countries planned a joint film production on the expedition of Admiral Cheng Ho (Zheng He) "to illustrate the centuries-long cultural ties between Indonesia and China". A report in the *Jakarta Post* says that cultures from China have had "a tremendous impact" on Indonesian cultures (*Jakarta Post* 2007*a*; Taufiqurrahman 2007).

If hostility between non-Chinese and Chinese Indonesians is as deep-seated and intense as is sometimes suggested, one might expect a dramatic backlash to these developments. I may be ill-informed about this, but as far as I am aware, they have not (or not yet) caused a ripple. I do not mean to go to the opposite extreme and to suggest that relations between China and Indonesia (or between ethnic Chinese and non-Chinese Indonesians) have always been without friction. Even if present-day ministerial spin-doctors would like it to be true, that would be absurd. The issue here is one of balanced, conscientiously fair representation.

Nor am I suggesting that anti-Chinese violence did not occur in 1965 or 1998. Of course it did. But, to reiterate, in both cases the overwhelming majority of those who *died* as a result of violence were *pribumi* (indigenous) Indonesians, not ethnic Chinese. It is misleading, if not mischievous, to suggest otherwise. As I wrote in *Indonesian Chinese in Crisis:*

> In general ... the most characteristic form of anti-Chinese violence in the immediate post-coup years was not killing, violence to the person or incarceration, but damage to property, such as the despoiling, looting and burning of shops, schools, houses and cars (Coppel 1983, p. 58).

COMPARING 1965 AND 1998

Three decades later, from mid-1996 and climaxing in May 1998, there was also widespread and massive anti-Chinese violence which again largely took the form of destruction of property. There were some important differences, however.

One of the most important differences was in the extent of coverage of the anti-Chinese violence in the media and in academic writing. There was little such coverage in the media at the time in 1965 and little academic writing about it (Coppel 1983; Mackie 1976, 1980). In contrast, the 1998 anti-Chinese violence received saturation coverage in the media (especially the new electronic media through the World Wide Web) and a quite remarkable amount of academic attention. For a sampling of the literature in English, see Ang 2002; Coppel 2001; Heryanto 1999; Kusno 2003; Leksono 2001; Lochore 2000; Purdey 2002, 2005, 2006a and b; Sai 2006; Sidel 2001, 2007; Siegel 1998; Tan 2006; Tay 2000, 2006; and Wibowo 2001. It is not, I suggest, the extent of the coverage of the 1998 violence that is surprising. The violence took place in the major urban centres, including the capital Jakarta, in full view of the world electronic media. It was a culmination of months of rising tension and precipitated in the resignation of President Soeharto after he had been in power for more than three decades. What calls for explanation is the relatively slight coverage of the violence in general in 1965 and the tendency among many (especially in the media) to identify the Chinese as the victims of it. The first question may owe much, in the case of Western representations, to the Cold War environment and an unwillingness in the liberal democracies to acknowledge that the massacres might have been deliberately carried out by anti-communists who were politically motivated. It was easier to pass off such massive violence in racial or primordial terms (centuries of enmity between indigenous Indonesians and ethnic Chinese) or to put it down to a supposedly inherent Indonesian/Malay propensity to run *amuck* (and to note that the origin of this English word is the Malay/Indonesian word *amok* or *amuk*).

A second major difference between the 1965 violence and the more recent violence was the horrific gang-raping of women in 1998. This element was a major contributor to the outrage expressed around the world, especially among ethnic Chinese overseas. Unlike those who were killed, the rape victims were indeed mostly ethnic Chinese women. One of the most inflammatory aspects of the reporting of the 1998 gang-rapes was the posting of pictures of the bodies of brutally tortured women on websites (and circulated as attachments in email messages). These bodies were identified as being those of ethnic Chinese women who had been raped in the May violence, and they were reproduced in the press as such. In fact, a number of the pictures were of non-Chinese women in East Timor who had been tortured by Indonesian military and militia members there. These pictures had been on public display on the website of the East Timor International Support Centre (ETISC) long before May 1998. When it was disclosed that the pictures were "fakes" (in other words, that they were not pictures of the bodies of ethnic Chinese women at all), it was used as ammunition by those who denied that the May 1998 rapes of ethnic Chinese women had occurred at all against those who sought to establish as fact that they had (Sai 2006; Tay 2006). The controversy within and outside Indonesia then raged around this issue.

IMPORTANCE OF THE FRAMEWORK OF ANALYSIS AND REPRESENTATION

This illustrates again the widespread and distorting tendency to treat violence against ethnic Chinese in isolation from other outbreaks of violence. Where were those who might take up their cudgels in defence of the East Timorese women whose bodies were so publicly portrayed in these images and were the victims of this brutal sexual violence? A discourse of sexual violence against ethnic Chinese women that overlooks similar violence against other women in Indonesia amounts to special pleading. It is not so widely known outside Indonesia that the occurrence of the May 1998 rapes was the trigger for the establishment by President Habibie of the National Commission on Violence Against Women (*Komnas Perempuan*), which put on its agenda sexual violence against women elsewhere in the archipelago, including Aceh and East Timor (Tan 2006).

My point is that the interpretation of violence depends crucially on the framework within which it is represented. If the framework is one of an age-old indigenous enmity against Chinese, one is led towards a particular kind of conclusion; if it is one of military and militia brutality towards a civilian population, it takes you in another direction. This is actually part of a much bigger question. In what cases of violence in which there are ethnic Chinese victims do the circumstances justify us calling the violence "anti-Chinese"? If indigenous employees who feel exploited in their working conditions beat up their ethnic Chinese employer, is this "anti-Chinese" violence or is it violence based on class? If indigenous Muslims burn down a Christian church where the congregation includes some or many Chinese Christians, should we regard that as "anti-Chinese" violence or is it violence against Christians? I would suggest that there are no *a priori* answers to these questions. Nor are they necessarily either/or questions in the way that I have posed them here. There may be elements of class, ethnicity, and religion intermingled in the one case, and the incident may have been provoked or manipulated by others for political purposes. Each case needs to be examined in the light of the available evidence. As Mackie (1976, pp. 129–37) pointed out, the factors creating a predisposition towards group antagonisms, those which operate to restrain the expression of hostility, and those which precipitate violence in situations of tension, are multiple and complex.

It can also be very difficult to know how superficial or deep-rooted a particular factor may be. For example, the sixth of Mackie's precipitating factors involved "the open expression or flaunting of cultural and ethnic differences" such as the *barongsai* (lion dance) procession which he said was "provocative", "a public demonstration or assertion of Chineseness *on Indonesian soil*" (his emphasis) and "an affront to Indonesian nationalism" which could trigger anti-Chinese violence, at least in "times of acute tension" (136). In the Soeharto era, the public expression of Chinese culture was officially banned and Chinese Indonesians were told that "activities celebrating Chinese New Year (*Tahun Baru Imlek*) should be carried out internally among the family or individually" (Coppel 2002, pp. 213–26). Since 1998 this ban has been overturned to such an extent that Chinese New Year is now, as indicated above, an Indonesian national holiday and its festivities are broadcast live on national television, and even mainstream Indonesian political parties have used the Chinese lion dance (*barongsai*) in their election campaigns. There is now even a national *barongsai* festival (*Jakarta Post*, 2007c). The situation could change under President Susilo Bambang Yudhoyono's successor, of course; and one can easily imagine circumstances at present where performance of the *barongsai* could have a provocative, triggering effect (for example, if performed without prior consent in front of a mosque during the holy fasting month of Ramadan). Context is all-important.

Another of Mackie's precipitating factors was the state of relations with China (135) particularly, as he put it, "if Peking's reaction is one which Indonesians regard as provocative, threatening or interfering" as in 1959–60 and 1965–67. On the other hand, he wrote, "the fact that relations between the two governments were becoming closer was an important consideration [in May 1963], even though Peking said and did nothing to embarrass the Sukarno government", because "one of the motives of some instigators of the anti-Chinese riots in Bandung and elsewhere seems to have been to damage relations with China ..." If one looks at the situation today, the major fault lines in the world international order are no longer those between the communist and anti-communist blocs, where an anti-communist Indonesian military could perceive the ethnic Chinese in Indonesia as a potential fifth column for a communist China. The major international fault lines are now located more in the Middle East and the "war against terror". China has forsworn interference in Indonesian domestic affairs and is not perceived in Indonesia as a threat to Islam. If anything, a new Jakarta — Beijing axis (*poros*) may be in the making, with military and cultural agreements underway, and the Chinese economic juggernaut may be seen, as it is in Australia, as a motor for domestic economic growth.

ANTI-CHINESE VIOLENCE AFTER SOEHARTO

With these introductory remarks and caveats out of the way, I come at last to the question of anti-Chinese violence in Indonesia since the fall of Soeharto. *What* anti-Chinese violence? In his recently published book, *Riots, Pogroms, Jihad* (2007), John Sidel has asserted that "the familiar repertoire of anti-Chinese riots and church burnings disappeared from the stage of Indonesian public life" after 1998 with the exception of a few "so-called anti-Chinese riots" in Purworejo and Karawang in the months following the transfer of power in Jakarta (Sidel 2007, p. 2, 135; see also Sidel 2001, p. 59). Arguing that this is "an important change worthy of examination", he wrote:

> For contrary to suppositions of deep-rooted "ethnic hatred" or "economic resentment", the rising tide of unemployment, inflation, and hardship for ordinary Indonesians across the country and the easing of authoritarian restrictions on popular mobilization did not combine in 1998–99 to spell a return to anti-Chinese riots, much less an escalation in the frequency or violence of such disturbances (Sidel 2007, p. 136).

Why not? Sidel's explanation is embedded in a complex argument about shifts in the forms of religious violence in Indonesia from riots (1995–98) to pogroms (1999–2001) to jihad (2000–04). I am not going to explicate that argument here other than to draw attention to what he said about the first phase ("riots") when there were what he calls "so-called anti-Chinese disturbances" in which "crowds attacked, destroyed and burned shops, supermarkets, department stores, goods, and other property owned by Chinese Indonesians; Catholic and Protestant churches and other houses of worship; and police stations and other government buildings" (Sidel 2007, p. 1). Sidel's repeated use of the word "so-called" in this context, as well as in relation to the Purworejo and Karawang riots after May 1998, suggests that he may be reluctant to acknowledge ethnicity or race as a factor when ethnic Chinese are victims.

Jemma Purdey has no such reluctance. In her recently published book, *Anti-Chinese Violence in Indonesia, 1996–1999* (2006), she observed that "[t]heir ethnicity means that Chinese Indonesians are always vulnerable" (Purdey 2006*a*, p. 30). For her, although "the 'anti-Chinese riot' [may have] largely disappeared from government and public rhetoric" as Sidel suggested, "events of violence against Chinese did not cease". According to her, the "national rhetoric may have changed, but local realities had not" (Purdey 2006*a*, p. 211).

Once again, we find that context can colour the analysis. These are two excellent and sophisticated books, but their differing frameworks (religious violence in Sidel's case, anti-Chinese violence for Purdey) lead them to different conclusions. Despite these differences, however, they seem to be in underlying agreement that anti-Chinese violence has declined since Soeharto. Sidel may overstate the extent of the decline in the period of transition after May 1998, and indeed Purdey identifies a number of cases during that period other than those of Purworejo and Karawang to which he refers (Purdey 2006*a*, pp. 219–20). I think it is indisputable, however, that the incidence of anti-Chinese violence in Indonesia since then has been very slight. In fact, I have come across only two reported cases in the last seven years (which I will discuss below). As Sidel said, this decline is an important change worthy of examination, especially as there have been major and continuing outbreaks of other violence during this time. These have ranged from communal violence in Ambon (Maluku), Sampit (Central Kalimantan), and Poso (Central Sulawesi), to *jihadist* bombing attacks in Bali and Jakarta, to state-sponsored violence against alleged separatists in East Timor, Aceh, and Papua.

The exceptional cases of anti-Chinese violence to which I have referred above occurred in Jakarta (in 2000) and Makasar (in 2006). Both occurred on or close to the anniversary of the May 1998 violence. The May 2000 affair occurred in Glodok, Jakarta's Chinatown area. Rioters threw rocks at shopfronts, burned tables in the middle of the street, and clashed with police, who fired tear gas and engaged in close combat with the rioters. A BMW showroom, a McDonald's restaurant, and electronic stores were seriously damaged. A police spokesman said that more than one hundred people were questioned and eleven were arrested for inciting the rioters. Twenty policemen were injured and hundreds of police lined the streets after the mob fled. The incident was not only much smaller in scale than what had occurred two years earlier but its dynamics were also quite different in that ethnic Chinese were not the targets of the violence. The rioting was provoked by a pre-dawn police raid on illegal video compact disc sellers. Angry vendors and unemployed masses reacted violently to the raid. The police apparently did their best to protect the Chinese from the violence. What is left unexplained in this account is why the security forces chose to make their raid precisely on the second anniversary of the May 1998 incident (Firdaus 2000; Go 2000).

As reported in the media, a Chinese Indonesian man in Makassar allegedly tortured two indigenous female domestic servants, one of whom later died, sparking "anarchic student protests" on 10 May 2006. Protests continued the following day, but the students involved distanced themselves from the earlier "anarchic actions". The newspaper reports were coy in their description of what had actually occurred, but many Chinese-owned shops were closed (Editorial 2006; Hajramurni 2006*a* and *b*). This case is a classic example of the kind of violence which many Chinese Indonesians have come to regard as "normal" where Chinese Indonesians as a group are held responsible for the alleged crimes of an individual, and a rough, summary justice in the form of destruction of their property is administered by "anarchic" protesters. The reasons for this behaviour, which can be triggered by something as relatively trivial as a traffic accident, are not immediately obvious to people who live in societies governed by the rule of law. The *Jakarta Post* editorial opined:

> The riot in Makassar can be seen as an expression of anger and frustration with the current economic hardships faced by many people. The tortured maids are a symbol of the weak, while the suspect is a symbol of those who use their power to trample on the less fortunate.

A student activist reportedly claimed that the protest was "a spontaneous act of solidarity aimed at pressing the police to thoroughly investigate the case instead of making 'a backroom deal with the suspect'". Muhammad Darwis, a sociologist from Hasanuddin University, reportedly said:

> [T]he unfair treatment became the root of the locals' discontentment toward the Chinese-Indonesians, who slowly came to control the economic sector. The feeling was like a time bomb ready to explode ... especially since the local government nowadays also tends to keep its doors open for Chinese-Indonesian businesspeople.

Darwis, who was said to have conducted a study of social interaction between the Chinese and Makassar's Bugis people, blamed "exclusivity" among the Chinese Indonesians for their lack of interaction with the locals who were, he said, "an open community who can tolerate differences". He added that "there is also social jealousy since the Chinese-Indonesians, who are not as populous, control the economy and are favored (sic) by the administration" (Hajramurni 2006*b*).

There is much in this discourse that draws on a familiar repertoire from earlier incidents of anti-Chinese violence, giving each incident, in turn, a quality of re-enactment and, as it were, of "normality" (Purdey 2006*a*, pp. 207–09). It is also typical for both commentators and participants to set the event in a narrative of previous incidents. Indeed, it was recalled on this occasion that a similar event had occurred in Makassar in 1997 when "mobs set fire to buildings following the murder of a child by a Chinese-Indonesian" (Hajramurni 2006*a*). The *Jakarta Post* (Editorial 2006) drew attention to another precedent to the 2006 Makassar affair, namely the violence in Jakarta and elsewhere in May 1998:

> While the two riots were caused by completely different reasons, both were directly connected with Chinese-Indonesians. We raise the two upheavals because the May 1998 violence continues to haunt us, including our economy. Many citizens of Chinese descent are still too traumatized to return home after fleeing abroad following the tragedy eight years ago. It is happening again! That was the reaction of many people upon hearing about the violence in Makassar.

This kind of rehearsing of the script was also reflected in the rumours that there was an exodus of Chinese Indonesians from Makassar, emulating the exodus to Singapore, Hong Kong, and Australia that occurred in May 1998. The Mayor of Makassar denied that there was any exodus of Chinese Indonesians but admitted that they were "worried" (Hajramurni 2006*a*).

It is surely ironic that the pretext for violence against the Chinese Indonesian community in Makassar, falling as it did only a few days before the eighth anniversary of the May 1998 violence, should have been the alleged abuse of indigenous maids by an individual Chinese Indonesian employer. The most explosive issue in the attempts to uncover the facts of what occurred in May 1998 was the allegation that large numbers of Chinese Indonesian women had been raped. The allegation itself was strongly contested and the number of victims fiercely debated (Purdey 2006*a*, pp. 144–47). There is more than a hint in the reporting of the 2006 Makassar affair that the perpetrators of the violence there were, or at least believed themselves to be, justified in their actions since otherwise the abuse against the maids would have been ignored by the authorities because of the economic power of Chinese Indonesians. This "justification" itself is painfully ironic because the authorities have successfully resisted all attempts to have those responsible for the May 1998 rapes of ethnic Chinese women brought to justice.

MEMORY, HISTORY, AND JUSTICE *VS* AMNESIA, SILENCE, AND IMPUNITY

Every year people gather together in May to commemorate the 1998 violence. They hold vigils, rallies and marches, visit the graves of loved ones who died as a result of the violence, and call on the government to establish who masterminded the violence and to have them prosecuted. The commemoration in 2007 featured the launch of a book published by Solidaritas Nusa Bangsa (SNB — Homeland Solidarity) and Asosiasi Penasehat Hukum dan Hak Asasi Manusia Indonesia (APHI — Indonesian Lawyers and Human Rights Defenders Association). The book is 470 pages in length, with colour photographs, and its title is *Kerusuhan Mei 1998: Fakta, Data Dan Analisa* (The May 1998 Riots: Facts, Data and Analysis). The lead author, in a team of four, is Ester Indahyani Jusuf, a lawyer who is the tireless chair and driving force of SNB. The authors intended that the book should go beyond presenting facts, data, and analysis, as can be seen from its subtitle, *Mengungkap Kerusuhan Mei 1998 Sebagai Kejahatan Terhadap Kemanusiaan* (Uncovering the May 1998 Riots as a Crime Against Humanity), but they explain that this did not prove feasible because of concerns and promise that SNB will publish a complete legal analysis separately.

In an article published in the national daily *Kompas* on 13 May 2007, Ariel Heryanto pointed out that the violence in Jakarta nine years earlier had continued for days without any hindrance from the authorities, yet not a single person had ever been investigated, let alone prosecuted, for their part in the affair. He regretted what he regarded as a widespread misconception that what happened was racial violence vented by an "indigenous" majority on a Chinese minority. Although he did not deny that there was a racial element, given the prominence of ethnic Chinese victims, he preferred to focus on what he saw as an unconscious misogynistic sexism in society, especially among its mainly male leaders. This was a societal sickness that needed to be addressed, and to think of the May 1998 rapes as racial violence enabled most of the public to treat them as something that did not affect them.

The failure to bring to justice those who were responsible for the May 1998 violence is unfortunately not an isolated phenomenon in Indonesia (International Crisis Group 2001). Even after the passage of nearly half a century since 1965, none of those responsible for one of the worst massacres of the twentieth century has been held accountable for the crimes. Not only have most of those Indonesians who are believed to have committed gross violations of human rights not been prosecuted, but they have also held and continued to hold high office. As an article in the *Jakarta Post* on

18 May 2007 ('May 1998 Riots Remain Just Another Deadly Mystery') pointed out, high ranking military and police officers, who held important posts in Jakarta during the 1998 riots, have been left untouched, including the Jakarta Military commander Major General Sjafrie Sjamsoeddin, Jakarta Governor Major General Sutiyoso, and Jakarta Military Command chief of staff Brigadier General Sudi Silalahi. Sjafrie Sjamsuddin (now a Lieutenant General) is the Secretary General of the Indonesian Defence Ministry who signed the memorandum of understanding on defence and security matters in Beijing in April 2007; Sutiyoso (now retired Lieutenant General) is still the Governor of Jakarta; and Sudi Silalahi (now retired Lieutenant General) is Cabinet Secretary for President Susilo Bambang Yudhoyono.

It is understandable that the 1998 rape victims remain silent while these and other key military and political figures continue to hold positions of such influence. They know that it is extremely unlikely that any new government inquiry into the May 1998 violence will emerge, and are only too well aware of the risks of speaking out. The killing of Marthadinata, an eighteen-year-old member of the Volunteer Team for Humanity (TRuK), just before she was due to leave for the United States in October 1998 to testify about the rapes, was sufficient to intimidate TRuK members and must have added to the natural reluctance of rape victims to bear witness in public (Purdey 2006a, p. 146).

The May 1998 violence in Jakarta and other cities was a turning point for ethnic Chinese in Indonesia. Ignatius Wibowo (2001) argued that it "induced them to act", and he discerned three types of response: "exit", "voice", and "loyalty". By taking the "exit" option, they could either flee abroad or to some safer part of Indonesia or choose an "internal exit" by remaining and building higher steel fences around their houses. By adopting the "voice" strategy, they could campaign for the removal of discriminatory legislation and practices and agitate for the prosecution of the perpetrators of violence. He said that the overwhelming majority chose the residual category, "loyalty":

> [T]hey conducted their lives as usual and tried to make the best out
> of the existing situation. They did not protest the unjust situation, but
> hoped and believed that things would improve (Wibowo 2001, p. 143).

This quotation suggests passivity rather than action, but he included within the "loyalty" category those who form or participate in political parties.

Those who pursued the "voice" strategy have had considerable success. Most of the discriminatory legislation has been removed, and public demonstrations or assertions of Chineseness no longer seem to be regarded as provocative. A progress report on the extent of the change can be found in the October 2003 special issue ("Speaking Out: Chinese Indonesians after Suharto") of the journal, *Asian Ethnicity*. Those who have been trying to bring the perpetrators of violence to justice have had no such success, however. Although Komnas HAM (National Commission for Human Rights) re-opened investigations into the May 1998 violence in 2003, the attempt to have an Ad Hoc court established to hear evidence from witnesses came to nothing (Purdey 2006*a*, p. 217).

Purdey believed that the "absence of any institutional process of justice and healing for victims of the violence in May 1998 stands in the way of a resolution of the 'Chinese problem' in newly democratic Indonesia". As she pointed out, such a process in which "perpetrators show remorse for their actions and the state makes them accountable for crimes committed against humanity" is

> equally important for all victims of the New Order, including students killed at Semanggi in 1998 and 1999, Chinese Indonesian victims of May 1998, Muslim victims of Tanjung Priok in 1984 and the East Timorese who suffered in 1999. To fail to provide the opportunity for justice and to publicly remember these events is tantamount to saying that the suffering of these victims does not matter (Purdey 2006*a*, pp. 216–17).

I would want to add to this list the hundreds of thousands of victims of the violence in 1965 and 1966.

At this point we are forced to confront the magnitude of the task that faces justice and healing for the victims of violence in Indonesia. The scale is enormous and, unlike post-apartheid South Africa, the old regime has not been completely overthrown. As Mary Zurbuchen has written with reference to the 1965 violence:

> It is tempting to hope that through systematic examination ... Indonesia could engender a process of reconciliation and conflict resolution that would mitigate the continued violence and new communalism being witnessed at present. In reality, however, a formal process of truth-seeking may not lead to social healing ... In the post-Suharto proliferation of laws and legislation on human rights, official investigations, and national commissions on corruption and the judiciary, advocacy for a concerted attempt to revisit the past must compete with many other priorities in Indonesia's reform agenda (Zurbuchen 2002, p. 581).

I share her pessimism, and also her identification of the need to preserve the testimony of ordinary Indonesians "if the larger questions about Indonesia's 1965 mass killings and continuing patterns of communal and political violence, and how to prevent their recurrence, are ever to be answered" (Zurbuchen 2002, p. 581). The ongoing determination to expose the darker side of Indonesian history to the light of day by historians and activists such as Asvi Warman Adam, Budiawan, Hilmar Farid, Ester Jusuf, Kate McGregor, John Roosa, Hersri Setiawan, and Mary Zurbuchen gives me comfort that this may be more than a pious hope (Adam 2006; Budiawan 2004; Farid 2006; Jusuf et al. 2007; McGregor 2007; Roosa et al. 2004; Roosa 2006; Setiawan 2006; Zurbuchen 2005).

Concluding Remarks: What Can Be Done For The Future?

What else can be done to reduce the likelihood of anti-Chinese violence in the future? It is often suggested that an underlying cause is the perceived economic gap between indigenous and Chinese Indonesians. It is commonly and loosely said that ethnic Chinese control 70 per cent (or more) of the Indonesian economy. This is obviously an exaggeration, not least because great swathes of the economy have been in the large state sector, which has not been under Chinese control. A less extreme formulation is that they "control 70 per cent of the private, corporate, domestic capital (rather than the economy more widely)" (Backman 2001, pp. 88–89). On the other hand, at a 1999 conference in Canberra, Indonesian ambassador Wiryono cited figures attributed to James Riady that Chinese Indonesians controlled only about ten per cent of national wealth (Lloyd and Godley 2001, pp. 243). Whatever the reality of that lower estimate may be, public perceptions generally favour the higher figure.

Can something be done about it? I do not favour the notion of affirmative action for indigenous Indonesians, in part on principle because it would turn back the clock on the recent movement towards the removal of discrimination against Chinese Indonesians. It is also unsound because it treats all ethnic Chinese alike (whether rich, middle income or poor) on the one hand, and all indigenous Indonesians alike (whether rich, middle income or poor) on the other. There seems to me to be something inherently absurd about legislating for affirmative action in favour of more than 97.5 per cent of the population purely on the basis of their ethnicity and regardless of whether they are wealthy and educated or poor and nearly illiterate. It may seem utopian to propose that the gap between rich and poor could and should be alleviated by a system of taxation such as a capital gains tax and progressive income tax, but that is quite common in democratic societies with a well-established rule of law. Democracy and the rule of law may also seem utopian in the Indonesian context, but some progress has been made on both since the fall of Soeharto in 1998. Establishment of good governance and elimination of corruption through reform of government and the judiciary will make a system of taxation possible that is socially just; one which does not discriminate either for or against people on the basis of their ethnicity, but does so on the basis of their need and ability to contribute.

If Indonesians can succeed in making this admittedly difficult shift, the context will have changed to such a degree that, in the same sense, it is no longer thinkable to believe that it is provocative to hold the *barongsai* in public on Indonesian soil, "anti-Chinese violence" will be literally unthinkable.

References

Adam, Asvi Warman. *Soeharto: Sisi Gelap Sejarah Indonesia*. Yogyakarta: Ombak, 2004.

Ang, Ien. "Indonesia on My Mind: Diaspora, Internet and the Struggle for Hybridity". In *On Not Speaking Chinese: Living between Asia and the West*, pp. 52–54. London: Routledge, 2002.

Backman, Michael. "The New Order Conglomerates". In *Perspectives on the Chinese Indonesians*, edited by Michael R. Godley and Grayson J. Lloyd, pp. 83–99. Adelaide: Crawford House Publishing, 2001.

Budiawan. *Mematahkan Pewarisan Ingatan: Wacana Anti-komunis dan Politik Rekonsiliasi Pasca-Soeharto*. Jakarta: Lembaga Studi dan Advokasi Masyarakat (ELSAM), 2004.

Chin, Ung-Ho. *The Chinese of South-East Asia*. London: Minority Rights Group, 2000.

Chirot, Daniel and Anthony Reid, eds. *Essential Outsiders: Chinese and Jews in the Modern Transformation of Southeast Asia and Central Europe*. Seattle and London: University of Washington Press, 1997.

Coppel, Charles A. *Indonesian Chinese in Conflict*. Kuala Lumpur: Oxford University Press with ASAA, 1983.

──────. "Chinese Indonesians in Crisis: 1960s and 1990s". In *Perspectives on the Chinese Indonesians*, edited by Michael R. Godley and Grayson J. Lloyd, pp. 20–40. Adelaide: Crawford House Publishing, 2001.

──────. "Some Thoughts on the Size of the Ethnic Chinese Population in Indonesia". *Indonesian-studies Yahoogroup* (13 August) [accessed 2 July 2007].

──────, ed. "Celebrating Chinese New Year in Jakarta, February 1996: The View from the Internet". In *Studying Ethnic Chinese in Indonesia*, pp. 213–26. Singapore: Singapore Society of Asian Studies, 2002.

Cribb, Robert, ed. *The Indonesian Killings of 1965–1966: Studies from Java and Bali.* Clayton, Vic.: Centre of Southeast Asian Studies, Monash University, 1990.

Editorial. "Riot-prone Nation". *Jakarta Post*, 12 May 2006.

Farid, Hilmar. "Political Economy of Violence and Victims in Indonesia". In *Violent Conflicts in Indonesia: Analysis, Representation, Resolution*, edited by Charles A. Coppel, pp. 269–85. London & New York: Routledge, 2006.

Firdaus, Irwan. "Police Clash with Mob in Jakarta". *Associated Press* report, 13 May 2000 <http://www.geocities.com/~budis1/glodok2000/police_clash_with_mob_in_jakarta.htm/> (accessed 17 July 2007).

Go, Robert. "Riot Raises Doubts About Law and Order: Officials Stress the Jakarta Unrest Was Not Linked to the Violence against the Chinese in 1998, But Followed a Raid on Illegal Video-compact-disc Sellers". *Straits Times*, 17 May 2000 (accessed from LexisNexis Academic).

Hajramurni, Andi. "Makassar Calmer After Student Protests". *Jakarta Post*, 12 May 2006*a*.

———. "Makassar Violence Highlights Ethnic Tension in City". *Jakarta Post*, 15 May 2006*b*.

Heidhues, Mary Somers. "Indonesia". In *The Encyclopedia of the Chinese Overseas*, edited by Lynn Pan, pp. 151–68. Cambridge, Mass.: Harvard University Press, 1999.

Heryanto, Ariel. "Rape, Race and Reporting". In *Reformasi: Crisis and Change in Indonesia*, edited by Arief Budiman, Barbara Hatley, and Damien Kingsbury, pp. 299–334. Clayton: Monash Asia Institute, 1999.

———. "Asal usul Mei 1998". *Kompas*, 13 May 2007.

International Crisis Group. *Impunity versus Accountability for Gross Human Rights Violations.* Jakarta/Brussels: ICG Asia Report no. 12, 2 February 2001.

Jakarta Post. "More Chinese Tourists Expected to Visit Indonesia This Year". *Jakarta Post*, 2007*a* <http://www.thejakartapost.com/detailbusiness.asp?fileid=20070628.M05&irec=4> (28 June 2007) (accessed 29 June 2007).

———. "China, RI Look Into Joint Maritime Ops". *Jakarta Post* <http://www.thejakartapost.com/yesterdaydetail.asp?fileid=20070720.H07> (20 July 2007*b*) (accessed 13 August 2007).

———. "'Barongsai' festival to be held in Sragen". *Jakarta Post* <http://www.thejakartapost.com/Archives/ArchivesDet2.asp?FileID=20070716.H05> (16 July 2007*c*) (accessed 13 August 2007).

Jusuf, Ester Indahyani, Hotma Timbul, Olisias Gultom, and Sondang Frishka. *Kerusuhan Mei 1998: Fakta, Data & Analisa (Mengungkap Kerusuhan Mei 1998 sebagai kejahatan terhadap kemanusiaan).* [Jakarta]: Solidaritas Nusa Bangsa (SNB) & Asosiasi Penasehat Hukum dan Hak Asasi Manusia Indonesia (APHI), 2007.

Kieval, Hillel J. "Middleman Minorities and Blood: Is there a Natural Economy of the Ritual Murder Accusation in Europe?" In *Essential Outsiders: Chinese and Jews in the Modern Transformation of Southeast Asia and Central Europe*, edited by

Daniel Chirot and Anthony Reid, pp. 208–33. Seattle and London: University of Washington Press, 1997.

Kusno, Abidin. "Remembering/Forgetting the May Riots: Architecture, Violence, and the Making of 'Chinese Cultures' in Post-1998 Jakarta". *Public Culture* 15, no. 1 (2003): 149–77.

Leksono, Karlina. "The May 1998 Tragedy". In *Perspectives on the Chinese Indonesians*, edited by Michael R. Godley and Grayson J. Lloyd, pp. 55–60. Adelaide: Crawford House Publishing, 2001.

Lloyd, Grayson J. and Michael R. Godley, ed. "Summary of the Discussion". In *Perspectives on the Chinese Indonesians*, pp. 232–51. Adelaide: Crawford House Publishing, 2001.

Lochore, Laura. "Virtual Rape: Vivian's Story". In *Intersections: Gender History and Culture in the Asian Context*, 3 January 2000 <wwwsshe.murdoch.edu. au/intersections/issue3/laura3.html/>.

Mackie, Jamie, ed. "Anti-Chinese Outbreaks in Indonesia, 1959–68". In *The Chinese in Indonesia*, pp. 77–138. Melbourne: Thomas Nelson, 1976.

McGregor, Katharine E. *History in Uniform: Military Ideology and the Construction of Indonesia's Past*. Singapore: ASAA in association with NUS Press, 2007.

Pizzey, Jack. *Slow Boat from Surabaya: Through South-east Asia with Jack Pizzey*. Videorecording: written and narrated by Jack Pizzey, Episode 2, "Rich, Clever, Homeless". Phillip Emanuel Productions, 1988.

Purdey, Jemma. "Problematizing the Place of Victims in *Reformasi* Indonesia: A Contested Truth about the May 1998 Violence". *Asian Survey* 42 (4 July–August 2002): 605–22.

————. "Anti-Chinese Violence and Transitions in Indonesia: June 1998–October 1999". In *Chinese Indonesians: Remembering, Distorting, Forgetting*, edited by Tim Lindsey and Helen Pausacker, pp. 14–40. Singapore: Institute of Southeast Asian Studies, 2005.

————. *Anti-Chinese Violence in Indonesia, 1996–1999*. Singapore: ASAA in association with Singapore University Press, 2006*a*.

———— "The 'Other' May Riots: Anti-Chinese Violence in Solo, May 1998". In *Violent Conflicts in Indonesia: Analysis, Representation, Resolution*, edited by Charles A. Coppel, pp. 72–89. London & New York: Routledge, 2006*b*.

Roosa, John, Ayu Ratih, and Hilmar Farid, eds. *Tahun Yang Tidak Pernah Berakhir: Memahami Pengalaman Korban 1965: Esei-esei sejarah lisan*. Jakarta: Lembaga Studi dan Advokasi Masyarakat (ELSAM), 2004.

Roosa, John. *Pretext for Mass Murder: The September 30th Movement and Suharto's Coup d'état in Indonesia*. Madison, Wis: University of Wisconsin Press, 2006.

Sai, Siew Min. "'Eventing' the May 1998 Affair: Problematic Representations of Violence in Contemporary Indonesia". In *Violent Conflicts in Indonesia: Analysis, Representation, Resolution*, edited by Charles A. Coppel, pp. 39–57. London & New York: Routledge, 2006.

Setiawan, Hersri. *Kidung Para Korban: Dari Tutur Sepuluh Narasumber Eks-tapol.* Pakorba, Yogyakarta: Pustaka Pelajar, 2006.

Sidel, John T. "Riots, Church Burnings, Conspiracies: The Moral Economy of the Indonesian Crowd in the Late Twentieth Century". In *Violence in Indonesia*, edited by Ingrid Wessel and Georgia Wimhöfer, pp. 47–63. Hamburg: Abera, 2001.

———. *Riots, Pogroms, Jihad: Religious Violence in Indonesia.* Singapore: NUS Press, 2007.

Siegel, James T. "Early Thoughts on the Violence of May 13 and 14, 1998 in Jakarta". *Indonesia* 66 (October 1998): 75–108.

———. "Thoughts on the Violence of May 13 aand 14, 1998 in Jakarta". In *Violence and the State in Suharto's Indonesia*, edited by B.R.O'G. Anderson, pp. 90–125. Ithaca, NY: Southeast Asia Program, Cornell University, 2001.

Taufiqurrahman, M. "China, RI Tighten Cultural Connection". *Jakarta Post*, 28 June 2007 <http://www.thejakartapost.com/yesterdaydetail.asp?fileid=20070628.H08> (accessed 29 June 2007).

Tan, Mély G. "The Indonesian Commission on Violence against Women". In *Violent Conflicts in Indonesia: Analysis, Representation, Resolution*, edited by Charles A. Coppel, pp. 229–41. London & New York: Routledge, 2006.

Tay, Elaine. "Global Chinese Fraternity and the Indonesian Riots of May 1998: The Online Gathering of Dispersed Chinese". *Intersections: Gender History and Culture in the Asian Context*, 4 September 2000 <wwwsshe.murdoch.edu.au/intersections/issue4/tay.html>.

———. "Discursive Violence on the Internet and the May 1998 Riots". In *Violent Conflicts in Indonesia: Analysis, Representation, Resolution*, edited by Charles A. Coppel, pp. 58–71. London & New York: Routledge, 2006.

TGPF [Tim Gabungan Pencari Fakta]. "Final Report of the Joint Fact-Finding Team (TGPF) on the 13–15 May 1998 Riot, Executive Summary, 23 October 1998". In *Perspectives on the Chinese Indonesians*, edited by Michael R. Godley and Grayson J. Lloyd, pp. 332–60 (Appendex 2). Adelaide: Crawford House Publishing, 2001.

The, Siauw Giap. "The Chinese in Indonesia: A Review Article". *Kabar Seberang*, 7 July 1980, pp. 114–30.

Wang Gungwu. "Islam Versus Asia's Chinese Diaspora". Project Syndicate, July 2002 <http://www.project-syndicate.org/commentary/gungwu1> (accessed 27 June 2007).

Wibowo, Ignatius. "Exit, Voice and Loyalty: Indonesian Chinese after the Fall of Soeharto". *Sojourn*, vol. 16, no. 1 (2001): 25–46.

Wikipedia. "Chinese Indonesian". <http://en.wikipedia.org/wiki/Indonesian_Chinese> (accessed 17 July 2007).

Zurbuchen, Mary S. "History, Memory and the '1965 Incident' in Indonesia". *Asian Survey* 42, no. 4 (2002): 564–82.

———, ed. *Beginning to Remember: The Past in the Indonesian Present.* Singapore: Singapore University Press in association with University of Washington Press, 2005.

8

ETHNIC CHINESE AND ETHNIC INDONESIANS: A LOVE-HATE RELATIONSHIP[1]

Natalia Soebagjo

Almost ten years ago, ethnic Chinese became the systematic target and victims of mass rioting. Even if the May '98 riots were incited by as yet unidentified "*provocateurs*", they would not have developed so intensely and so quickly if there were no underlying anti-Chinese sentiment among the masses.[2] More than 10,000 were killed, including non-Chinese; primarily ethnic Chinese women were gang-raped; and losses of around US$187.5 million were incurred, but to this day no decisive action has been taken to follow up on reports and calls for accountability by the Indonesian Human Rights Commission and other NGOs. The authorities' disinterest in finding out the truth behind the riots only gives credence to the perception that the Chinese are dispensable.

Hence, to be able to begin to resolve the problem of the Chinese in Indonesia, we have to first accept the fact that there remains some ambivalence on how the non-Chinese and Chinese respond to each other. One cannot help but agree with social scientist, Dr Thung Yulan, who believes that "the recognition of the existence of the identity of 'Chineseness' of the ethnic Chinese is the necessary first step to take", in any attempt to accept the ethnic Chinese as part of the Indonesian make-up.[3] So far, the *pribumi* have only been able to do this very reluctantly.

The study of ethnic relations in Indonesia after the fall of Soeharto is now certainly more interesting, if not equally complicated. Whereas previously all talk on matters related to "SARA", namely ethnicity, religion, race, and inter-group differences, was repressed, in the current era of *Reformasi* it is a free-for-all: anyone can say anything about everything, including subjects that were once considered divisive and dangerous. In the post-Soeharto era of openness and freedom of expression, the pent-up primordial sentiments lurking ominously behind Indonesia's "unity" of ethnic diversity and religious fervour are let loose. Therefore, we are faced not only with the problem of continuing tension between ethnic Chinese and non-Chinese, but also of inter-group and intra-group ethnic tension and religious intolerance, such as what we have painfully witnessed in Maluku, in Poso, between the Maduranese and the Javanese, for example. On top of this, there is the problem of economic hardship and gaping socio-economic inequality. Amidst all this turmoil, the age-long "Chinese problem" has just become another item on the long list of problems Indonesia currently faces and an item going further down the list.

This freedom that the Indonesians are now enjoying, however, came at a price. As Soeharto began to lose his grip on power due to his inability to understand or control, much less influence, events swirling around him in the last few years of his rule, opposition forces emerged calling for his resignation.[4] The anti-Soeharto student movement in May 1998 in Jakarta suddenly erupted into anti-Chinese riots which shocked Jakartans who never believed that the violence they saw happening in the provinces would occur in the capital city, leaving thousands dead and more fleeing in fear and panic.

Hence, Soeharto's rule came full circle. His rise and fall were both marked by violence and bloodshed: the 1965 attempted coup ushered his entrance, and the 1998 May riots escorted his exit. Ethnic Chinese were the targeted victims of both episodes.

A LOOK BACK

A consequence of 1965 was the continued nurturing of anti-Chinese sentiments which had been festering, in some form or other, since 1740 when 10,000 Chinese were massacred in Batavia by colonial soldiers, and driven out of the walled city. Then, as in 1998, the Chinese quarter was burnt down and shops were looted, and the Chinese fled.

Under the Dutch colonial system, the status of ethnic Chinese was clear cut. They were "Foreign Orientals", just like those of Arab or Indian descent, a notch or more below the Europeans and Westerners, but above the indigenous people. After the 1740 Chinese Rebellion, their role was limited to keeping the colonial economic machinery going. They were organized under a "kapitan" who was answerable to the Dutch East India Company and who managed the affairs of the Chinese under his group. This system prevailed into the twentieth century and effectively established a system of ethnic segregation and ethnic division of labour.

The collapse of the Qing dynasty in 1911 and the subsequent rise of nationalist movements in China had a big impact on the Indies-born Chinese in the Dutch East Indies whom the Chinese considered as their citizens, but were also Dutch subjects under the Dutch Nationality Law. Developments on the Mainland split them into groups with different political orientations. The *totok* Chinese, later immigrants, were oriented towards the Mainland, whilst the *peranakan* Chinese were generally divided into those who supported the Dutch Indies, and those who were for the independent Indonesian nation slowly unfolding.

When an independent Indonesia became a reality in 1945, the *peranakan* Chinese were torn between two options: assimilate and be absorbed into, or maintain the *peranakan* Chinese identity, but integrate with the people of the new Indonesian state. The Chinese Union (Persatuan Tionghoa) was established to protect the interests of the Chinese minority in an independent Indonesia. The party believed that accepting Indonesian citizenship did not necessarily mean having to lose one's ethnic identity and called for equal treatment with other groups, regardless of their race, culture, and religion. The Union evolved into the Indonesian Chinese Democrat Party (Partai Demokrat Tionghoa Indonesia) whose members were split into those who placed hope in joining ethnic Indonesian political parties without losing their own ethnic identity, and those who thought it pointless to do so because they would still be considered a minority. The latter argued that because the Chinese were discriminated against, it was better for minority groups to unite and fight against discrimination.

The Chinese Democrat Party broke apart and a new socio-political organization was established: Badan Permusjawaratan Kewarganegaraan Indonesia, better known as BAPERKI (the Indonesian Citizens' Consultative Body). BAPERKI's integrationist approach was based on the premise that Indonesia was made up of different ethnic groups, of which Chinese was one, and that all ethnic groups should be treated equally. At first BAPERKI garnered a lot of support, but as it took on Leftist leanings, support for it fell. Its position was that discrimination against the minority Chinese could only be eradicated in a socialist society and so assimilation through compulsory name-changing and inter-marriage with the locals was futile. Yap Thiam Hien

(1913–89), a human rights advocate, also did not believe in the efficacy of name-changing and inter-marriage, but he also did not believe that socialism was the solution. The root of the Chinese problem, according to Yap, was the issue of majority-minority ethnic relations. He called for non-discrimination, the understanding and respect for other cultures, anti-racialism, and the protection of ethnic identity as a human right.

The assimilation approach adopted by the Lembaga Pembinaan Kesatuan Bangsa (LPKB) was an attempt to "force" ethnic Chinese to become Indonesians by assimilating into the indigenous community until the Chinese ethnic minority blends and disappears amongst the locals. The fault, so to speak, was not in the hands of the indigenous, but more in the hands of ethnic Chinese who tend to maintain their exclusive group identity with little affinity towards Indonesia. The pro-assimilation group believed that name-changing, mixed marriages, conversion to Islam, would help to hasten the natural process of assimilation. If BAPERKI sided with the communists, LPKB sided with the right-wing political forces and the anti-communist Armed Forces. Not surprising then that when Soeharto came to power, the assimilationist approach became the official New Order government approach towards finding a solution to the Chinese problem.[5]

Decades later and in an independent Indonesia where ethnic Chinese are already legally Indonesians, strains of the arguments posed by the political activists of the pre-independent days can still be discerned today.

Tjoe Bou San (1891–1925), editor-in-chief of *Sin Po*, blamed Dutch separatists' policies for separating ethnic Chinese from other ethnic groups, alienating them into a distinct minority, powerless in the face of both the Dutch and the indigenous people. Hence the *Sin Po* group favoured maintaining ties with China which may be in a better position to protect them. With the rise of China in the twenty-first century, are there ethnic Chinese in Indonesia who believe that their future would be more secure in China or elsewhere?

The late Phoa Liong Gie from Chung Hwa Hui believed that although the ethnic Chinese were not absorbed into indigenous society, they were nevertheless already partly integrated. Still, their interests differed from those of both the Dutch and the locals, and so ethnic Chinese should just stay neutral and serve whoever comes to power. Should ethnic Chinese of today's Indonesia remain neutral and stay low-key by not voicing their aspirations since their fate remains the same no matter who is in power?

Liem Koen Hian (1896–1952), founder of Partai Tionghoa Indonesia, followed developments in Indonesian local politics closely and felt that because the Chinese were living in Indonesia and, unlike the *totok* Chinese, had no intention of going back to China, they should anticipate being part of the Indonesian nation, including being Indonesian citizens. Over time he believed that ethnic Chinese could be absorbed into the indigenous Indonesian community. Time has passed, but to what extent have the Chinese who are now Indonesian citizens been absorbed into the indigenous society and considered part of the Indonesian nation?

SOEHARTO AND THE NEW ORDER

When Soeharto came to power in 1966 and wanted to create his New Order government, he was faced with the dilemma of wanting to capitalize on the business and commercial acumen of the Chinese to develop the economy after the carnage of 1965. But at the same time, he wanted to eliminate their perceived economic dominance.[6] This is a somewhat sympathetic assessment of Soeharto's motives. He soon discovered that the Chinese, being ethnically and economically distinct, were useful "buffers" between the elite and the public, not only in the area of trade and commerce, but also in times of social hostility.[7] They were an ethnic minority that was comparatively successful and, therefore, vulnerable, easy targets as scapegoats, and hence in need of protection for which the Chinese were forced to pay.

Like the colonial Dutch before him, Soeharto did indeed take advantage of the Chinese minority's economic prowess and even cultivated his own inner circle of Chinese tycoons, but in doing so, he fostered and strengthened the perception that the Chinese dominated the Indonesian economy.[8]

Soeharto's policies towards ethnic Chinese were opportunistic and expedient. When he wanted to develop small businesses and cooperatives, which were mainly owned and run by non-Chinese, he simply gathered together thirty-one Chinese owners of business conglomerates and invited them to his ranch in Tapos, urging them to transfer twenty-five per cent of the shares in their companies to cooperatives. During the 1998 financial crisis, the Jimbaran group of ninety-six tycoons, including Soeharto's own children, was asked to convert their U.S. dollar holdings to Indonesian Rupiah or to donate gold. The Chinese business tycoons who were by then deep in debt were reluctant, but apparently, thirteen Chinese tycoons had already been picked out by General Faisal Tanjung, Commander of the Armed Forces, for financial contributions, calling on their sense of nationalism and solidarity to Indonesia and stressing the fact that they were able to become rich because they were in Indonesia.[9] In the end it was not clear how much they actually contributed to both these calls, but moves such as these only strengthened the perception among the non-Chinese that the Chinese did indeed control the economy and were, therefore, indispensable to Indonesia's economic well-being but, at the same time, they also had a debt to pay to the nation which had given them the opportunity to enrich themselves.

This small group of ethnic Chinese tycoons who were useful to Soeharto as cash cows made life difficult for the majority of ethnic Chinese who were not in their league. Most Chinese are professionals, small shopkeepers, and traders. Based on the 2000 census, it is estimated that the number of ethnic Chinese is somewhere around 1.5 per cent of the population or about three million people,[10] yet it is this handful of super-rich which increases the animosity and resentment of the non-Chinese towards the rest of the ethnic Chinese, many of whom most likely also resent these tycoons for making their own acceptance into the community that much harder.

In hindsight, Soeharto's strong arm assimilation approach to solving the Chinese problem by stressing uniformity was successful in containing, but not eradicating, the problem. It has become very difficult to determine who, in fact, are ethnic Chinese in Indonesia. Self-identification was used in the 2000 Census, but many ethnic Chinese no longer identify themselves as Chinese. They no longer have Chinese names, do not speak Mandarin or any of the dialects, do not celebrate Chinese festivals, and often do not even have the physical traits of the Chinese. In short, they have no affinity with Chinese culture and history, nor with Mainland China. They identify themselves as Indonesians, but it is often the indigenous Indonesians who remind them or point out to them that they are, in fact, Chinese. According to I. Wibowo, this is because "Chineseness" has been "frozen" into a fixed state of permanence: anyone with yellow skin, slit eyes, straight hair is a Chinese.[11]

An analysis of the 2000 Population Census also concluded that out of approximately 1.50 per cent of the total population who are ethnic Chinese, only 93,717 (0.05 per cent) are foreigners.[12] The remaining 1.45 per cent are Indonesian citizens. Legally, ethnic Chinese in Indonesia are Indonesian citizens, whether or not they have assimilated or not. There should no longer be any ambiguity.

The May '98 Riots, however, opened a Pandora's Box. It shocked many ethnic Chinese into the realization that they were Chinese after all, and no matter what their citizenship, no matter how many generations they have lived in Indonesia and, worse, no matter what they have contributed to the community or even the country, they could still very easily become targets and victims of political power struggles and economic downturns.

POST MAY '98

The consequence of May '98 and the fall of Soeharto was the ushering in of a new phase in Indonesia's history. The nation at the time was most badly hit by the Asian financial crisis, forcing its leaders and people to re-evaluate the Soeharto years and to undergo a restructuring of economic and political institutions to ensure a more democratic, economically sustainable, and socially just future. Indonesia embarked on a period of soul-searching and its people began to question what it means to be "Indonesian" amidst political turmoil, economic hardship, ethnic conflict, and secessionist movements. They were given the opportunity to recreate the Indonesian "nation". After decades of being denied their political and cultural rights, ethnic Chinese found themselves able to assert themselves in the public domain and given the opportunity to participate in the rebuilding process. The rights taken away from them by Soeharto were being returned to them piecemeal.

In September 1998, President B.J. Habibie carried out legislative reforms to end the official use of the labels "*pribumi*" and "*non-pribumi*". A year after the riots, he issued a Presidential Instruction allowing the teaching of Mandarin Chinese. He also abolished a regulation which required the Chinese to produce the SBKRI, the certificate of citizenship introduced in 1958 and which effectively discriminated against the Chinese because no other ethnic group is required to have such a document as legal evidence of citizenship. This was not the first time this has been done. In 1996 there was already a Presidential Instruction to that effect, but it was not consistently implemented.

Efforts to abolish the use of the SBKRI have repeatedly failed because it is a source of unofficial income for bureaucrats. It is estimated that billions of Rupiah per annum can be unlawfully gained this way. In 2003, for example, the cost of obtaining an SBKRI ranged between Rp. 2 million to Rp. 7.5 million (US$235 to US$882). Although the SBKRI is clearly discriminatory, one wonders, however, that if such a document were also required of ethnic Indian or Arab in Indonesia, would they not also be victims of extortion, given that corruption is endemic in Indonesian society?

In 2006, the Citizenship Bill was signed, and according to the Bill, anyone born on Indonesian soil, no matter what their parents' status, is considered to be an Indonesian citizen. Yet even with the Citizenship Bill, ethnic Chinese still have problems in obtaining ID cards and passports because the lower level bureaucracies still require the SBKRI, claiming that there are no implementing regulations in place and, therefore, the regulations stipulated in the State Gazette inherited from the Dutch still apply.

B.J. Habibie is credited for paving the way for political liberalization and the subsequent proliferation of political parties, including ethnic Chinese political parties, but his attitude towards the Chinese was insincere. Although he expressed regret towards the victims of the May '98 riots, he was driven primarily by the need to restore business confidence, rather than genuine sympathy. Granted, it was Habibie who set up a Joint Fact Finding Team two months after the riots, but the government had no choice but to do it given the scale and intensity of the riots, as well as the pressure from both local and international communities. Unfortunately, the Team's findings were later dismissed by the government. In March 1999, Habibie even had the gall to claim that "he didn't have a full picture of what happened" that fateful May.[13]

Habibie's sentiments towards the Chinese were revealed in his comments in a July '98 interview with *The Washington Post* in which he said, "If the Chinese community does not come back because they don't trust their own country and society, I cannot force them, nobody can force them … But do they really think we will then die? … Their place will be taken by others."[14] It was clear that, for Habibie, the Chinese are dispensable. It was also clear that the government only wanted the Chinese for their capital and for them to return and get back to doing what they are supposedly best at: business.

Such comments raised questions in people's minds regarding Habibie's sincerity and concern towards the Chinese. Nevertheless, calling for the end of the usage of the terms *"pribumi"* and *"non-pri"* was alone already a major step that Habibie made in the right direction.

The one president whose sincerity was never questioned was Abdurrahman Wahid, affectionately called Gus Dur. Long before he became the fourth president in 1999, he had already been championing equal treatment for ethnic Chinese. After the riots, he became a founding member of GANDI, the Anti-Discrimination Movement in late 1998. One of his creative initiatives as Chairman of Nahdlatul Ulama (NU) in the early 1990s was the cooperation with Summa Bank to establish a small-scale credit branch and a bank branch in Sidoarjo, East Java. The intention was not only to provide credit facilities for micro- and small-scale traders, but also to show that NU, as one of the largest grass roots Islamic movements in Indonesia, was able to cooperate with a Chinese bank owned by Edward Soeryajaya, son of Astra's William Soeryajaya. Unfortunately, the cooperation was prematurely ended because Bank Summa ran into management problems.

To many Chinese, Gus Dus is like a father figure, "Bapak Tionghoa". It was Gus Dur who in 2000 revoked Presidential Instruction no. 14/1967,[15] which effectively reinstated the cultural and religious rights of the Chinese. In 2002, Megawati reinforced this by declaring Chinese New Year a national holiday.

A REAWAKENING

The atrocities during the final years of Soeharto's power and the subsequent reform era reawakened the Chinese identity in both negative and positive ways. It was a horrific realization that our nation building process was flawed and that the Chinese were still considered as "them", and easy, even legitimate, targets, but at the same time, it stirred their consciousness into action and into claiming their rights.

There is cautious optimism about the fact that the Chinese now are able to express their cultural identity. Come each February or thereabouts, all major cities are decked in red to celebrate *Imlek*, and the sound of drums accompanying lion dances deafen in the shopping malls, to the glee of Chinese and non-Chinese alike. Extensive media coverage adds to the frenzy. There are now numerous Chinese-language newspapers as well as television programmes and radio stations in Mandarin. Mandarin courses are easily available and very popular amongst non-Chinese also who realize its importance for doing business and taking advantage of Mainland China's economic rise.

It has become acceptable to express one's Chinese identity, but what is the reaction to this? For some Chinese, this recognition of their ethnic and cultural identity is a positive development as it accords them the same recognition as the eleven other ethnic groups which comprise more than 1.5 per cent of the Indonesian population.[16] Being Chinese is no different to being a Javanese, a Batak, or a Balinese. For others, it makes little difference in that the acceptance of the Chinese by the dominant non-Chinese group is only superficial. To them, the discrimination, the stereotyping, the negative image of the Chinese still exists despite official statements saying otherwise, so keeping a low profile is, therefore, the best option. There is also the feeling that the display is a case of "too much, too soon" which some fear could lead to a backlash from the non-Chinese community too accustomed to accusing the Chinese of being "exclusive" and unwilling to integrate with the rest of society.

At the national celebration of Chinese New Year in 2007, for example, President Susilo Bambang Yudhoyono still had to reiterate the fact that Indonesians of Chinese descent were an integral part of the country's identity, that they had contributed as much to the country's struggle for independence and development as other ethnic groups and, therefore, there must no longer be any more discrimination, or unfair treatment towards them. Religion and ethnicity should not be the basis for discrimination.[17] Only a few months before that, however, his Vice-president, Jusuf Kalla, had appeared in the studios of Metro TV and asked Chinese businessmen not to consider, "this country, this nation, as a hotel" and flee when conditions are bad. Instead, they should have a sense of ownership with the country and participate in development efforts and that there is no reason to invest their capital overseas. He added that trust should be developed amongst the Chinese themselves. When questioned about a guarantee for their safety, all he could say was that Indonesia is much safer than before.[18] Clearly, the mindset of some in the ruling elite has not changed. The onus is on the Chinese to be pro-active and make themselves part of the Indonesian nation. Rarely is inclusion and acceptance perceived as being a joint responsibility of both the Chinese and the non-Chinese.

In defining what is the Indonesian nation, its founding fathers Soekarno and Hatta often quoted French philosopher Ernst Renan who defined a nation as "a soul, a spiritual principle ... A nation is a large-scale solidarity, constituted by the feeling of the sacrifices that one has made in the past and of those that one is prepared to make in the future. It presupposes a past; it is summarized, however, in the present by a tangible fact, namely consent, the clearly expressed desire to continue a common life."[19] A nation defined as such, as "the desire to continue a common life", was meant to overcome Indonesia's ethnic and religious diversity as it is not defined based on race, ethnicity, religion, language or, most importantly, geography. What if the past sacrifices of the Chinese in Indonesia are not recognized as such in the present? Can they then be expected to make the same sacrifices in the future? What happens, however, if there is no sense of solidarity among the diverse ethnic groups? How can this sense of nationhood be achieved if the minority is not acknowledged or recognized as being part of the same history? As Wang Gungwu so aptly asked, "Whose history should they (the Chinese) choose if they cannot determine their own history? Can they deny history and create their own history?"[20]

With political liberalization, the Chinese in Indonesia now have the opportunity to create their own history for a better future. One Chinese who is trying to do so is Lieus Sungkarisma. When asked why he set up the Partai Reformasi Tionghoa Indonesia in June 1998, he explained that,

> We see the reform era as giving every citizen the opportunity to freely express his opinion, to form alliances, and to come together ... We use the term 'reform' to mean two things. Internally, to reform the attitude and characteristics of the Chinese who have not yet been accepted by the wider public. Externally, we also ask the wider public to reform themselves so that if a Chinese has integrated with Pancasila, then they have to be accepted as part of the Indonesian nation.[21]

Nurdin Purnomo, a Chinese businessman, also set up the Partai Bhineka Tunggal Ika, which tried to appeal to a wider audience, beyond just ethnic Chinese.

Not all the Chinese were in favour of the creation of ethnic-based parties as it was considered a step back in the nation building process. Some preferred to enter politics through nationalist-based parties, such as Partai Demokrasi Indonesia-Perjuangan, Golongan Karya, Partai Amanat Nasional, and even the NU-affiliated Partai Kebangkitan Bangsa. Not surprisingly, the Chinese-based parties did not fare too well in the elections. Nevertheless, in the 1999 general elections four ethnic Chinese managed to win seats in the House of Representatives. In 2004, as many as 172 Chinese Indonesians across the country ran for legislative seats or as regional representative council candidates. Four of the thirty-eight Jakarta DPD candidates were of Chinese descent.[22] The point to note is that given the opportunity, there are ethnic Chinese who are willing to play an active role in Indonesian politics, just like anyone else.

Those who did not want to enter the political arena, became indirectly politically involved by becoming activists in a range of non-governmental organizations, humanitarian groups, and clan associations, thereby participating in the lively development of Indonesia's civil society, be it working for the interests of ethnic Chinese or for universal issues such as human rights and equality. Admittedly the majority will just want to lay low and "go about their business quietly, without participating in any organizational activity, political or otherwise." [23] This may be so, but at least now they have the option to do otherwise. The trepidation holding them back remains today because the indigenous Indonesians, as much as the Chinese, are still unable to think beyond the confines of their own biases fuelled by previous government policies which fostered hostility between them. The biases and the discriminatory policies feed on each other.

The obvious solution is to break the vicious circle. At the state level, discriminatory policies are slowly being revoked and on 19 July 2007, the draft bill for the Elimination of Racial and Ethnic Discrimination was passed.[24] How the bill will be implemented will be the true test. Once passed, however, the Chinese will have to seek a new rallying point and be forced to look into issues with wider relevance. As Christine S. Tjhin, a researcher of the Centre for International and Strategic Studies, observed, the issue of anti-discrimination has been a dominant theme in the political discourse of the Chinese. She puts forward two possible reasons: political inexperience or the narrowness of political thinking. The former can be solved with time and greater participation in mainstream politics, but the latter only reveals the low quality of the politics.[25]

Already in 2004, the persistent complaints about the SBKRI were beginning to annoy. Megawati had told the Chinese to unite and stand up against the bureaucrats who asked them to show their SBKRI. "... Don't just complain and comply, if you are asked tell them that it's not needed, it takes two hands to clap", she graphically said.[26] A few days later, Minister for Justice and Human Rights, Yusril Ihza Mahendra, told them to stop asking for special treatment by refusing to show proof of citizenship when applying for passports. "Even the *pribumi* are asked, why shouldn't the Chinese be asked too?" he said.[27] The message given is that if the Chinese want to be treated equally, they need to speak up and do something about it. They also reveal that the past strategy of quiet compliance adopted by the Chinese to avoid trouble is no longer the answer.

In the business arena, the financial crisis led to the crumbling of the older conglomerates into smaller entities and with new business conglomerates in the making, some of which are indigenous companies. More companies have gone public with listings on the stock exchange and small-medium enterprises are being encouraged to develop. With continuous calls for greater transparency, fairness in competition, anti-trust and anti-corruption measures, as well as a critical media it would be more difficult to build up a crony *cukong* system which worked so well in Soeharto's favour. The Chinese are now no longer the only rich ones. Non-Chinese government officials, politicians, and businessmen and women have also become very wealthy, be it through lawful or unlawful means. There is also greater media coverage of the poor Chinese in Tangerang and elsewhere, dispelling the myth that all Chinese are super-rich business tycoons. Indonesians are beginning to discover that there are Chinese in all walks of life, not just in business. According to Megawati, if Chinese want to become civil servants or join the military, they are free to do so because there is no discrimination, but she questions whether they would be keen to take up such hardship vocations.[28]

There is also growing realization and awareness that ethnic Chinese in Indonesia, just like the non-Chinese, are a diverse mix of individuals. It is no longer relevant to categorize the Chinese into the straight-forward categories of "*peranakan*" or "*totok*", primarily because as time passes, we no longer know who the *totok* Chinese are. If mastery of the Chinese language is a criteria for being considered a "*totok*", nowadays more and more people, including non-Chinese, are learning the language. If being China-oriented is another criteria, then with diplomatic ties between Indonesia and China resuming and with China's spectacular rise, increasingly more people are keen to know more about China as a regional, if not international, power which cannot be ignored. When the May riots broke out, few, if any, fled to China for sanctuary. Many went to Bali and to Singapore where visas are not needed. In an increasingly globalized world, therefore, the whole world is open to ethnic Chinese and non-Chinese alike to seek opportunities for a better and more secure future which may or may not be in China. Markets now determine individuals' orientation, not just government policies and cultural regimes. An increasing number of people have become global citizens.

CALM BEFORE ANOTHER STORM

Given recent developments, have relations between ethnic Indonesians and ethnic Chinese changed after May 1998? The answer, unfortunately, is still unclear. The jury is still out on this one. We cannot delude ourselves into thinking that there is no differentiation between the Chinese and indigenous Indonesians. There remains a separating line.

Purdey concluded that after six decades of independence, "Chinese Indonesians remain second-class citizens, with economic privileges but few political rights."[29] This is slowly changing but unless Indonesians — Chinese and non-Chinese alike — are able to shed the misperceptions and stereotyping, create a more equitable society, overcome corruption, improve governance, and tighten law enforcement as part of its long "to do" list, it will take longer to delete the separating line.

Solving the "Chinese problem" is, however, part of solving the as yet unresolved challenge of Indonesia's ongoing nation building process. Not only has Indonesia witnessed anti-Chinese violence, but also communal violence in Kalimantan, Sulawesi, and Maluku and, most recently, secessionist demands in Papua and Maluku have come to the fore again. As Pahler observed, "Now people of different ethnic, religious, cultural, and also linguistic backgrounds as well as of different socio-economic abilities live close together in comparatively small areas. Their integration was in many cases unsuccessful."[30] Hence, the integration of diverse ethnic groups into one unified nation state is a challenge the Indonesian people are still grappling with. Indonesia, not only faces tension between ethnic Chinese and indigenous Indonesians, but also tension between indigenous Indonesians themselves. Nation building is an ongoing, dynamic process, but to achieve the ideal of "unity in diversity", Indonesians have to accept the fact that they live in a plural and multicultural environment in order to formulate and implement the kind of state policies needed to mitigate the tension.

Even though anti-discrimination laws are already in place, it is still difficult to foresee a future when we will no longer hear of ethnic Chinese being victimized by the bureaucracy and having to pay more for the cost of birth certificates, produce legal documents which they need not have, or pay for their sense of security. This is because we are unable to estimate or measure the depth and extent of the hostility and resentment still felt towards the Chinese.

In the meantime, if we assume political stability in Indonesia can be achieved and sustained, there is still hope for growing tolerance and acceptance of the differences. The Chinese in Indonesia now have greater opportunity to define their role in society from the community level right up to the national level. The onus, however, is not on the Chinese alone. If the Chinese are expected to break away from the mindset of the past, so too are indigenous Indonesians. In order to create a new future together, both parties have to play their part. Should there be another political power struggle or another downturn in the economy and violence erupts once again, there should be a greater sense of solidarity among the diverse peoples of Indonesia.

Notes

1   Paper presented in a seminar on Ethnic Chinese in Indonesia in an Era of Globalization, jointly organized by the Institute of Southeast Asian Studies (ISEAS), Chinese Heritage Centre (CHC), and NABIL Foundation in Singapore, 19 July 2007.

2   I. Wibowo, ed., "Penutup: Kapan Ke-Cina-an akan Berhenti", in *Harga yang Harus Dibayar: Sketsa Pergulatan Etnis Cina di Indonesia* (Jakarta: PT. Gramedia Pustaka Utama, 2000).

3   Thung Ju Lan, "Susahnya Jadi Orang Cina: Ke-Cina-an sebagai Konstruksi Sosial", in *Harga yang Harus Dibayar: Sketsa Pergulatan Etnis Cina di Indonesia*, edited by I. Wibowo (Jakarta: PT. Gramedia Pustaka Utama, 2000).

4   R.E. Elson, *Soeharto: A Political Biography* (Cambridge: Cambridge University Press, 2001), pp. 267–96.

5   See Leo Suryadinata, *Pribumi Indonesians, the Chinese Minority and China* (Singapore: Heineman Asia, 1992).

6   Jemma Purdey, *Anti-Chinese Violence in Indonesia, 1996–1999* (Singapore: Singapore University Press, 2006), p. 20.

7   Ibid., p. 25.

8   It is unclear how much of the economy is in the control of the Chinese. In his 1995 study, *Overseas Chinese Business Networks in Asia*, Michael Beckman stated that: "Sino-Indonesians control approximately 73 per cent of listed firms by market capitalization. At the end of 1993, Sino-Indonesians (who

constitute just 3.5 per cent of all Indonesians) controlled 68 per cent of the top 300 conglomerates and nine of the top ten private sector groups." This 70 per cent figure or higher seems to be the popular belief. In March 1998, when anti-Chinese violence was raging, in a visit to Japan, B.J. Habibie claimed that the Chinese who only make up 3 per cent of the population, control 90 per cent of the economy.

9   Kees v. Dijk, *A Country in Despair: Indonesia Between 1997 and 2000* (Jakarta: KITLV Press, 2001), p. 104.

10   Leo Suryadinata, Evi Nurvidya Arifin, and Aris Ananta, *Indonesia's Population: Ethnicity and Religion in a Changing Political Landscape* (Singapore: Institute of Southeast Asian Studies, 2003), p. 101.

11   I. Wibowo, ed., "Penutup: Kapan Ke-Cina-an akan Berhenti", in *Harga Yang Harus Dibayar: Sketsa Pengulatan Etnics Cinadi Indonesia* (Jakarta: P.T. Gramedia Pustaka Utama, 2000).

12   Ibid., p. 76.

13   Purdey, *Anti-Chinese Violence in Indonesia, 1996–1999*, op. cit., p. 180.

14   Ibid., p. 175.

15   Presidential Instruction no. 14/1967 banned the practice of Chinese religion, beliefs, and customs, including the prohibition of Chinese characters, which at the time was deemed a hindrance to assimilation.

16   These ethnic groups are the Javanese, Sundanese, Malay, Madurese, Batak, Minangkabau, Betawi, Buginese, Bantenese, Banjarese, and Balinese. *Indonesia's Population: Ethnicity and Religion in a Changing Political Landscape*, op. cit., p. 31.

17   "SBY Pledges Fairness for Chinese", *Jakarta Post*, 25 February 2007.

18   "Jangan jadikan Indonesia sebagai 'Hotel'", *Media Indonesia Online*, 11 October 2006.

19   Translated by Dr Harsja W. Bachtiar in "Integrasi Nasional Indonesia", *Wawasan Kebangsaan Indonesia: Gagasan dan Pemikiran Badan Komunikasi Penghayatan Kesatuan Bangsa"* (Jakarta: BAKOM-PKB Pusat, 1994), p. 29, as "Nasion adalah suatu jiwa, suatu asas spiritual … Ia adalah suatu kesatuan solidaritas yang besar, tercipta oleh perasaan pengorbanan yang telah dibuat di masa lampau dan yang oleh manusia-manusia yang bersangkutan bersedia dibuat di masa depan. Nasion mempunyai masa lampau, tetapi ia menlanjutkan dirinya pada masa kini melalui suatu kenyataan yang jelas: yaitu kesepakatan, keinginan yang dikemukakan dengan nyata untuk terus hidup bersama."

20   Wang Gungwu, "Orang Etnis Cina mencari sejarah", in *Harga yang Harus Dibayar: Sketsa Pergulatan Etnis Cina di Indonesia*, edited by I. Wibowo (Jakarta: P.T. Gramedia Pustaka Utama, 2000).

21   Sungkarisma, Lieus, "Selama 32 Tahun Kita Salah", in *Kapok Jadi Non-Pri: Warga Tionghoa Mencari Keadilan*, edited by Alfian Hamzah (Bandung: Zaman Wacana Mulia, 1998).

22 "Chinese Indonesians Rising to Political Stage", in *Jakarta Post*, 25 March 2004.
23 Tan, Mely G., "The Ethnic Chinese in Indonesia: Trials and Tribulations", in *Tribute to Rev. DR. Eka Darmaputra* (Publisher unknown).
24 "RUU PDRE Tak Wadahi Kebutuhan Masyarakat", *KOMPAS*, 5 July 2007.
25 Christine S. Tjhin, "Partisipasi Politik Tionghoa dan Demokratisasi", posted on HKSIS <http://groups.yahoo.com/group/budaya_tionghoa/message/6916> on 14 October 2006.
26 Glori K. Wadrianto, "Presiden: Tindak Tegas Peminta SBKRI", posted on *KOMPAS Cyber Media*, 10 August 2004.
27 Glori K. Wadrianto, "Yusril: Warga Tionghoa Jangan Tuntut Keistimewaan", posted on *KOMPAS Cyber Media*, 12 August 2004.
28 "Pemerintah Tidak Diskriminatif terhadap Etnis Tionghoa", posted on *KOMPAS Cyber Media*, 14 September 2004.
29 Purdey, *Anti-Chinese Violence in Indonesia, 1996–1999*, p. 218.
30 Klaus Pahler, representative of the Konrad Adenauer Stifting, noted this observation in his introduction of a compilation of papers and discussion materials presented during the "International Workshop on Ethno-Religious Conflicts in Indonesia Today" conducted by the Center for Languages and Cultures, State Institute for Islamic Studies, Jakarta which was published as *Communical Conflicts in Contemporary Indonesia* (Jakarta: Pusat Bahasa dan Budaya, IAIN Jakarta & The Konrad Adenauer Foundation, 2002), p. xi.

References

Barton, Greg. *Gus Dur: The Authorized Biography of Abdurrahman Wahid*. Jakarta: Equinox Publishing (Asia) Pte. Ltd., 2002.

Communal Conflicts in Contemporary Indonesia. Jakarta: Pusat Bahasa dan Budaya (The Center for Languages and Cultures), IAIN Syarif Hidayatullah in cooperation with The Konrad Adenauer Foundation, 2002.

Elson, E.R. *Soeharto: A Political Biography*. Cambridge: Cambridge University Press, 2001.

Hamzah, Alfian, ed. *Kapok Jadi Nonpri: Warga Tionghoa Mencari Keadilan*. Bandung: Zaman Wacana Mulia, 1998.

Heidhues, Mary Somers. *Southeast Asia: A Concise History*. London: Thames & Hudson, 2000.

Jahja, H. Junus, ed. *Nonpri di Mata Pribumi*. Jakarta: Yayasan Tunas Bangsa, 1991.

Ong, Aihwa. *Flexible Citizenship: The Cultural Logics of Transnationality*. Durham: Duke University Press, 1999.

Purdey, Jemma. *Anti-Chinese Violence in Indonesia, 1996–1999*. Honolulu: University of Hawaii Press, 2006.

Ricklefs, M.C. *A History of Modern Indonesia since c.1300*. London: The Macmillan Press Ltd., 1994.

Suryadinata, Leo. *Pribumi Indonesians, The Chinese Minority and China*. Singapore: Heinemann Asia, 1992.

————. *Negara dan Etnis Tionghoa: Kasus Indonesia*. Jakarta: LP3ES, 2002.

————. *Chinese and Nation-Building in Southeast Asia*. Singapore, Marshall Cavendish, 2004.

Suryadinata, Leo, Evi Nurvidya Arifin, and Aris Ananta. *Indonesia's Population: Ethnicity and Religion in a Changing Political Landscape*. Singapore: Institute of Southeast Asian Studies, 2003.

Van Dijk, Kees. *A Country in Despair: Indonesia between 1997 and 2000*. Jakarta: KITLV Press, 2001.

Vatikiotis, Michael R.J. *Indonesian Politics under Soeharto: Order, Development and Pressure for Change*. London: Routledge, 1993.

Wang, Gungwu. *Only Connect! Sino-Malay Encounters*. Singapore: Times Academic Press, 2001.

Wawasan Kebangsaan Indonesia: Gagasan dan Pemikiran Badan Komunikasi Penghayatan Kesatuan Bangsa. Jakarta: BAKOM PKB Pusat, 1994.

Wibowo, I., ed. *Harga yang Harus Dibayar: Sketsa Pergulatan Etnis Cina di Indonesia*. Jakarta: P.T. Gramedia Pustaka Utama in cooperation with Pusat Studi Cina, 2000.

————. *Retrospeksi dan Rekontekstualisasi Masalah Cina*. Jakarta: P.T. Gramedia Pustaka Utama in cooperation with Pusat Studi Cina, 1999.

9

RELUCTANT INTERNATIONALIZATION: THE CASE OF THE SALIM GROUP

Marleen Dieleman
The late Wladimir Sachs

Introduction

Globalization has become a keyword for managers today, and many companies claim to be global as they increasingly do business across borders. Globalization can be understood as the phenomenon occurring as a result of the perceived contraction of time and space. Companies often start activities abroad because it can bring advantages such as more economies of scale, access to global networks and technologies, and learning from locally different product markets. Within business circles an important globalizing trend is the break-up of the value chain, where different steps in the production process take place in different locations. Western companies have taken the lead in building up international investments and sales, but in recent years companies from emerging markets have started to follow suit.

The Indonesian economy under President Soekarno could be characterized as closed, but under President Soeharto, Indonesia became increasingly embedded in the global economy. Exports rose from the 1980s onward, and foreign direct investment surged in the period up to the Asian crisis. Soeharto was responsible for remarkable economic growth during his presidency, which made Indonesia a sizeable consumer market. The economic growth also facilitated the parallel emergence of many home-grown business groups, the largest of which are often owned by families of Chinese descent (Robison 1986). Business groups, or conglomerates, exist around the world, but are particularly common in emerging markets, including in Southeast Asia (La Porta 1998; Claessens et al. 2000). Many of those emerging market business groups consist of numerous separate companies active in a range of industries, often under the control of a family, or a coalition of families (Granovetter 1995).

While during Soeharto's New Order the economy was relatively open, many trade barriers existed to protect local industries. Especially well-connected business groups, such as those of Soeharto's children and a few Indonesian Chinese groups benefited from a favourable regulatory environment. In the period after the Asian Crisis however, as a result of IMF demands, many of the existing protectionist measures benefiting those businesses close to the Soeharto regime have been abolished, thereby moving a step more in the direction of an open market economy. In an era of globalization and the integration of markets, one would also expect that Indonesian Chinese business groups would follow suit and ride the waves of globalization.

To what extent have these Chinese Indonesian large businesses internationalized, and how global are these companies? Theories of what is sometimes called the Chinese Family Firm (CFB) mostly assume that there is something particularly "Chinese" about these companies that makes them successful. The dominant discourse is that this *Chineseness* stems from Confucian values which exercise influence on the business behaviour of migrant Chinese business families. For example, ethnic Chinese are argued to be particularly dynamic (Kraar 1994; Kao 1993; Yeung 2000) and are thought to create very flexible organizational structures (Redding 1990, 1995). The diaspora nature of these successful immigrant enterprises is argued to facilitate a high degree of internationalization (Granovetter 1992; Rauch and Trindade 2002). Some authors have gone as far as to call ethnic Chinese firms "transnational" enterprises (Douw et al. 1999; Liu 2001), or have termed them "ungrounded empires" (Ong and Nonini 1997). Talking more generally about Asian business groups, Mathews (2006) argued that these domestically grown "dragon multinationals" are more likely to be successful in an era of globalization than Western firms due to their network-like flexible structure and their familiarity with alliances with other firms or groups, and other authors also talked about the globalization of ethnic Chinese firms (Yeung 2000; Carney 2005).

This chapter critically examines the existing rhetoric on the transnational ethnic Chinese firms in Indonesia. Using the example of the Salim Group, one of the largest ethnic Chinese groups in Indonesia, this chapter shows how companies struggle to become more international due to various forms of path dependency. It examines the interplay between the explicit intent of corporate leaders to shape a global company, and the internal and external obstacles to reaching this goal. The chapter proceeds as follows. It first sketches the background of the globalization of large firms and, in particular, the rise of ethnic Chinese multinationals from Southeast Asia, and explores the theoretical explanations for this phenomenon and argues that there is a substantial disagreement between authors focusing on the flexible and dynamic "ethnic Chinese" enterprise, and the international business literature which tends to focus on the obstacles to internationalization. Subsequently, the chapter explores both views by using the case study of the Salim Group, one of the larger ethnic Chinese family conglomerates from Indonesia. The case narrative is analysed in the findings section. The chapter ends with conclusions and recommendations for further research.

INTERNATIONALIZATION AND GLOBALIZATION OF ETHNIC CHINESE GROUPS FROM SOUTHEAST ASIA

Globalization of businesses is often associated with increased cross-border investments, acquisitions, and sales. Recent reports show an increase in such cross-border flows on a worldwide scale. Large multinationals play an important role in the globalization of markets, accounting for the majority of cross-border investments and mergers and acquisitions. Thomas Friedman, in a best-selling book, has described globalization with the idea that "the world is flat". Not all academics agree that the world is flat. They point out that most of the large multinationals are oriented towards their home market, and if they are international, they often concentrate on a certain region (for example, the European Union, or America) rather than being global (Rugman and Verbeke 2004). Only those very few companies that have substantial overseas sales and assets can be called global firms.

While virtually all of the global companies in the previous decade were Western multinationals, a new trend is now emerging where multinational companies from developing countries are increasingly gaining influence. Not only are multinationals from developing countries a rising category, foreign direct investment into developing countries also more often stems from other developing countries. A well published example of this is the extensive

Chinese foreign direct investment in Africa. Large companies from developing countries are, therefore, increasingly entering the "global" business world, and are a category worthy of more scholarly attention.

A recent United Nations Conference on Trade and Development (UNCTAD) investment report (2006) defined transnational companies (TNCs) as those companies with considerable foreign sales and assets as a percentage of total sales and assets. While the top hundred TNCs worldwide consists of only four Asian companies, the top hundred TNCs from developing countries consists of seventy-seven Asian companies, clearly showing the cross-border activities and growth of Asian multinational firms. Among those Asian firms from Southeast Asia, many are run by ethnic Chinese. Table 9.1 gives an indication of some of those large ethnic Chinese firms.

These figures support the idea that ethnic Chinese companies in Southeast Asia are increasingly turning into global companies (e.g. Ahlstrom et al. 2004). How can one explain the rapid rise of ethnic Chinese multinationals in Southeast Asia? Academic experts on ethnic Chinese firms in Southeast Asia emphasize the embedding in personal networks between diaspora Chinese in Asia, based on common surnames, clans, or dialect groups (e.g. Backman 2001; Granovetter 1992; Lever-Tracey 2002). For this reason, authors often prefer to speak of ethnic Chinese business networks rather than of ethnic Chinese businesses (Chan 2000; Hamilton 1991; Gomez and Hsiao 2001). These personal networks often function across borders. Some researchers argue that networks based on dialect groups of ethnic Chinese continue to be an important factor influencing their business networks (Liu 1998). Chinese migrants have set up voluntary organizations, often based on dialect groups, to fulfill functions such as preserving culture, providing mutual assistance, and creating regional trade networks, and these organizations continue to flourish. Some authors argue that the intra-ethnic Chinese networks offer a competitive advantage as they cross borders and facilitate internationalization (Granovetter 1992; Rauch and Trindade 2002). Anecdotal evidence of business connections between large ethnic Chinese tycoons are given in many semi-popular books, for example in Weidenbaum and Hughes' book, *The Bamboo Network*, the title of which refers to the flexible networks of ethnic Chinese in Asia (Weidenbaum and Hughes 1996).

Cross-border minority group networking can also explain why so many ethnic Chinese tycoons have invested in China (e.g. Brown 1998), usually also in their places of birth. Provinces with many migrants in southeastern China, such as Fujian and Guangdong, have received an enormous amount of foreign direct investment in recent decades. The ties with one's place of birth are termed *qiaoxiang ties*, referring to a sojourner's village or hometown, and

Table 9.1
Selected Large "Ethnic Chinese" Companies in Southeast Asia
(ranked by market capitalization, in millions of dollars)

Company	Country	Industry	Market Value	Sales	Geographic Scope
Singapore Press Holdings	Singapore	Publishing	4021	581	Regional
City Developments	Singapore	Hotels	3928	1408	Global
Genting	Malaysia	Hotels	3541	1223	Regional
IOI Corporation	Malaysia	Agri/fisheries	3032	1314	Global
Shin Corp.	Thailand	Telecom	2725	493	Regional
YTL Power Intl.	Malaysia	Utilities	2643	891	Global
Venture Corp.	Singapore	Electronics	2550	1889	Global
YTL Corp.	Malaysia	Utilities	2189	1160	Global
Fraser and Neave	Singapore	Drinks	2170	2039	Global
Want Want Holdings	Singapore	Food	1637	524	Regional

Source: UNCTAD 2006, p. 161.

have been the subject of analysis in a number of books and research projects (Douw et al. 1999). Researchers emphasizing the intra-ethnic networking skills often see ethnic Chinese family businesses as a transnational form of management, which is not necessarily linked to or rooted in a nation (Dahles 2005; Ong and Nonini 1997; Yeung 2000). Migrant businesses often face official or unofficial discrimination, and some researchers argue that one of the reactions is that these groups tend to start "portable" lines of business that can easily be transferred to other places (Bonacich 1973). It is not unusual to find minorities that function as commercial elites in emerging markets. The success of these minorities is often attributed to having developed systems to deal with hostile environments, such as social networks, intra-ethnic trust, low transaction costs, or the pooling of capital (Davis et al. 2001; Portes and Sensenbrenner 1993; Xin and Pearce 1996), and this successful approach eventually makes them 'essential outsiders' (Chirot and Reid 1997).

The literature on the internationalization of large firms takes a very different path. Academics studying the internationalization of businesses often note the difficulties of such business activity due to cultural differences (Hofstede 1991), and lack of knowledge of, and networks in, local markets. This has been summarized with the concept of the liability of foreignness (Zaheer 1995). In addition to the difficulties associated with operations abroad, there is also considerable difficulty in changing the organization in order to develop business beyond the home market. Companies trying to develop capabilities for operating on a global scale often face barriers to change inherent in the set-up of the company and the knowledge and routines built up over time. The fact that corporate history matters, and limits the number of choices that the company can implement, is often referred to as administrative heritage (Bartlett and Ghoshal 1989) and sometimes called "path dependence". Administrative heritage refers to the physical heritage (the assets of the firm) as well as to the cultural heritage of a firm, such as the mentalities and knowledge embedded within the company. While many researchers who are specialized on ethnic Chinese firms point to their dynamism and flexibility, which makes them suitable to operate in a globalized world, a few of these authors have started to criticize these theories and have pointed at the administrative heritage of ethnic Chinese firms that hindered their further development (Carney 1998; Carney and Gedajlovic 2003; Ahlstrom et al. 2004).

If we look at Table 9.1, the idea that ethnic Chinese firms are a driving force behind a global breed of Asian multinationals seems to be supported. However, companies from the largest country in Southeast Asia in terms of population, Indonesia, are conspicuously absent from this list. Logically speaking, there can be two reasons for the lack of Indonesian companies on this list. Either the list is not accurate, or there are indeed no large and global companies in Indonesia. If indeed large Indonesian companies are lagging behind when it comes to globalization of their businesses, the question as to what could be the reasons behind this is relevant. These questions are the topic of this chapter. In order to explore in more depth how Indonesian Chinese businesses cope with globalization, this chapter takes a single case study approach. It presents a study of the Salim Group, one of the largest ethnic Chinese business groups from Indonesia, and examines its patterns of internationalization.

Methodology

Case research is often used to explore patterns of corporate development in an in-depth manner, with a particular focus on the "how" and "why" questions relating to certain phenomena. Case research normally seeks to combine different sources of information, and various points of view. Within the context of Indonesian Chinese business groups, such a more holistic approach is particularly valuable as Indonesian business groups are not always transparent, and relying on a single source of data (e.g. annual reports) may give limited or even misleading information. Within Indonesia, Indonesian Chinese business families, and particularly those families that became successful and connected with the political elite, may not wish to make known publicly which assets they control for fear of expropriation.

While case studies offer many advantages in view of the richness of data and possible new insights emerging from them, they also pose various methodological problems, such as limited generalizability. However, if the researchers are disciplined and sensitive to potential pitfalls, case research allows for the development of new hypotheses and concepts that can advance future theory development. In particular the use of "extreme" cases has been promoted as a good strategy to come to new insights on topics which are understudied (Eisenhardt 1989).

The Salim Group was selected on theoretical sampling principles. While statistical sampling aims at selecting a representative sample from a population, theoretical sampling selects cases based on whether the phenomenon of interest is "transparently observable" (Eisenhardt 1989). The Salim Group was the largest and most prominent group in Indonesia, and it was in a position to engage in internationalization due to its substantial access to capital and resources. Furthermore, direct access to this group for research purposes was possible, which was seen as a unique situation.

The case study is a rich, longitudinal, exploratory study of a corporate group within its institutional context, covering a period from its inception in 1938, to 2005. The research was carried out from 2003–07 using a variety of sources, including fifty-seven interviews, sixty-nine annual reports (covering ten years), media sources, secondary literature, and corporate documentation. It consciously had some overlap between data collection and analysis to strengthen emerging themes (Glaser and Strauss 1967) and emphasized triangulation (Yin 2003) or trying to obtain the same information from a variety of sources. The condensed story below is available in more detail in a book on the Salim Group (Dieleman 2007).

THE CASE OF THE SALIM GROUP

The Emergence of a Domestic Business Model

The Salim Group was set up by a Chinese migrant by the name of Liem Sioe Liong (hereafter, Liem), and was first a family trading venture located in Central Java. The family trading business was set up under the colonial Dutch occupation of Indonesia (Twang 1998), an era in which the economy was geared towards exportation of commodities, such as sugar or rubber. While Liem started with import and export trade, he was not really shaped by the dominant commodity export model of colonial enterprises. When Liem's activities were still small, the Pacific War brought fundamental changes to Indonesia, and when the Indonesian leaders subsequently proclaimed independence, Liem decided to stay, and sided with the new nationalist leadership (Soetriyono 1989). Because of Liem's relationship with a local army unit, he achieved stability and income as a supplier, a position in which he was lucky enough to partner with a relative of Soekarno, as well as to meet Soeharto, who was later to replace Soekarno after a bloody regime change that crushed the Communist party.

Supplying goods such as textile and soap to the army, the foundations were laid for a business model in which Liem produced and traded products for the domestic market, rather than for export markets. During the Soeharto period this model was intensified. The coincidence of a close relationship with a long-term dictator of a large country profoundly changed the Salim Group's outlook. When Soeharto came to power in 1965, Liem had already built a substantial set of business activities, despite high inflation and economic decline during Soekarno's rule. Soeharto soon realized that achieving strong economic growth was an essential aspect of political legitimacy; and he created the conditions for a thriving economy in which private capital was encouraged and international trade allowed, although key industries such as oil remained in government hands. With foreign capital nationalized by Soekarno and private business constrained, few successful and substantial businesses had existed in post-colonial Indonesia. Along with a few other Chinese businessmen, Liem was among the favoured ones enlisted by Soeharto to help Indonesia develop into a modern economy — and Liem took full advantage of his skills, relations, and the opportunities offered to him.

In the context of a rapidly growing domestic economy, policies to stimulate import substitution industrialization and close connections with the political leadership, the Salim Group developed its domestic business model and focused on making products for Indonesian masses, such as food, cement, cars, and financial services. In the formative period of the Salim Group — and many other Indonesian Chinese conglomerates that emerged in the Soeharto era followed this pattern — a strong business model was established that focused on producing for the needs of the local population. In doing this, the group worked closely with the government, for example in setting up steel production in the 1980s, jointly with the Indonesian government (Sato 1993). At the same time, the government also aligned itself closely with Salim, for example by placing Soeharto's family members on boards, or occasionally bailing out Salim companies in times of acute need. Salim, for its past, was expected to offer its capital and resources to help Soeharto develop the Indonesian economy, but also personally, for example to contribute to Soeharto's charitable foundations.

This business model meant that Salim, first and foremost, acquired knowledge of local, rather than international markets, and that it became strongly embedded in the Indonesian economy where it had most of its capital tied up in profitable industrial enterprises. Its links with local politicians, particularly Soeharto, increased its embeddedness in the local context. The fact that the Salim Group was deeply rooted in the Indonesian economy can perhaps be captured in a motto that Liem wanted to pass on to his children: "We plant a tree with the purpose of it growing big. What you should not do is to move the tree, which has already grown, to another place" (Tempo 1984).

Early Internationalization

In the 1970s, the Salim Group started its first steps on the path of internationalization. This consisted of both starting activities abroad and bringing to Indonesia foreign partners. First, it acquired loans for its Indonesian cement factories from the Bangkok Bank, also run by an ethnic

Chinese family in Thailand, thus tapping the regional ethnic networks. Second, it formed joint ventures with various Western and Japanese companies in order to acquire capital and technology for producing goods in Indonesia, such as cars, cement, food, and chemicals. It used these ventures to upgrade its capabilities and raise local production standards to international quality levels. A Western partner of the Salim Group at the time said:

> The Salim Group sought Western partners in order to acquire technological capabilities. For example, they wanted to develop a new baby food product but they ran into quality problems in their food production. We assisted them with the production process and the operation of new machinery, but time and time again the samples were rejected because of quality problems, which irritated them. Later they managed to master the production process.

In 1975 the Salim Group, which had already grown into one of the largest Indonesian groups, started to invest in Hong Kong and Singapore, according to Anthony Salim, son of the founder and heir to the family business, in order to "balance the portfolio". Any large company that is closely linked to a particular regime, and that benefits from these links, runs a high political risk when this regime is replaced. Long-term dictatorships, such as that of Soeharto's, are the exception rather than the rule, and it is perhaps this lucky long period of relative stability, economic growth, and close political connections, that allowed the Salim Group to witness such unprecedented corporate growth.

In a country such as Indonesia, where the rule of law is rather weak in comparison to the rule of man, a regime change could easily involve confiscation of property or capital. Such a situation occurred, for example, when Soekarno decided to nationalize foreign companies, as well as the Oei Tiong Ham Group, the largest firm in Indonesia in the period around World War II. In view of the real risks of regime change and asset confiscation, it is rather sensible that the Salim Group attempted to moderate these risks by investing abroad. In Hong Kong, their businesses were grouped under First Pacific, a company listed on the Hong Kong Stock Exchange and with investments in various businesses and industries in Asia. The company was run by a Filipino CEO while the Salim family and their partners occupied several seats on its board and maintained control through their ownership stakes. In Singapore too, several businesses (many of them under a legal entity called KMP) were established in food, property, and real estate. In an interview with the author, Anthony Salim, current CEO of the Salim Group and son of Liem, said: "Of course we started to balance our portfolio. We have no pretension to hide that we have started to invest outside Indonesia since 1975, when we created our Singapore and Hong Kong companies."

Several of those foreign companies also produced goods or offered services targeted at local markets, such as QAF in Singapore, or PLDT in the Philippines. Aside from a few businesses in the Riau Archipelago that targeted nearby Singaporean consumers, supplying to them meat, orchids, and other food-related products, most Salim companies have not been strong in exporting, even if the Soeharto government started to stimulate exports from the 1980s onwards. Some of the smaller companies exported after first satisfying domestic demand, but most companies produced for Indonesian consumers.

When China opened up for investment, Liem and one of his long-time partners, Djuhar, invested in their home town in Fujian, China, building several factories and infrastructure facilities there. Djuhar later explained to a journalist:

> When we started this in 1987, Fuqing had no factories and no industrial workers. There were no conditions for them — no hotel and only a few antiquated telephones. We had to put in the infrastructure — roads, telecommunications, hotels and a pier ... Our aim was to do something for our home town, provide work for its people, and raise living standards (*South China Morning Post* 1997).

The Chinese Indonesians have always been regarded with considerable suspicion in Indonesia, particularly because a few of them became business tycoons who controlled many large companies. This criticism was also voiced towards the Salim Group, especially when it came to investments abroad. Investing money in other countries would, according to popular opinion, shows the lack of loyalty of the Chinese to Indonesia. There was a strong public outcry against investing "Indonesian" money in China, the homeland of ethnic Chinese. This was also the case with Liem's investments in China, which came to be labelled as capital flight.[1] As a consequence, the group kept a very low profile when it came to investing in China, and it carefully grouped these investments under separate legal entities, often located outside Indonesia, and until recently, in privately owned companies.

> Recently he came under strong criticism for multi-million dollar investments in his home province in China. "Where can I go?" asked Mr Liem. "If I invest abroad, they call it capital flight; if I invest in Indonesia they say I want a monopoly." (*Financial Times* 1995).

With the economic growth China experienced over the last decade, it became an attractive market to invest in, especially for members of the Chinese diaspora that had an advantage in terms of language and cultural proximity. On the other hand, Anthony Salim mentioned the cultural problems he had when investing in China:

> Once you are successful in one country, it does not mean that you are successful in another ...

> We have experience that if you try to put Indonesian management in China, it does not work. We need Chinese people in China, but with Indonesian values; Indonesian ways of doing things.

Because of these problems Anthony Salim considered the success of the Chinese businesses "mixed".

The Soul of the Salim Group

Over the years, the foreign companies, and in particular, First Pacific, grew substantially, thereby increasing the value of Salim's non-Indonesian assets. While the Salim Group indeed invested considerable amounts of money outside Indonesia, this was still modest compared with their investments in Indonesia. The Indonesian companies continued to do well, and most companies went through considerable expansion and organic growth in the period 1975–95. The growth of the Salim Group within Indonesia was such that the Salim Group came to have important positions in many industries, making it a powerful player that could not be ignored. After twenty years of internationalization, in 1995, the Salim Group was still very much an Indonesian rather than a global company. Figure 9.1 shows the degree to which the Salim Group obtained its income from domestic or foreign sources and shows that about a third of the income stemmed from non-Indonesian activities. Even if the Salim Group was embedded in global capital markets, worked extensively with Western and Japanese partners, it has never abandoned its business model, which is to produce domestically for local masses.

An analysis of boards of listed Salim companies abroad showed that many of those were managed by professional CEOs, while the Salim family and partners held various positions on the supervisory board. The large Indonesian company boards especially had many Salim insiders, showing where the Salim Group leadership focused their attention.

**Figure 9.1
Internationalization of the Salim Group:
Composition of Sales According to Origin**

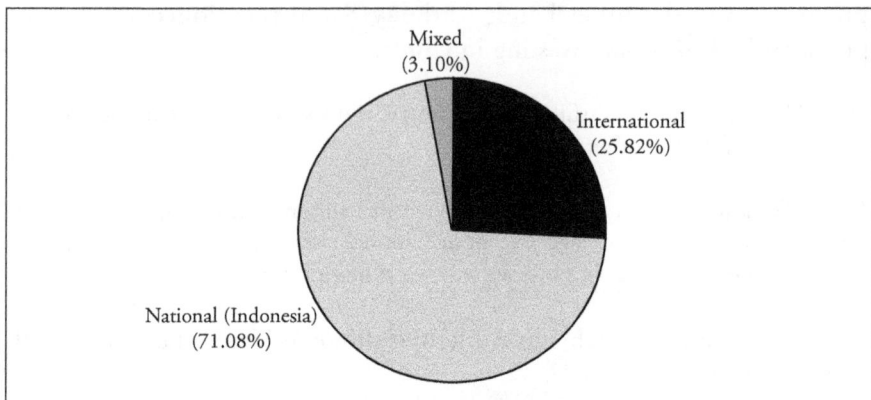

Mixed
(3.10%)

International
(25.82%)

National (Indonesia)
(71.08%)

Source: Adapted from Salim Group brochure, 1995/1996.

The Asian Crisis

In the period up to the Asian Crisis, many local conglomerates, including the Salim Group companies, benefited from import tariffs that shielded its businesses from international competition. In particular, the well-connected companies, such as the Salim Group, benefited from favourable state interventions. An example of this was the bailout of the Salim company, Indocement, in 1985, by the government, when it was facing problems paying its debts. This national context that favoured Soeharto's cronies was increasingly inviting criticism from the IMF and the World Bank, which promoted a liberal free trade model with low or no protection of local industries and players. When the Asian Crisis came to Indonesia, Soeharto was eventually forced by the IMF to curb the protectionist policies favouring friends and family members. In the early phases of the Asian Crisis, the IMF imposed on Indonesia several economic policies that meant a change in the business environment for the Salim Group companies, some of which suffered from lowering tariffs on imports that competed with locally produced Salim Group products.

By the time the crisis reached its full scale, Soeharto's position became precarious and he eventually resigned. The demise of Soeharto's order had severe consequences for the Salim Group. Having been so powerful, and so closely associated with Soeharto, the Salim family was seen as a symbol of this regime. The group became a target for public anger, and the family house — as well as several branches of the Salim-owned Bank Central Asia (BCA) — was set on fire. BCA, the largest privately owned bank in Indonesia, had two of Soeharto's children on its supervisory board, and was subsequently the victim of a bank run that depleted its resources, and it was later nationalized.

The fall of BCA marked a new period for the Salim Group. A new government, espousing anti-corruption policies, took over from Soeharto and recapitalized the bank, demanding from the Salim family full repayment, as well as a fine for the violation of certain banking laws. The total amount fixed by IBRA, the government entity in charge of bank restructuring, was approximately US$5 billion. The Salim family complied, thereby earning praise from friends and enemies alike, and handed over 107 companies to the Indonesian government to pay off its debts. The government officials that dealt with Salim Group assets told the author that they themselves were also surprised to see what companies the Salim Group owned. Generally speaking, the companies that surrendered to the government tended to have complicated holding structures, making it complicated to establish with certainty who the owner was.

"The companies acquired by IBRA were never directly owned by Anthony Salim", said an IBRA employee.

The situation after the Asian Crisis was extremely hostile for all ethnic Chinese, and in particular, for the Salim family which was taken as a symbol of everything that was bad in the Soeharto regime. In addition to being in a hostile context, many of the Salim companies suffered from high debt-to-equity ratios, and some of them were even technically bankrupt or without working capital. In addition to this, as Indonesians had less to spend, the demand for local products plunged, adding extra problems to the already suffering Salim companies. The new government pressurized the foreign Salim Group partners to withdraw, even if this was against their wishes:

> The government was not fond of Salim, and forced them out of our joint venture. ... We did not want the Salim Group to exit from our cooperation, we were unhappy with this development. When you do business in a country like Indonesia you need to find a local champion, who can solve problems when they occur, and with good relations with the government (Western Partner of the Salim Group).

> Finally the government told me, we are now in control, and even though we know you have a deal with Anthony Salim, we don't want you to

have a 50/50 partnership with him, because he is not very much liked any more in Indonesia. Make it a minority share. I told them I need a local partner with knowledge. So finally I ended up, against my wish, buying 65% of the company while Anthony Salim had 13% (Western Partner of the Salim Group).

The Salim Group was thus faced with considerable problems in its home market, on which it relied heavily. The foreign Salim companies also suffered, but the effects of the Asian Crisis were most severe in Indonesia. Although it could probably have opted to withdraw from Indonesia altogether, the Salim family did not do this. In choosing what companies to hold on to and what companies to hand over to the government, it became very clear that the Salim Group wanted to hold on to its large Indonesian companies: Indofood, Indocement, Indosiar, Indomobil, and a few others. In order to achieve this goal, the Salim family sold off various foreign companies in Singapore and the Philippines and it shuffled Indofood offshore by transferring the family's shares to First Pacific Company in Hong Kong, which they also controlled. Other companies were secretly acquired again after they were given to the government, which subsequently sold them to interested parties. This strategy did not work in the case of Indocement, which the Salim family initially wanted to hold on to. The company was eventually controlled by HCG, a German cement multinational, who took majority ownership as a result of government interference. This strategy again confirmed that the Salim Group's soul was very much in Indonesia.

Internationalization Resumed

After a few years of coping with the Asian Crisis, the Salim Group started to take its first steps towards growth, albeit not at the rate achieved before the crisis. Based on interviews with Anthony Salim, we learn that the internationalization strategy of the group was changed. Anthony Salim again aimed to balance his portfolio, but this time he realized that he needed to become more international than ever before. He aimed at achieving a portfolio of companies with fifty per cent being inside Indonesia and fifty per cent outside, thus reducing the dependence on Indonesia, which would, however, still remain the most important market.

In view of the low value of the Rupiah in and immediate after the Asian Crisis, some of the Salim companies stepped up their efforts to export — a logical strategy when you have loans in foreign currency, and when your local competitiveness is boosted by a low local currency. The large Salim companies, such as Indofood, Indomobil, and Indocement, however, never gained much experience with export markets and their foreign sales remained very low, when compared with total sales.

Rather than focusing on being a global company, Anthony Salim modestly saw himself as operating in the "fresh water" rather than in the "big sea". He opted to become a strong player within the Asia-Pacific region, thereby capitalizing on his knowledge and connections rather than moving into unknown territory. He saw an axis of opportunity between Australia, ASEAN, and China. In the words of Anthony Salim:

> Salim will be able to arbitrage between China, Asia, and Australia. How we define [it] is very wide. That is the game. There will be a north-south axis in Asia. ... This equation will hold almost 2 billion people. And 2 billion rich people, because they have a growth of 4–8% or so in a few years ... that's as big a market as America if you put that together.

If there was an opportunity to link these countries, for example, the Australian expertise in agribusiness with the Chinese and Indonesian markets, then lucrative business could be achieved. In this manner, a new strategy for the Salim Group was envisioned which continued the focus on domestic businesses, but which controlled the entire value chain that might involve different locations in Asia.

A few steps were taken to realize this strategy. One of the examples of this strategy was the acquisition of a minority share in listed Australian company Futuris. Futuris had a wheat division, and Indofood was one of the largest wheat importers for its noodles. Following the acquisition of this minority stake, Anthony Salim was appointed on the board of directors of Futuris in March 2003.

In China, the group paid US$500 million for a 45 per cent stake in the COSCO property group. According to Anthony Salim, these acquisitions fit in a strategy where the Salim Group aims at mediating on the axis between Australia-ASEAN-China. Also, several Salim-controlled companies were listed on the Singapore Stock Exchange.

The Salim Group perceived its key competence in a mediation role with good knowledge of local markets. In taking this approach, the Salim Group aims for regionalization rather than globalization. Whether the strategy of a 50/50 per cent mixed portfolio will materialize and how long it will take Anthony Salim to achieve this goal remains to be seen in the coming years.

Findings

The Salim Group is clearly one of the Indonesian companies with the resources and managerial capabilities to establish operations abroad. It did internationalize for the last few decades, but this internationalization has always remained very partial. While the group had global ambitions before the Asian Crisis, it now focuses on increased internationalization, but on a regional scale within the Asia-Pacific region. In the case of the Salim Group, one can observe several types of path dependency.

First, the group developed a domestic business model focusing on products for a large consumer base and stuck to it, even when the government started providing incentives to establish export industries instead of import substitution industries. Profiting initially from army connections and the pent-up demand after the economy recovered from the detrimental policies implemented during the Soekarno era, this model made sense in the historical setting in which the Salim Group emerged. In a large and fast-growing market such as Indonesia, this domestic business model offered excellent business opportunities in many industries. When the import-substitution industrialization phase ended and the government started to promote exports, the Salim Group stayed with their local-for-local model instead of adapting to new circumstances. After all, much of their capital was fixed in their industrial enterprises, which were doing well, so the Salim Group leadership spent most of their money in their already successful businesses and in establishing similar businesses that produced for local markets. Although the Salim Group maintained some organizational characteristics that made it flexible and quick to act on emerging business opportunities, the basic domestic business model remained the same, both in Indonesia and abroad.

Second, the Salim Group's soul remained in their domestic businesses, which were established in close connection with Soeharto. Although the Salim family pursued internationalization strategies for several decades, this has never changed their fundamental dependence on Indonesia. Before the Asian Crisis, after two decades of internationalization about twenty-five to thirty per cent of the sales came from international operations, showing how much the Salim Group was part of the Indonesian economy, in which the Group played a major role. When the Asian Crisis occurred, the Salim Group decided to sell many of their international companies to save their Indonesian enterprises, showing again how much the group was oriented towards Indonesia. Given the political pressure to dissolve the Salim Group during the crisis, why did they not try to hold on to their foreign companies instead of their Indonesian enterprises? Apparently their investments in social capital, in fixed assets, and their market knowledge were specific to Indonesia, and it was not easy to leave this market behind. The Asian Crisis has shown that the Salim Group was unable to disentangle itself from the Indonesian domestic context. Contrary to a company such as Philips, which closed its doors in the Netherlands during the Second World War and continued doing business by moving its headquarters to the United States, the Salim Group was unable or unwilling to do so. It appeared that rather than being transnational, the company was actually strongly attached to Indonesia. Anthony Salim would now like to change this dependence in a local context and he has invested heavily in other Asian countries. But he still wants to have fifty per cent of the business in Indonesia.

The Salim Group study shows how companies become strongly embedded in a domestic economy and develop resistance to change over time. The national and historical context played a central role in defining the basic business model of the Salim Group. It has always been a domestic player in large emerging market industries, deeply embedded in the Indonesian context, combining business acumen and relationship capabilities. Other Southeast Asian markets such as Singapore or Malaysia were smaller than Indonesia, making internationalization a more logical option than within the fast growing, large consumer market of Indonesia. There were always ample opportunities for growth in Indonesia, so the Salim Group stuck to its domestic business model. Changing this fundamental strategic orientation is a slow process.

The Salim Group was intricately linked to the Soeharto regime, and it operated on an understanding of give and take with Soeharto. While the government occasionally stepped in to help Salim, the Group was also expected to extend financial and operational support to Soeharto's ventures, or those of his family. This close alliance clearly benefited the Salim Group and contributed to its ascent to become Indonesia's largest conglomerate. But the success of this alliance also led the Salim Group in the direction of domestic growth. The Indonesian companies were well protected and successful and, therefore, there was little reason to focus considerable resources abroad. Although the Salim Group "balanced" its portfolio, its soul really was in the Indonesian companies, some of which were intricately linked with Indonesia's Soeharto regime.

The Salim Group case also shows how the hostile domestic context for ethnic Chinese business families had an impact on the structure of the organization. Due to public criticism of capital flight and the fear of asset expropriation, the Salim family had built a conglomerate in which ownership was opaque. As a consequence, even the government did not have a clear idea of which companies the Salim family controlled. Rankings of the largest transnational companies take market value or sales as a key indicator and only companies listed on stock exchanges are taken into account. Since the Salim Group is not a single legal entity, and does not publish any consolidated corporate data, the chances that a company of this form will end up in any "top 100" are modest, even if its total sales exceeded all ethnic Chinese companies mentioned in Table 9.1. Many Indonesian companies show similar dispersion of ownership and, as a consequence, it is hard to estimate the shape of the entire conglomerate.

UNCTAD's list of the largest transnational companies uses an indicator for how international the company is. The fact that the Salim Group is not ranked, even if it was considered one entity, is entirely justified. The Salim Group, while scoring high on size, still scores relatively low on international sales and assets, and for this reason does not (yet) deserve a place in the list of the largest emerging market transnational firms.

While this chapter has highlighted the obstacles to internationalization of the Salim Group, it must be noted that these obstacles are not unusual. Every large company that tries to globalize can only do so by putting in considerable effort and resources. Becoming a transnational company is not an easy undertaking, contrary to what the theory on "transnational ethnic Chinese business networks" suggests. Other global firms have experienced similarly slow internationalization processes. Only in 2007 did General Electric, one of the world largest global firms, announce that, for the first time, it achieved fifty per cent of its sales outside the United States.

Conclusions and Recommendations for Future Research

This chapter explored the internationalization patterns of large ethnic Chinese businesses, using the case study of the Salim Group. The first conclusion of this study is obvious for anyone familiar with doing business abroad: internationalization takes considerable time and energy. A company as large as the Salim Group, which was involved in global networks of ethnic Chinese and Western/Japanese alliances, internationalized extremely slowly and partially. While all companies suffer from path dependence, the Salim Group perhaps faced more obstacles than others. It developed a local-for-local business model from the very beginning, a model that was successful for decades. The home market was large and grew rapidly, so profits rose year after year. As a consequence of this success, only partial attention was paid to internationalization. The soul of the Salim Group remained in its Indonesian businesses, whereas the foreign businesses served to "balance the portfolio". The Asian Crisis made Salim's dependence on Indonesia clear once more, and Anthony Salim now aims at increased internationalization, which is a logical step, given the level of political risk and uncertainty in Indonesia.

All things taken into account, the Salim Group cannot be considered a global player. The group is moving towards a regional business model, but is still heavily dependent on the home market. The theories that consider ethnic Chinese firms "footloose" and speak of transnational enterprises are clearly not applicable to the Salim Group. The Salim Group turns out to resemble patterns that are normal in every large firm: it is hard to detach the company from its administrative heritage and increased internationalization requires sustained action from corporate leaders and the allocation of substantial financial and managerial resources. While there is considerable fear in Indonesia that companies such as Salim could simply relocate to other countries and withdraw their funds, or that they engage in "*ersatz* capitalism" rather than in value-adding activities (Yoshihara 1998), this analysis shows that this may not be justified.

In order to explain the behaviour of ethnic Chinese family firms, it is not sufficient to take into account theories that claim that ethnic Chinese firms tend to build companies that are agile and flexible, and that they, due to their migrant past, have a natural and ready-made diaspora business network that facilitates internationalization. One should also consider theories of path dependence that can explain why companies face such difficulties when it comes to implementing strategies of internationalization.

Is the transnational Indonesian Chinese company a myth? The answer to this question appears to be tentatively positive when one considers the corporate history of the Salim Group. The Oei Tiong Ham Concern, another large Indonesian Chinese firm, displayed a similar dependence on Indonesia. When this company, the largest in Southeast Asia, was nationalized by the Soekarno regime, it had already internationalized for decades and built substantial activities abroad. But the Indonesian headquarters remained its nervous system, and when this was taken out, the company never regained its former glory: it could hardly survive once the home market activities were closed (Post 2006). While these are just two cases, the deconstruction of the myth of the transnational Indonesian Chinese conglomerate merits further scholarly attention. More research on other Indonesian Chinese firms should shed light on whether the Salim Group is a unique case when it comes to its reluctant internationalization, or whether the patterns observed here can be found in a broader range of companies.

Note

[1]   Although different definitions of capital flight exist, I prefer to think of this phenomenon as the transfer of liquid assets (money or valuables that can easily be converted into cash) across borders. When a company invests in factories abroad, I prefer to call this foreign direct investment, rather than capital flight.

References

Ahlstrom, D., M.N. Young, E.S. Chan, and G.D. Bruton. "Facing Constraints to Growth? Overseas Chinese Entrepreneurs and Traditional Business Practices". *Asia Pacific Journal of Management* 21 (2004): 263–86.

Backman, M. *Asian Eclipse: Exposing the Dark Side of Business in Asia*. Singapore: John Wiley, 2001.

Bartlett, C. and S. Ghoshal. *Managing Across Borders: The Transnational Solution*. Harvard Business School Press, Boston, 1989.

Bonacich, E. "A Theory of Middleman Minorities". *American Sociological Review* 38, no. 5 (1973): 583–94.

Brown, R.A. "Overseas Chinese Investments in China — Patterns of Growth, Diversification and Finance: The Case of Charoen Pokphand". *The China Quarterly* 155 (1998): 610–36.

Carney, M. "A Management Capacity Constraint? Obstacles to the Development of the Overseas Chinese Family Business". *Asia Pacific Journal of Management* 15 (1998): 137–62.

———. "Globalization and the Renewal of Asian Business Networks". *Asia Pacific Journal of Management* 22 (2005): 337–54.

Carney, M. and E. Gedajlovic. "Strategic Innovation and the Administrative Heritage of East Asian Family Business Groups". *Asia Pacific Journal of Management*, vol. 20, no. 1 (2003): 5–26.

Chan, K.B., ed. *Chinese Business Networks, State, Economy and Culture*. Singapore: Prentice Hall, 2000.

Chirot, D. and A. Reid. *Essential Outsiders: Chinese and Jews in the Modern Transformation of Southeast Asia and Central Europe*. Seattle: University of Washington Press, 1997.

Claessens, S., S. Djankov, and L.H.P. Lang. The Separation of Ownership and Control in East Asian Corporations. *Journal of Financial Economics* 58, no. 1/2 (2000): 81–112.

Davis, K., M.J. Trebilcock, and B. Heys. "Ethnically Homogeneous Commercial Elites in Developing Countries". *Law and Politics in International Business* 32, no. 2 (2001): 331–61.

Dieleman, M.H. *The Rhythm of Strategy: A Corporate Biography of the Salim Group of Indonesia*. Amsterdam: Amsterdam University Press, 2007.

Douw, L.M., C. Huang, and M.R. Godley, eds. *Qiaoxiang Ties: Interdisciplinary Approaches to "Cultural Capitalism" in South China*. London: Kegan Paul, 1999.

Eisenhardt, K.M. "Building Theories from Case Study Research". *Academy of Management Review* 14, no. 4 (1989): 532–50.

Financial Times. "Leaders of Indonesia's Big Business Return Fire: Bureaucracy and a Lack of Transparency Irk the Mostly Ethnic Chinese Tycoons". 1 September 1995, p. 4.

Gomez, E.T. and H.H.M. Hsiao, eds. *Chinese Business Networks in Southeast Asia: Contesting Cultural Explanations, Researching Entrepreneurship*. Richmond, Surrey: Curzon Press, 2001.

Granovetter, M. "Economic Institutions as Social Constructions: A Framework for Analysis". *Acta Sociologica* 35 (1992): 3–11.

———. "Coase Revisited: Business Groups in the Modern Economy". *Industrial and Corporate Change* 4 no. 1 (1995): 93–130.

Hamilton, G., ed. *Business Networks and Development in East and Southeast Asia*. Hong Kong: Centre for Asian Studies, University of Hong Kong, 1991.

Hofstede, G. *Cultures and Organizations: Software of the Mind*. London: McGraw-Hill, 1991.

Kao, J. "The Worldwide Web of Chinese Business". *Harvard Business Review* 2 (1993): 24–36.

Kraar, L. "The Overseas Chinese: Lessons from the World's Most Dynamic Capitalists". *Fortune*, 31 October 1994, pp. 91–114.

La Porta, R., F. Lopez-de-Silanes, and A. Shleifer. "Corporate Ownership Around the World". *Journal of Finance* 54 (1999): 471–518.

Lever-Tracy, C. "The Impact of the Asian Crisis on Diaspora Chinese Tycoons". *Geoforum* 33 (2002): 509–23.

Liu, H. "Old Linkages, New Networks: The Globalization of Overseas Chinese Voluntary Associations and its Implications". *China Quarterly* 155 (1998): 582–609.

———. "Social Capital and Business Networking: A Case Study of Modern Chinese Transnationalism". *Southeast Asian Studies* 39, no. 3 (2001): 358–83.

Mathews, J. "Dragon Multinationals: New Players in 21st Century Globalization". *Asia Pacific Journal of Management* 23, no. 1 (2006): 5–27.

Ong, A. and D. Nonini. *Ungrounded Empires: The Cultural Politics of Modern Chinese Transnationalism*. New York: Routledge, 1997.

Portes, A. and J. Sensenbrenner. "Embeddedness and Immigration: Notes on the Social Determinants of Economic Action". *American Journal of Sociology* 98, no. 6 (1993): 1320–51.

Post, P. "Paradise Lost: Fates and Fortunes of the Oei Tiong Ham Concern, 1930s–1960s". *NIOD Working Paper*, 2006.

Rauch, J.E. and V. Trindade. "Ethnic Chinese Networks and International Trade". *Review of Economics and Statistics* 84, no. 1 (2002): 116–30.

Redding, G.S. *The Spirit of Chinese Capitalism*. Berlin: Walter de Gruyter, 1990.

———. "Overseas Chinese Networks: Understanding the Enigma". *Long Range Planning* 28, no. 1 (1995): 61–69.

Robison, R. *Indonesia, the Rise of Capital*. Australia: Allen & Unwin, 1986.

Rugman, A.M. and A. Verbeke. "A Perspective on Regional and Global Strategies of Multinational Enterprises". *Journal of International Business Studies* 35 (2004): 3–18.

Sato, Y. "The Salim Group in Indonesia: The Development and Behavior of the Largest Conglomerate in Southeast Asia". *The Developing Economies* 31, no. 4 (1993): 408–41.

Soetriyono, E. *Liem Sioe Liong, Kisah Sukses*. Jakarta: Indomedia, 1989.

Tempo. "Liem Buka Suara". 31 March 1984.

Twang, P.Y. *The Chinese Business Elite in Indonesia and the Transition to Independence 1940–1950*. Kuala Lumpur: Oxford University Press, 1998.

UNCTAD. *World Investment Report 2006: FDI from Developing and Transition Economies: Implications for Development*, no. E.06.II.D.11, 2006.

Weidenbaum, M. and S. Hughes. *The Bamboo Network: How Expatriate Chinese Entrepreneurs are Creating a New Economic Superpower in Asia*. New York: The Free Press, 1996.

Xin, K. and J. Pearce. "Guanxi: Good Connections as Substitutes for Institutional Support". *Academy of Management Journal* 39 (1996): 1641–58.

Yeung, H.W.-C. "The Dynamics of the Globalization of Chinese Business Firms". In *Globalization of Chinese Business Firms*, edited by H.W.-C. and K. Olds. London: Macmillan, 2000.

Yoshihara, K. *The Rise of Ersatz Capitalism in South East Asia*. Singapore: Oxford University Press, 1998.

Zaheer, S. "Overcoming the Liability of Foreignness". *Academy of Management Journal* 38, no. 2 (1995): 341–64.

10

IS THERE A FUTURE FOR CHINESE INDONESIANS?

Jamie Mackie

What kind of future can be foreseen in the decades ahead of us, or hoped for, by the Chinese Indonesians (or Sino-Indonesians, as I feel they would be better named, by analogy with terms such as Sino-Thai and Sino-Americans)? Will it be smoother than the bumpy ride they have experienced since 1945, or even more troubled and insecure? Nobody can possibly know, of course; but some guesses may be better than others and it is worth trying to work out which factors are likely to influence the outcome most strongly. Moreover, the task of trying to analyse how far current trends are likely to persist or change in the years ahead (even those rooted far back in the past) is itself a challenging, and at times, controversial, exercise, yet crucial for any serious attempt to think about their future.

For that purpose, my aim here is to start by looking at some of the currently observable trends that are likely to exert an impact on the future course of ethnic relations affecting the situation of the Sino-Indonesians (or SI, as I will refer to them henceforth), then to assess what may be the most probable determinants of any future course of events relevant to that, the least desirable as well as the most; finally to consider what factors are likely to influence *pribumi* attitudes towards the SI and, conversely, what kinds of responses and attitudes are likely to emerge among the SI themselves.

Before embarking on those substantive issues, however, I must say something about my use of some of the terminologies here and about the basic reasoning that underlies my own approach to this subject.[1] Even the adjective "Chinese" or the term "Sino-Indonesian" can be problematic since in the last resort, it must be a matter of self-identification by the person(s) concerned, as was found by the designers of the 2000 Census in Indonesia when they had to formulate a question about the ethnicity of its respondents for the first time since the 1930 Census. It is not just a matter of one's name or language, or religion, or socio-cultural characteristics — what Geertz usefully called "primordial loyalties" — although these are often used as rough markers for various purposes.[2] On the other hand, self-identification is not simply a matter of subjective choice; descent or ancestry is a crucial, even inescapable, factor in the equation. Many *pribumi*, perhaps most, are inclined to see the issue simply in racial terms, unfortunately, and in many cases even to regard the SI still as *asing* (aliens), not "real Indonesians" (*asli*), without adequately recognizing that nearly all of them are now Indonesian citizens, born and educated in Indonesia, and that they now identify themselves as Indonesians rather than Chinese, albeit of a distinctive ethnic stock. Yet their Chinese ancestry and cultural background is still a source of great pride to most of them, which they are reluctant to abandon — just as Americans and Australians of British ancestry were a few generations back, or those of Italian, German, or Polish ancestry (and others) in the U.S., who retain varying degrees of pride in their ethnic background and culture. Becoming more and more American or Australian over the years has not entirely eliminated that.

The old notion of a "melting pot" which would fuse them all into broadly homogeneous Americans or Australians in a process of "assimilation" has long ago been abandoned as fallacious. Assimilation is a word which literally implies "making similar" in some vague, but overarching sense, an almost impossible dream for impoverished immigrants in most cases. The many groups of "hyphenated" Americans, Australians, or Canadians (and similar immigrant groups in many other countries in this era of mass international migration) who retain their sense of ethnic origins while becoming full-fledged and loyal citizens of the country they have settled in — a process called "multiculturalism" in some countries, although it is not an entirely satisfactory term, and hardly appropriate at all to Indonesia's unique nation building operation — provide us with better examples of how such groups can be absorbed into the wider society of their new land than do such terms as "melting-pot" or "assimilation". The notion of "hybridity" is a feature of many countries worldwide in this age of globalization (although in varying proportions and with widely differing degrees of smooth adjustment or socio-cultural stress) which provides us with better terminology for thinking about and discussing these issues.[3]

The difference between assimilation and integration as the most suitable idea to describe the process of absorption of the SI into Indonesian society was debated extensively in the 1950–60s between Baperki, a leftist organization consisting almost solely of SI and closely associated with the PKI (Communist Party), and the anti-Communist LPKB which advocated full-scale assimilation into Indonesian life in all respects.[4] The latter, made up of relatively well-educated and already "Indonesianized" members of the SI minority (essentially *peranakan*), urged the use of Bahasa Indonesia rather than Chinese dialects, adoption of Indonesian nationality, and the use of Indonesian names. Baperki replied that conforming with such a policy might be possible for the wealthier SI who had been educated in Indonesian, but was not a practical demand to make of poorer Chinese-speaking Chinese who had no reason to learn Indonesian and, in many cases, could not afford to do so. When President Soekarno finally threw the weight of his support behind Baperki and integration of the SI, the doctrine of assimilation faded into the background for several years. But the pendulum swung back strongly in favour of assimilation after the Gestapu coup attempt of 1965 and the emergence of General Soeharto's strongly anti-communist government, which banned Baperki along with the PKI, and soon proceeded to fashion a new set of doctrines regarding the SI which were openly assimilationist in character.[5]

The policy adopted by President Soeharto in 1966–67 rested on two main pillars. One was to draw a sharp distinction between WNI (Indonesian nationals) and *Cina asing* (aliens, with either PRC or Taiwan citizenship or, "stateless"), with the expectation that most SI would now prefer to opt for the former status. The other was to use the term "assimilation" as the socio-cultural goal to be achieved and to limit the open expression of Chineseness in a number of ways. No real debate on the integration-assimilation issues of the kind that had occurred a few years earlier was permitted and the label "assimilationist" was applied blandly to Soeharto's approach for the next thirty years, although it was neither discussed nor implemented with much consistency, while a great deal of barely covert discrimination against the SI was practised. On the other hand, Soeharto's increasing reliance on a small number of SI *cukong* (cronies), later to become the great *konglomerat* which dominated most of the more lucrative spheres of the Indonesian economy from the 1980s onward, seemed to have little or nothing to do with the goal of achieving effective assimilation. It certainly aroused a great deal of *pribumi* antagonism towards his whole approach to what was commonly called "the Chinese problem" — that is, the fact that such a small minority of the population controlled such a disproportionate share of its corporate wealth.

Hence it was not surprising that when the downfall of Soeharto occurred in 1998 against a backdrop of alarming anti-Chinese violence in May 1998 (and also before and after), along with a general revulsion against many of his policies, there was also a backlash against the doctrine of assimilation from both sides. Many *pribumi* now hope for action of a Malaysia-style affirmative-action policy with the aim of dismantling the conglomerates, and to provide a more level playing field in the business sphere. The SI, on the other hand, were hoping for an end to anti-Chinese discrimination and more genuine acceptance as citizens of Indonesia, with equal rights to those of the *pribumi*. But instead of using the label "integration" for the new policies with its lingering leftist overtones, the term *pembauran* (literally "mixing", but with implications close to *de facto* assimilation) came into widespread use, which had the advantage of implying neither of those two contentious terms and yet pointing in the general direction of a healthily integrated society. Most Indonesians could at least feel they understood in broad terms what it meant. We must hope that the idea of *pembauran* will provide an adequate basis for the future pattern of accommodation of the SI into Indonesian society, since unless it succeeds, their future, is likely to involve continuing tensions and strains.

INTERMARRIAGE PATTERNS AMONG SINO-THAIS AND SINO-INDONESIANS: ILLUMINATING CONTRASTS

My basic approach to the problems confronting us here will derive in large part from the revealing contrasts and similarities I see between the status of the SI in Indonesia, and the Sino-Thais in Thailand, earlier in their history, and today, and probably well into their futures also. Here I will be drawing on a comparison first made by G.W. Skinner in 1960.[6] Focusing on the much greater degree of social integration of the Sino-Thais into the society of Thailand (or "assimilation" as he then described it, perhaps a shade too optimistically) than had occurred up till then in Indonesia's more troubled circumstances, Skinner provided an approach to the problem which went far beyond the common explanation that Islam represents an obstacle to smooth integration of the ethnic Chinese in Indonesia, whereas Buddhism does not in Thailand. (That is, of course, part of the story, but by no means the whole of it.) Skinner put the stress more on the fact that in Thailand there had long been quite a high degree of intermarriage between the leading families of Chinese immigrant communities and the families of prominent Thai leaders ever since the late eighteenth century, with the result that the foremost Chinese families (not yet called Sino-Thai) came to be drawn into Thai society and to adopt Thai language and cultural characteristics — or, as Skinner put it, to be gradually assimilated towards Thai-ness.[7] And later other Chinese immigrants followed in their footsteps, intermarrying with Thai women and also merging into Thai society to varying degrees. That set of processes has now been going on for many generations in Thailand, with the result that the line of distinction between Sino-Thai and "real" ethnic Thai has become so blurred that it is often difficult to tell which group some of them might be identified with. Hence, while it is generally said that the Sino-Thai population is about ten per cent of the total, it is usual to add "give or take two to three per cent" because of the extent of that blurring due to so many intermarriages. Similar but slightly different processes have also been occurring in the Philippines, but because the situation there has been complicated by historical circumstances, my focus here will be confined to Thailand.

But nothing like that has yet occurred in Indonesia, where the historical background reveals an utterly different pattern of absorption or integration of the SI into the various regional communities. It warrants our attention here in thinking about the future, precisely because the pattern of intermarriage was so different from that of Thailand, and will probably not change rapidly or radically for many years to come. There had been some tendency in the eighteenth century for members of Chinese settler communities to marry local women, and for their leaders to marry into aristocratic Javanese families, as in Thailand, but that process almost ceased in the nineteenth century as the Dutch took control over most of Java and reduced the power of local rulers and the aristocracy severely. Further, they imposed regulations to separate the Chinese from the "native" population by residential segregation within the "Chinatown" sections of the larger cities. Hence there was no strong incentive for Chinese leaders to identify closely with the society around them, as in Thailand. In fact, the more ambitious Chinese looked more towards a Dutch way of life than a Javanese one, learning the Dutch language, going to Dutch schools, and often adopting modern Dutch business practices. (Marriage to Dutch women occurred only rarely, however.)

During the Indonesian struggle for independence, only a handful of Chinese supported the Indonesians and many clung to the Dutch, something that was held against them for many years afterwards. Only since about the 1970s has there been some tendency for a few younger, middle-class SI to marry Indonesians, but the number has not been large so far. (Those who have done so appear to have met their spouses either at school or Christian churches, not necessarily a plus in the eyes of some Muslims.) Intermarriage will probably increase in the decades ahead, but not to any great extent in the immediate future. Thus Indonesia seems likely to lag far behind Thailand and the Philippines in this respect and the blurring of lines of ethnic separation that has occurred there will take even longer.

The comparison between Thailand and Indonesia with respect to the patterns of socio-cultural integration of ethnic Chinese in both countries deserves much closer examination than it has yet had, for the Thai experience provides the best example, in my view, of the path that Indonesia could be encouraged to follow over the decades ahead of us (albeit with some differences). We can safely assume that if the SI follow a trajectory broadly similar to that of the Sino-Thai towards integration into the local community, they are likely to experience a reasonably tolerable future. The trajectories observable in the other countries of Southeast Asia are very different and do not provide such promising examples to think about as Thailand's does — neither Malaysia, Singapore, or the Philippines which are all radically different, nor the special cases of Vietnam, Cambodia, and Burma.[8] I do not want to overstate the similarities of the Thai and Indonesian cases, for there are other factors to be taken into account. The most obvious of these is that the Sino-Thais represent a much larger proportion of the country's population and have dominated its commercial life for much longer, and to an even greater extent, than the two to three per cent of SI has ever done, often in close collaboration with wealthy or influential ethnic Thai partners or protectors. Furthermore, it is hard to discern in Thailand anything like the *pribumi* "proto-capitalist class" striving to mobilize political backing for measures to constrain the economic activities of the SI. And the strongly anti-Chinese attitudes of some Muslim groups in Indonesia have had no parallel among even the most activist Buddhists in Thailand. So it cannot be expected that the trajectory of integration of the SI will closely resemble that of the Sino-Thai in the decades ahead of us, even though I think theirs is a more appropriate case to study and learn from than the almost unique situation in Malaysia or the much-touted (but badly misleading) "model" of the melting pot in the United States.[9]

RECENT TRENDS

1. Generational Change: Indonesianization and De-Sinification

Between 1945 and 2005, the character of the ethnic Chinese minority in Indonesia changed radically. For more than a decade after 1945, only a small fraction of them, the locally-born, had Indonesian nationality (still an unsettled and complex legal issue at that time), many had been born in China, and even those who had been born in Indonesia, probably well over 65 per cent at that time, were torn between identifying themselves as Indonesians or as Chinese nationals in the immediate aftermath of the Communist revolution in China. But by 2005, nearly all the SI had been born in Indonesia, most of them since independence (apart from a tiny handful of very old pre-1950 immigrants from China, virtually all such immigration had ceased entirely after 1949); they were predominantly Indonesian citizens and had received their education there, mostly in Indonesian-language schools after 1967 and nearly all, except the diminishing *totok* fraction, would probably have thought of themselves primarily as Indonesians, no longer as Chinese.[10] The fact that diplomatic relations between Jakarta and Beijing were suspended between 1967 and 1990 and personal contacts almost entirely forbidden, meant that the process of de-Sinification was far-reaching among the younger generation. Some minor changes to their legal status that have occurred since the fall of President Soeharto in 1998 may have improved their situation slightly, while the effects of China's dramatic opening up to trade with the outside world since about 1990, and the "charm offensive" by Beijing to allay fears in Southeast Asia, have changed the international context radically. But it has also generated talk at times of a revival of solidarity amongst the worldwide diaspora of the Chinese overseas.[11] How far that has modified the mindset of younger-generation SI towards re-Sinification — or may be expected to do so in the years ahead if People's Republic of China (PRC) comes to exert more active economic and political leverage across Southeast Asia as its wealth and power increase — is a question I cannot answer but, I suspect, not much. On the other hand, the revival of interest in Chinese language teaching among the SI and other manifestations of Chinese culture suggest that the previous de-Sinification process may slow down slightly, although probably not radically.

2. Ethnic Consolidation: A Blurring of *Totok-Peranakan* Differences?

The division of ethnic Chinese into the two sharply different groups of *totok* and *peranakan* over the last century or so of colonial rule has become less marked over recent decades with the cessation of immigration from China since the 1940s. It has not yet disappeared entirely on a linguistic plane, however, and will no doubt persist into the future for some time, although with diminishing social significance as the number of China-born and

Chinese-speaking SI diminishes. In effect, this will mean that the entire SI population is gradually becoming more *peranakanized* and closer in its cultural and social character to the rest of the Indonesian population. That must surely have the effect of facilitating the *pembauran* process and reducing the likelihood of tensions such as those that occurred in the 1960s. It is another aspect of the Indonesianization process mentioned above.

3. Legal Status, Nationality Problems, and Discriminatory Measures

There will soon be few, if any, SI who have not become Indonesian nationals, although the various legal anomalies which have taken years to sort out may still pose problems for a small number. Hence one of the most contentious issues of the 1960s which aroused a lot of suspicion about the supposed "loyalty" of the SI to Indonesia will have faded into the background. Unfortunately that does not mean we can assume that all forms of discrimination against them by the various government agencies they have to deal with will quickly come to an end for we still hear many allegations that the enactment of laws and regulations abolishing earlier forms of discrimination against them are simply not being implemented as intended. Can we foresee whether such discrimination will diminish in the years ahead, or perhaps intensify? I would like to think there may be good reasons to believe it will diminish gradually as the *pembauran* process gains strength. But there are many factors and attitudes involved here, on both sides, so any predictions at this stage would be too risky to attempt.

4. SI Economic Dominance and the Widening Wealth/ Income Gap

The social and economic problems created by the steadily increasing economic dominance of the SI over their *pribumi* rivals, in bad times such as 1997–98 as well as good, and the contrast between the very great wealth of some of them and the general poverty of so many ordinary Indonesians, are so well known that there is little need to elaborate on them here. These problems are frequently invoked as one of the principal factors behind much of the antagonism towards them that underlies the prejudiced views, discrimination, and periodic outbreaks of violence against them.[12] The SI have often been characterized, as have other Southeast Asian Chinese elsewhere, as "pariah entrepreneurs" or "economic animals" who have achieved their success mainly through the corruption-prone patron-client relationships they have built up with local rulers or officials in what are intrinsically patrimonialist political systems.[13] The most notable cases of this were the dozen or more *cukong* associated with President Soeharto in his early years, who nearly all became immensely wealthy in due course.

Whether or not their predominance will persist over the decades ahead, or suffer from the kinds of adverse attitudes towards them prevailing in the past, is simply unforeseeable. But several point of relevance here are worth bearing in mind.

First, it cannot be assumed that the political and economic circumstances that so greatly favoured the big SI conglomerates during the thirty years of Soeharto's presidency will be equally beneficial to them over the next thirty. They then enjoyed the immense advantages of highly favourable treatment from an extraordinarily powerful president, a singularly patrimonialist, patronage-based form of government, and a long period of sustained and rapid GDP growth when capital accumulation (in large part from rent-seeking activities) was relatively easy. None of these conditions applies in the post-Soeharto era. (Nor did they apply during the previous twenty years before Soeharto assumed power, when ethnic Chinese businessmen faced much greater difficulties, even after Dutch dominance of the economy was ended by the nationalization of all Dutch enterprises in 1957–58, leaving them as the dominant entrepreneurial talents in Indonesia. But the preference given to state enterprises during Soekarno's 1959–65 phase of "Guided Democracy" and "Guided Economy" meant that few SI businessmen were becoming exceptionally wealthy yet. Moreover, they then faced relatively little effective competition from *pribumi* rivals, as they do to a much greater extent today.) So it is not impossible that the rise of the wealthy group of *cukong* in the Soeharto era may appear in due course to have been a temporary aberration.

It would be absurdly premature to imply, on the other hand, that the big conglomerates that emerged in the Soeharto era will not retain the same dominance of key sectors of the Indonesian economy that they achieved before 1998. They are too smart to be written off as incapable of adapting to changing circumstances, for that is one of the things that virtually all Southeast Asian Chinese seem to be remarkably good at doing in almost any business environment. But the political and economic context they must work in today is significantly different and in some respects less favourable than it was in the New Order years. There are a few signs, too, that economic policy is gradually being reformed in the direction of a more open and competitive environment — and one, moreover, in which there is now a handful of *pribumi*-owned large-scale enterprises competing against the SI, with strong official backing. The picture is complicated by the tangled party politics of the post-1998–99 liberalization of the political system, the decentralization of far greater powers and revenues to regional authorities, and to the new forms of "money politics" that have emerged.[14]

Second, it is worth remembering that only since 1989–90 has the Jakarta Stock Exchange come back to life after several earlier decades of torpidity, with the result that big business in Indonesia is becoming increasingly corporatized. That is likely to result in a greater degree of cross-ownership of shares in large as well as small public companies. How far that will dilute the ownership of the larger SI conglomerates remains to be seen. If it happens, it will almost certainly be a long, slow process. But it could be the most promising route towards any goal worth considering as one of the most desirable solutions to the problem of SI economic dominance.

Third, it is likely that what might be called the catch-up effect will benefit at least some of the smarter and longer-established *pribumi* businessmen, the younger, better-educated ones especially, if the economic climate becomes more favourable over the next decade or so. Far more of them are becoming well acquainted with the ways of big business in a modern computerized economy than their predecessors were thirty years ago. If that happens, we might be close to crossing a major watershed between the one-sided pattern of rivalry between SI and *pribumi* business firms in the past, and something that may be distinctly different in the years ahead. It should be a much healthier state of affairs in many respects, although perhaps a more difficult life for the SI than hitherto.

5. Residential Desegregation and Resegregation and the Widening Gap in Incomes and Wealth

Because so little attention has been paid by anyone writing on the socio-economic status of the SI to the extent of residential desegregation that occurred after the end of the colonial era away from the chinatowns established by the Dutch or, to the more recent tendency towards a form of partial resegregation that has been occurring as wealthy SI move into suburbs occupied exclusively or predominantly by other SI, the implications for successful *pembauran* of both processes have been overlooked. The extent of the two tendencies cannot be measured in any precise way, but the trend deserves close consideration, especially for its future implications.

The Dutch had required that the Chinese reside in specified urban areas (*wijken* — in effect, Chinatowns) in an attempt to minimize contact between the Chinese and "the natives". They also tried to limit the extent to which they could reside in rural areas, without total success, although only in a few areas did the Chinese live and work as farmers or fishermen among the locals, most notably in Riau, Kalimantan Barat, and Bangka-Billiton.[15] But after independence, both SI and well-to-do *pribumi* started moving into new middle-class suburbs such as Kebayoran and Kemang (and Menteng after the Dutch were ejected suddenly in 1957–58) and similar suburbs in Surabaya, Bandung, and other towns. That process could be described as a form of residential *pembauran* of an essentially beneficial kind, for it enabled both groups to get to know each other better and to meet socially more often. While the old Chinatowns remained, many of the wealthier and upwardly mobile SI moved away from them into the newer suburbs.

But that process seems to have been reversed over the last decade or so as the development of housing centres, built either exclusively for the SI, or for the very wealthy, has resulted in pockets of residential segregation that are bound to have retrograde social consequences, as they reinforce notions about SI exclusivity and exorbitant wealth that badly need to be reduced, not aggravated. If *pembauran* is ever to succeed in its various aims, residential segregation of that kind is surely one of the worst social pathologies that Indonesia needs to avoid. How that should be done is certainly a very complex and difficult question; I can only hope it will be tackled, preferably by the SI themselves in some way, without the government just resorting to measures involving overt racial discrimination. But it is not easy to be optimistic on that score.

6. The Demographic Aspect: Is The SI Population Declining?

This is a controversial and unresolved question. Crude estimates of the size of the SI population, which are based unreflectingly on the surprisingly low 2000 Census figure, might give rise to a belief that its numbers are not only much lower than had been previously believed, but could even appear to be declining fast and terminally because of declining SI fertility levels. Leo Suryadinata and his colleagues have made a revised calculation that the number is probably between three and four million (that is, 1.5 to 2 per cent of the total population), which I suspect may still be on the low side.[16] I take the view that we simply cannot draw any firm conclusions from those census figures because we have no real idea as to how high the level was of under declaration of their Chinese ethnicity by large numbers of SI (or "category jumping" in technical jargon) so soon after a time of intense fears of anti-Chinese antagonism, following the turbulent events of 1998.[17]

This is not the place to go into that issue in any detail, but because of its centrality to our thinking about the future of the SI, I must explain my reasons for preferring a figure of around 2.5 per cent, which implies about five million in 2007. I am inclined to disregard the 2000 Census results entirely and look instead at the three key variables determining the size of the SI population since 1930, which is the most reliable estimate we have (1.23 million, or 2 per cent of the total), or 1961 when a meticulous calculation was made by Skinner on the basis of what was then known from earlier registration figures for aliens and about SI birth and death rates. He estimated that they then numbered about 2.45 million or roughly 2.5 per cent of the total. Unless the decline in SI fertility rates (that is, birth rates, in effect) since then has been well above the national average — unlikely, in my view — or the level of SI out-migration has been far higher than we are aware of, I see no reason to conclude that the SI population has declined much below the 1961 figure of 2.5 per cent, since the SI death rate has almost certainly been well below the national average, due to easier access to better medical services. The whole question certainly deserves further investigation. But the important point here is that we can confidently assume that the SI population will not decline into insignificance due to the above demographic determinants in the course of this century.

FUTURE DETERMINANTS OF THE SITUATION

1. Local Politics and Economic Factors

There is much that needs to be explored under this heading, but I will confine myself to one very general observation. The dramatic swing since 1998 from the highly authoritarian Soeharto regime with its intense concentration of both political power and financial resources in the hands of the president, towards a much more dispersed pattern of power distribution under the *demokrasi dan reformasi* regime that has developed since then, with unprecedented powers and financial resources now allocated to the *daerah* (regions), has created an entirely new political system that is unlikely to be reversed by another strong man like Soeharto, either a military man or any other. That could make the future more problematic for the SI, insofar as many of them were beneficiaries from Soeharto's patronage system, but will probably find life far more unpredictable in the more open and competitive political environment that has emerged since 1998–98. Some of the most retrograde features of the former patrimonialist regime still persist and the "money politics" of the new regime, although of a very different stamp from the pre-1998 brand, seems even more blatant and all-pervasive. But the more competitive character of the economic policies now being adopted and the shift towards a far more decentralized power structure will almost certainly change things greatly for wealthy SI.

2. The International Context: Regional and Global

We have seen how in the 1960s the international politics of the Cold War played an important part in exacerbating the problems faced by ethnic Chinese throughout Indonesia, especially the role of the PRC and its relations with the PKI at a time of very turbulent domestic politics. Beijing's attempts to exert greater influence in Southeast Asia had the effect of making life much more difficult for the SI because its interference was strongly resented and the political leverage it could exert was, in fact, very limited. This was followed by more than twenty years when external factors exerted relatively little influence, since diplomatic relations with the PRC were "frozen" until 1990, and the Cold War was becoming less relevant to Southeast Asia. But the great increase in China's influence in the region since the 1990s, politically as well as economically, which seems almost certain to continue far into the future, may well have the effect of making her "the paramount power" once again for the first time in nearly six hundred years.[18]

How that may affect the position of the SI, either favourably or adversely, is not easily predictable. What caused problems for them in the 1960s was not so much that they were torn individually by divided loyalties to either Jakarta or Beijing (as before 1942) in the Cold War politics of that turbulent decade between Indonesia or China, but rather that they inevitably came under suspicion from the authorities and hostile demagogues on the ground that their loyalty to Indonesia was unreliable. In such troubled times it was very easy for their enemies to mobilize popular hostility against them. Might that kind of situation recur?

Something similar could conceivably occur again in the decades ahead if the international situation becomes threatening, especially if conflict between the United States-Japan-Australia axis and the ASEAN states gives rise to a serious political polarization among the nations of East and Southeast Asia; but I think the risk is relatively low. Indonesia would probably do its best to avoid taking sides in any such conflict, although the domestic as well as the international politics involved could become quite nasty, with doubts again being raised about the loyalty of the SI by their enemies.

Here again, it is the domestic political context that is likely to be crucial, providing scope for demonization of the SI as scapegoats, rather than that they may be called upon personally to make difficult choices. Beijing has apparently become well aware by now that it would be most unwise to try to invoke support of any kind from the Southeast Asian Chinese, or to try to intervene to defend their interests if they come under attack as in the 1960s or 1999.

Of greater concern to the SI may be the international politics of the "war on terror" if it intensifies, of any resurgence of militant Islamic *jihadi* activity in the region were to create a wider escalation of violence there by *JI* or *al Qaeda* elements. If any such political turbulence occurs, the SI might find themselves targeted as scapegoats yet again by their rivals and enemies, or execrated by Muslim extremists as so often in the past. It could become a very disturbing prospect for them. But will it happen?

3. The "China" Factor

Quite apart from the international relations scenarios sketched above, there are three other aspects of the rise of China as a major power in the politics of Southeast Asia that may impinge upon the situation of the SI in potentially awkward ways. One is that it could have a retrograde effect by reversing the general trend towards de-Sinification and Indonesianization that has been an important factor behind the *pembauran* process over the last half-century. That could play into the hands of their enemies and derail any hope of further improvements towards real *pembauran*.

Another is the possibility of a recurrence of the sort of call for worldwide solidarity among the Chinese like the 1991–92 "Greater China" flurry of excitement, especially if it evoked a strong response among the SI. I would like to think that is unlikely and that Beijing would have the good sense to discourage any such move; but in the tangled international politics of the next few years, one cannot be entirely sure.

Finally, the big SI conglomerates are now doing business in China and building up political linkages there in a way that was almost impossible in the Soeharto era. That may be harmless enough and even beneficial to Indonesia if they behave with good sense; but if they allow their narrow personal interests to clash with the broader interests of Indonesia in general or, the delicate situation of the SI community, in particular, it could give rise to problems. It could become very different from the pre-1998 situation and the politics involved may require very sensitive handling.

4. The Impact of Globalization

We cannot ignore the potential effects on the position of the SI in the ongoing globalization of markets, capital flows, new technologies, and especially, of rapid communications and transport in the decades ahead of us, although it is easy to be carried away by speculations about such matters. Some of the effects of globalization could prove highly beneficial to the SI, insofar as many of them tend to have the educational advantages and cosmopolitan experience (as well as personal or family contacts worldwide) to benefit most from it all. Whether or not there may be any downside to it as far as the *pembauran* process is concerned, or in terms of the attitudes of the *pribumi* to the SI and vice versa, is something we can only guess at this stage. But Indonesia's future will clearly be affected by the changes sweeping across the globe that will make the future very different from the past in diverse ways.

PRIBUMI ATTITUDES: WELCOMING, RESISTANT, OR DISCRIMINATORY?

It is risky to offer any confident predictions or sweeping generalizations here. Too little is known about the range and intensities of popular attitudes in this area. In various parts of Indonesian society, there are many people who would favour the smooth integration of the SI into the communities in which they reside, while in other parts, we can find extremists who want to stir up hatred towards them for all sorts of dubious reasons. Good and bad are mixed up in constantly shifting proportions, as in every country, yet in the middle there are much larger numbers of Indonesians of moderate, but often muddled opinions on these matters, ranging across a wide spectrum, whose views are inclined to fluctuate in response to changing circumstances. Not enough opinion polling has been done to give us an accurate picture of the distribution of various attitudes; so the pictures formed in the minds of most people derive mainly from partisan reports about the various outbreaks of anti-Chinese violence that have occurred from time to time, which tend to highlight the more negative side of the picture at the expense of the more positive. Recent studies on such violence by Coppel, Purdey, and Sidel — and the many Indonesian accounts they have drawn on — provide us with some clues to current attitudes, but much more needs to become known about their spread, intensity, and inevitable complexities.

It has long been well known, unfortunately, that hostility towards ethnic Chinese in Indonesia has been strongest in some Muslim circles, most notably in the Sarekat Dagang Islam, and its successor, the Sarekat Islam, in the early twentieth century, and more recently in the fierce words and actions of some radical Muslim groups since the fall of Soeharto. This has worrying implications for the future of the SI insofar as it seems more likely that the strength and militancy of those groups will increase in the years ahead rather than decline in influence — but there is little that the SI can do to prevent that, except to hope that the basic moderation and reasonableness of the mainstream Muslim organizations in Indonesia will act as a buffer of some sort. (Perhaps greater efforts should be made by them in the religious domain, although I cannot imagine how — and it seems unlikely that the answer lies in urging more SI to convert to Islam, which has not been very successful so far in either winning many converts, or deflecting Muslim resentments). But the national and international politics of Islamic extremism in Indonesia and other parts of the Muslim world have become so entangled in the "war on terror" that any predictions on how it will all play out in the years ahead are highly speculative.

Several other factors that have had a bearing on the levels of hostility or relative tolerance experienced by the SI over recent decades need to be kept in mind in any thinking about their future. One is that in times of governmental breakdown or extreme weakness, outbreaks of anti-Chinese violence or overt hostility are more likely to occur, as in 1945 and 1965–67. By contrast, during the three decades when the Soeharto regime was strongly in control, anti-Chinese violence was relatively infrequent — and local military commanders who failed to crack down on it promptly and firmly were often penalized for their laxity.[19] The May 1998 violence in Jakarta, and to some extent elsewhere, was in part an anti-Soeharto outburst as well as anti-Chinese, at a time of virtual paralysis of the central government, although the political dynamics of all that was too complex and controversial to be typecast briefly. And we must remember that even the turbulence of the mid-1960s involved a tangled mixture of anti-PRC hostility as well as fear of the PKI and of international communism more generally, which came to be focused on the local Chinese as a potential "fifth column" sympathetic to China's expressed aim of expanding its influence in Southeast Asia via local Communist parties. It is hard to imagine a repetition of anything like that scenario in the near future.

ATTITUDES AND THINKING AMONG THE SINO-INDONESIANS

Much will depend, I feel, on the wisdom and foresight contained within the ideas and expectations that develop among the SI themselves about what their position in Indonesian society is likely to be in ten, twenty or fifty years' time. There was a slight flurry of comment about that in 1998 after the fall of Soeharto when the first steps in the direction of *demokrasi dan reformasi* occurred, but it tended to be focused mainly on questions about how to remedy the various discriminatory measures and practices applying to the SI under the Soeharto regime and on the best forms of political action to adopt in the new environment of democracy — that is, whether to set up a specifically SI party similar to the old PTI in the 1930–40s, or to try to exert some influence from within the existing parties, and if so, which? Not much attention was given, as far as I could see, to the other side of the coin: what to do about remedying the disproportionate wealth of such a small ethnic minority. There was some discussion on what alternatives there might be to Soeharto's advocacy of assimilation as the appropriate signpost towards the future in Indonesia and some echoes of the early 1960s debates between advocates of assimilation and integration as the most appropriate objectives to aim at. But most of that discussion ran into the sands as the term *pembauran* took over as the preferred term to use, since it conveniently avoided any need to make a choice between those two divergent concepts. That was not a bad thing in some respects since it deflected away any serious political divisions of a possibly explosive issue. But it had the adverse effect that the deeper questions that need to be addressed about how the SI should see themselves fitting into Indonesian society have largely been bypassed. I am not aware of much discussion within the SI community about those most basic questions since then. Yet it is surely essential that there should be, for three reasons.

One is that, just to think in terms of clinging to the status quo as it has developed during and since the Soeharto era, is probably a dangerous and unsustainable strategy. The widening gap between increasingly wealthy SI and much poorer *pribumi* does not fit well into anyone's notions of what *pembauran* signifies as a socio-cultural objective, especially if the trend towards residential segregation along the lines mentioned above becomes worse. New thinking by younger-generation SI that goes beyond the old clichés about assimilation or the melting pot or some form of multiculturalism is going to be needed — and they will have to be formulated in ways that will be acceptable to both the SI themselves and (thereafter) the rest of the Indonesian population. That will not be easy and I do not presume to have any useful suggestions towards such solutions, except to urge that market forces and government regulations must be combined to work towards rather than against, a desirable outcome. The solutions will have to come from other Indonesians and the SI themselves, probably after a prolonged process of *musyawarah dan mufakat* (consultation and consenses in the public domain.

Second, as those comments imply, whatever solutions are advanced will have to be based on a set of socio-economic trade-offs acceptable to both sides, the *pribumi* as well as the SI. I cannot help thinking that this will require the wealthier SI business firms and their owners to play the leading part in finding new ideas about how large and powerful SI organizations such as the Soeharto-era conglomerates, which still dominate the business landscape, can make a far greater contribution towards reducing, rather than continually widening, the wealth gap that has developed since the 1960s, between them and their *pribumi* rivals. If they cannot do so, there is a danger that forceful measures may be taken to do it for them — and against them. It is an inherently unhealthy situation, probably an unsustainable one in the long run. But resolving it will be an immensely difficult task, just as the worldwide gap is between the super-rich and the poor in most countries, even the wealthiest. Yet it is the unusual ethnic dimension that makes it uniquely dangerous in Indonesia. So it will require that the best and brightest people on both sides of the ethnic divide get together first to talk about what options may be best for exploring in Indonesia's unique circumstances.

Third, the relative lack of any clearly recognized set of SI community leaders in recent years, who might be able to mobilize other members to contribute to the search for new answers to these profoundly difficult and politically fraught problems, is a big obstacle to easy progress here. Here again, the comparison with Thailand is illuminating. Indonesia has had no equivalents in recent years to the Lamsam and Sophonpanich families (and several others) who have generally provided a high degree of community leadership, as well as economic eminence, in Thailand, throughout much of the last century. Neither Liem Sioe Liong nor William Suryadjaja, the two major *towkays* (big businessmen) of the New Order period, nor any of the twenty or so other major *konglomerat*, ever played anything like that sort of community leadership role. And I am not aware of any others who might be emerging as such in the post-Soeharto era. Whether that is a good or bad thing is for others to decide. I merely mention the difference as a phenomenon of some relevance to the capacities of the various SI communities to act cohesively and with some foresight as to where their best interests lie. If they are simply fragmented and rudderless in the face of the challenges ahead (as they were to some extent in the 1945–49 years and the 1960s), the chances that a path of wisdom and foresight will be taken are likely to be slim.

A Tentative Conclusion

My answer to the title question will be: yes, the SI will certainly have a future, and with some luck, a smoother one than previously, if they seriously address themselves to making the *pembauran* process work much better so as to reduce the rough edges of inter-ethnic frictions; but perhaps not, if it does not improve. I doubt that their circumstances will become so bad that many will feel they should try to migrate, and I suspect that most will, in fact, continue to be much wealthier than most Indonesians — which is essentially what the central problem here is all about.

It is highly unlikely that they will lose their identity as a distinctive group within Indonesian society (something that has certainly not happened yet in Thailand, despite the far greater extent of socio-cultural integration there over several generations), although I think it more likely that their sense of a strongly Chinese cultural identity will continue to erode — just as my own Scottish one has over two generations — as family links to China dwindle. Nearly all will soon just regard themselves as Indonesians first and foremost, provided that the rest of the Indonesian population proves to be ready to accept them as such.

That is, of course, the great unknown factor in the equation here. And it will probably take several generations before the sense of ethnic difference and the tensions associated with it will fade into insignificance. In Australia it took nearly two hundred years for the disadvantaged Catholic Irish to become fully at ease in an Anglo-Protestant social ambience, and the problem was far less complex because the latter were on top; and Asian immigrants have also been able to achieve a fairly smooth process of *pembauran* there over the last thirty years, to an astonishing degree. It can happen, but it needs ideas and leadership. Throughout the world, the patterns of difference of this kind (called multiculturalism or multiracialism in some cases) are being modified gradually and in some cases alleviated — another aspect of globalization — although they are still poisonous and even explosive in some cases. Indonesia's problem is by no means the worst in the world; but it is a stubborn and difficult one. We must simply hope for the best — and give a lot more thought and frank discussion to the question of how to bring that about, and not just leave it to the accidents of chance and history.

Notes

[1] I must clarify here that the title of this talk was proposed to me by the conference organizers; it is one I would not otherwise have dared to undertake.

But the challenge was a stimulating one. My qualifications for expressing any opinions on this subject are not that I am a Sinologist, nor especially knowledgeable about Sino-Indonesians, but simply that I have been interested in their predicament and prospects for many years, ever since I first worked in Jakarta in the 1950s. But I have also had the great advantage of being able to learn much about them from various graduate students I have been associated with in Australia, notably Leo Suryadinata and Charles Coppel — although they are in no way responsible for, nor necessarily in agreement with, the views expressed here.

2   On "primordial loyalties", see Clifford Geertz, "The Integrative Revolution: Primordial Loyalties and Civil Politics in the New States", in *Old Societies and New States*, edited by Geertz Glencoe (The Free Press, 1963).

3   "Hybridity is a concept that confronts and problematizes boundaries although it does not erase them. As such hybridity always implies an unsettling of identities." Ien Ang, "Together-in-Difference: Beyond Diaspora, Into Hybridity", *Asian Studies Review* 27, no. 2, June 2002, p. 146.

4   On the 1960s integration-assimilation controversy, see Mary F. Somers Heidhues, "Perananakan Chinese Politics in Indonesia" (Ithaca, Cornell Modern Indonesian Project Interim Reports Series, 1964); also, *The Encyclopedia of the Chinese Overseas*, edited by Lynn Pan (Singapore: The Chinese Heritage Centre, 1998), pp. 165–68.

5   Charles Coppel, *Indonesian Chinese in Crisis* (Kuala Lumpur: OUP, for the Asian Studies Association of Australia, 1983).

6   G.W. Skinner, "Change and Persistence in Chinese Culture Overseas: A Comparison of Thailand and Java", *Journal of the South Seas Society*, vol. 16, 1960; also Skinner, "The Chinese Minority", in *Indonesia*, edited by Ruth McVey, for Human Relations Area Files (New Haven, 1963).

7   It has been argued that Skinner "overemphasized the forces of assimilation which ... have colored his perception of the Chinese in Thailand ... Assimilation as defined in the Amercan sociological and anthropological literature has not taken place", according to Chan Kwok Bun and Tong Chee Kiong, "Rethinking Assimilation and Ethnicity: the Chinese in Thailand", in *The Chinese Diaspora: Selected Essays*, edited by Wang Ling-chi and Wang Gungwu (Singapore: Times Academic Press, 1998). I have summarized the key point of their argument and set out my own views on "assimilation" (along with Ien Ang's very interesting suggestion that we think rather in terms of "hybridity") in my piece on "Thinking about the Chinese Overseas", *The American Asian Review*, vol. xxi, no. 4 (winter 2003): 1–44.

8   The situation in Singapore is entirely non-comparable as it is essentially an ethnic Chinese city state, while in Malaysia, the Chinese segment of the population is many times greater than in Indonesia — over one-third of the total around the time of independence and now declining towards a quarter. In the Philippines, the position of the ethnic Chinese is even more complex and non-comparable.

In Cambodia, although the Chinese had merged into the host society almost as smoothly as the Sino-Thai had done in Thailand, they have had a dreadfully hard time under, and since, the Pol Pot regime took oppressive measures against nearly all town dwellers and "bourgeois elements" in the 1970s, reducing the Chinese population there by more than half. Likewise in Vietnam, the Chinese suffered severely from the ideological conflicts of the Vietnam war era, which forced many to leave the country.

9   It was significant that although the relevance of the Malaysian and U.S. "models" of accommodation of ethnic minorities was mentioned at the Singapore conference which gave rise to this book, the significance of the Thai experience was almost entirely ignored.

10 For the best information on the current situation facing the SI, see *The Encyclopedia of the Chinese Overseas*, 2nd ed. (Singapore: Chinese Heritage Centre, 2006); and Leo Suryadinata, *Understanding the Ethnic Chinese in Southeast Asia* (Singapore: Institute of Southeast Asian Studies, 2007).

11 On the 1991–92 flurry of "Greater China" speculation, largely economic in focus, but also more broadly political and embracing the worldwide diaspora, including Southeast Asia, see the special edition of the *China Quarterly*, December 1993, especially Wang Gungwu, "China and the Chinese Overseas", pp. 926–46.

12 In her study of anti-Chinese prejudice and violence in Indonesia, Jemma Purdey observes that the thesis that the SI are targeted for violence "solely because of their economic role, without regard to their political and legal situation" is misguided. "Their ethnicity means that Chinese Indonesians are always vulnerable" and "a complex layering of sentiments motivates an act of violence against [them]; jealousies, misdirected frustrations, and racialised prejudice. Prejudice is not enough on its own to bring about violence." See her exemplary analysis of these complex issues in *Anti-Chinese Violence in Indonesia, 1996–1999*, (Singapore University Press in association with the Asian Studies Association of Australia Publication Series, 2006); also relevant is Charles Coppel, ed., *Violent Conflict in Indonesia: Analysis, Representation, Resolution* (London and NY: Routledge, 2006).

13 Because corruption is such a universal and multifarious phenomenon, almost drained of meaning by overuse with reference to Indonesia, it seems to me more informative to utilize the word patrimonialism (that is, a system of government based on the use of patronage to ensure the loyalty of subordinates) as the basic malady Indonesia has suffered from under President Soeharto and his successors. In his classic 1979 article on the subject, Harold Crouch wrote that Soeharto upheld his authority largely "through the distribution of patronage. He was able to reward loyal supporters and win over potentially dissident officers with appointments to civilian posts that offered prospects of material gain"; see "Patrimonialism and Military Rule in Indonesia", *World Politics*, vol. 31, no. 4 (1979): 461–87.

[14] Good accounts of the Indonesian domestic politics surrounding the fall of Soeharto and the anti-Chinese rioting of May 1998 and the swing towards *demokrasi dan reformasi* thereafter are given in Kevin O'Rourke, *Reformasi: The Struggle for Power in Post-Soeharto Indonesia* (Sydney: Allen & Unwin, 2002); and Edward Aspinall and Greg Fealy, eds., *Local Power and Politics in Indonesia: Decentralisation and Democratisation*, Indonesia Update Series (Singapore: Institute of Southeast Asian Studies, 2003).

[15] On Chinese farmers in rural areas of Indonesia, see Mary Somers-Heidhues, "Chinese Settlements in Rural Southeast Asia", in *Sojourners and Settlers: Histories of Southeast Asia and the Chinese*, edited by Anthony Reid (Sydney: Allen & Unwin, 1996). A strong argument that they often became well integrated into their surrounding communities was advanced about the Chinese in the Tanggerang area, near Jakarta, by Go Gien Tjwan, *Eenheid en verscheidenheid in een Indonesiasch Dorp* (Amsterdam University, Sociologisch-Historisch Seminarium voor Zuidoost Azie, 1966).

[16] Leo Suryadinata, Evi Nurvidya Arifin, and Aris Ananta, *Indonesia's Population: Ethnicity and Religion in a Changing Political Landscape* (Singapore: Institute of Southeast Asian Studies, 2003).

[17] Jamie Mackie, "How Many Chinese Indonesians?", *Bulletin of Indonesian Economic Studies*, vol. 41, no. 1, April 2005. G.W. Skinner, "The Chinese Minority", in *Indonesia*, edited by Ruth McVey (New Haven, 1963).

[18] Milton Osborne, in "The Paramount Power: China and the Countries of Southeast Asia" (Lowy Institute Paper, Sydney, no. 11, 2006, p. vii), writes that "China's relations with the countries of SE Asia have changed substantially, even dramatically, over the past decade" and "China has become a power whose interests cannot be ignored".

[19] After the many troubles suffered by the SI during the tense power struggles of 1965–67, there were only a few episodes of serious anti-Chinese violence over the next thirty years of Soeharto's rule after he was firmly established in office, notably two quite exceptional outbursts in Bandung in 1974, and Solo in 1980.

INDEX

www.ingramcontent.com/pod-product-compliance
Lightning Source LLC
Chambersburg PA
CBHW021541260326
41914CB00001B/113